D0265579

MANAGING CHANGE

MANAGING CHANGE

second edition

Edited by
Christopher Mabey
and
Bill Mayon-White

Published in association with
The Open University

P·C·P
Paul Chapman
Publishing Ltd

Copyright selection and editorial material © The Open University 1993.
All other material copyright as credited.

All rights reserved

Paul Chapman Publishing Ltd
144 Liverpool Road
London
N1 1LA

Apart from any fair dealing for the purposes of research or
private study, or criticism or review, as permitted under the
Copyright, Designs and Patents Act, 1988, this publication may be
reproduced, stored or transmitted, in any form or by any means,
only with the prior permission in writing of the publishers, or
in the case of reprographic reproduction in accordance with the
terms of licences issued by the Copyright Licensing Agency.
Inquiries concerning reproduction outside those terms should be
sent to the publishers at the abovementioned address.

British Library Cataloguing in Publication Data

Managing Change. – 2Rev. ed
I. Mayon-White, Bill
II. Mabey, Christopher
658.406

ISBN 1–85396–226–0

Typeset by Inforum, Rowlands Castle, Hants
Printed and bound by
The Cromwell Press Ltd
Broughton Gifford, Melksham, Wiltshire

H 9 8 7 6

CONTENTS

ACKNOWLEDGEMENTS

We are grateful to those listed below for permission to reproduce copyrighted material.

Ch. 1, Andrew Pettigrew and Richard Whipp, (1991) *Managing for Competitive Success*, pp 104–137, Blackwell, Oxford.

Ch. 2, Charles C. Snow, Raymond E. Miles and Henry J. Coleman Jrn., (1992) Managing 21st Century Organizations. Reprinted by permission of publisher, from *Organizational Dynamics*, Winter © 1992. American Management Association, New York. All rights reserved.

Ch. 3, Sue Dopson and Rosemary Stewart, (1990) What is Happening to Middle Management? *British Journal of Management*, Vol 1 pp 3–16 © 1990 by John Wiley and Sons Limited. Reproduced by permission of John Wiley and Sons Limited.

Ch. 4, Russell L. Ackoff, The art and science of mess management, *Interfaces,* Vol 11, no 1, pp 20–26 © 1981, The Institute of Management Sciences.

Ch. 5, Gerry Johnson, (1988) Processes of Managing Strategic Change, *Management Research News*, Vol 11, No 4/5 pp 43–46. Reprinted by permission of Barmarick Publications.

Ch. 6, James Brian Quinn (1980), Managing Strategic Change, *Sloan Management Review*, Vol. 21, no. 4, pp 3–20. Copyright © 1980 by the Sloan Management Review Association. All rights reserved.

Ch. 7, David A. Nadler (1980) Concepts for the Management of Organizational Change, from Michael L. Tushman and William L. Moore (eds) *Readings in the Management of Innovation.* Copyright © 1988 by Ballinger Publishing Company. Reprinted by permission of Harper-Collins Publishers Inc.

Ch. 8, Excerpts from Why Change Programs don't produce change by Michael Beer, Russell A. Eisenstat and Bert Spector (1990) *Harvard Business Review*.

Nov/Dec pp. 158–166. Copyright © 1990 by the President and Fellows of Harvard College, all rights reserved.

Ch. 9, Derek Pugh, (1978) Understanding and Managing Organisation Change, *London Business School Journal*, Vol. 3, no. 2, pp 29–34.

Ch. 10, David Coghlan (1988), In Defence of Process Consultation, *Leadership and Organisation and Development Journal*, Vol 9, no, 2, pp 27–31.

Ch. 11, Excerpts from Dorothy Leonard-Barton and William A. Kraus (1985) Implementing New Technology, *Harvard Business Review* Nov/Dec. Copyright © 1985 by the President and Fellows of Harvard College; all rights reserved.

Ch. 12, Bill Mayon-White (1990) Problem-solving in small groups: team members as agents of change, from Colin Eden and Jim Radford (eds) *Tackling Strategic Problems – The role of group decision support* pp 78–89, © (1990) Sage Publications Ltd.

Ch. 13, Arthur A. Owen (1982), How to Implement Strategy, *Management Today,* July, pp 51–53.

Ch. 14, Colin Price and Eamonn Murphy (1987), Organizational Development in British Telecom, *Training and Development*, July, pp 45–48.

Ch. 15, Leonard D. Goodstein and W. Warner Burke (1991), Creating Successful Organization Change, (1991). Reprinted by permission of publisher from *Organizational Dynamics,* Spring © 1991, American Management Association, New York. All rights reserved.

Ch. 16, Paul Iles and Randhir Auluck (1990), Team Building, Inter-Agency Team Development and Social Work Practice, *British Journal of Social Work*, Vol 20, No 2 pp 151–164 © 1990 British Association of Social Workers. Reprinted by permission of Oxford University Press.

Ch. 17, Graham Benjamin and Christopher Mabey, (1990), A Case of Organisation Transformation, *Management and Education Development*, Vol 21, Part 5 pp 327–34. This article was first published in *Management Education and Development.*

Ch. 18, G. Walsham (1992), Management Science and Organisational Change: a Framework for Analysis, *Omega International Journal of Management Science*, Vol 20 no. 1 pp 1–9, Pergamon Press Ltd, Oxford.

Ch. 19, Excerpts from Jeffrey Pfeffer, Understanding power in organizations, in *Managing with Power* (1992). Harvard Business School Press, Boston. Copyright © 1992 by the President and Fellows of Harvard College; all rights reserved.

Ch. 20, Nigel Nicholson, Organizational Change, from *Arbeits- und organisations-psychologie, Internationales Handbuch in Schlüsselbegrissen.* Psychologie Verlags Union, Munich. First published in English in this volume. © 1992 Nigel Nicholson.

Ch. 21, Gareth Morgan (1986) Organizations as Political Systems, from *Images of Organization*, pp 185–194, reprinted by permission of Sage Publications Inc.

Ch. 22, Peter Marris (1974), The Management of Change, from *Loss and Change* Routledge, London pp 147–159.

PREFACE
TO THE SECOND EDITION

Preparing a second edition of any volume is a task which is usually deferred indefinitely; however the Open University policy of updating its courses on a regular basis ensures that its texts remain fresh and relevant. In the six years which have passed since the first edition was published in 1986, this collection of readings has found a market beyond its intended Open University student readership. MBA and DMS students in the conventional universities appear to have welcomed the easy access to readings on change which this volume provides. The topic itself has grown in importance as organizations in both the public and private sectors struggled to cope with change. During the 1980s the principal challenges were privatization on the one hand and growth on the other. More recently, the deep economic recession in the UK has switched the pressures for change to those of downsizing, cost control, and survival.

The selection of papers in this new edition reflects all of these factors, with the needs of the Open Business School student being given top priority. In this edition, we have dropped some of the company specific studies which, although topical in 1986, had become dated and, in their place, included new material which will, we hope, prove to be more enduring. Another challenge which we addressed as editors was that of restructuring the readings to reflect the dominant strands of the distance learning course, of which this volume is a key part, and to echo some of the main bodies of work in this field. Change is a topic which straddles and encompasses the conventional boundaries between academic disciplines and the functional divisions within organizations. Change is thus truly an interdisciplinary topic, which is reflected in the selection of papers for this volume. In this edition we have included material from authors working on strategy, on organizational development, on systems theory, and in mainstream management, each presenting perspectives on change which reflect the biases and interests of the different groups. The student of management, and of change in particular, needs to be aware of these biases and to ensure that she/he takes care to filter these influences. In this new edition we have tried to bring together a balanced selection and to group the papers appropriately. Inevitably, our selection and structure will not suit all readers, but the structure does echo and reflect the organization of the distance learning texts which this volume accompanies. Some 10,000 students of management have worked their way through the original course and their views and those of the course tutors are reflected in the 'old favourites' which survived our review exercise. These papers seem to have found a place as classics on our topic.

The choices are personal and eclectic, but bring out views on change which are not sufficiently strongly argued in much of the mainstream literature. Thus, both in this selection and in the body of the course, we are arguing for a move away from the dominant theme of prescriptive approaches, and instead argue for a greater awareness of the importance and subtlety of process, people and teams in change settings. All too frequently, rigid plans and carefully crafted strategies have been discredited, destroyed and left spinning in the wake of the continuous, rapid and unrelenting changes which have characterized organizational life during the turn of the decade. Today's manager requires a range of skills, but none more so than the ability to sense how best to plan and manage change under a range of different circumstances.

This collection has been assembled to give such a manager ready access to a rich vein of contemporary change-management literature. We recognize that some readers will be the reluctant recipients rather than the enthused arbiters of change initiatives. Some will be planning change at a strategic level, but many will be wrestling with the frustration of implementing change at ground floor level. Some will be preoccupied with the task of technically complex change interventions, but most will also be immersed in the turbulent process of introducing changes and making them stick. For some, the focus will be their whole organization, for others it will be their immediate team. Hopefully, all will find something of relevance here from each section of the book.

Change has been a theme surrounding the team responsible for the original course which was first presented in 1987. Since then, two of the principal authors have left The Open University – Bill Mayon-White for the International Ecotechnology Research Centre at the Cranfield Institute of Technology, and Lewis Watson for the Information Systems Group at the Shrivenham Campus of the Cranfield Institute of Technology. Meanwhile, the Open Business School itself has grown rapidly, to become one of Europe's leading providers of management education. The stewardship of the Diploma level course, Planning and Managing Change, has passed to Christopher Mabey, recruited to the School of Management in 1989 from Rank Xerox, where he was responsible for management development in the UK. The course, in fact, has stood the test of time well and the revision now being prepared embraces much of the original philosophy and approach. Hence, it has been possible for us to forge an alliance of the old and the new in editing this volume and working together on the revised course. It will take its place within the Open Business School family of courses which now cover the full range of Certificate, Diploma and Master of Business Administration.

Also indicative of the rapidly changing environment is the School's collaboration with providers of management education in Eastern Europe. For example, this reader and the accompanying course have been translated into Hungarian by our colleagues Istvan Kiss and Imre Kornyei at Eurocontact in Budapest.

Formal acknowledgements to the original authors and copyright holders are given elsewhere, but as editors we are grateful to all of these for co-operation with us over the necessary editing which we have introduced, and to Marie Stanley for her care in smoothing the passage of this revision.

Christopher Mabey, Bill Mayon-White
Milton Keynes and London

September, 1992

PART 1:

Imperative of Change

PART 1:
IMPERATIVE OF CHANGE

The four papers in this, the first section, set out to explore some of the issues which generate and drive change and make change such a challenge for managers everywhere. They range from the chapter from Pettigrew and Whipp's longitudinal study of change in large organizations, through to Snow's work with his colleagues, where we find an examination of the drivers which will structure organizations over the coming decade and into the next century. These set up the economic and other external factors which are, by definition, outwith the control of managers. The second pair of papers look at what is going on inside today's companies and government agencies, with the study by Dopson and Stewart examining the 'delayering' phenomenon and the role of the middle manager, contrasted with the classic Ackoff paper on 'mess management' and problem solving in organizational settings.

Snow, Miles and Coleman describe the features and introduce examples of 'network organizations'. They suggest that these flat structures, with a federal structure of interconnected groups sharing common goals for a range of products and services, are appealing for the sense of ownership, creativity and local control which such arrangements engender. Their arguments are extended in the Pettigrew and Whipp material and in the Dopson and Stewart article.

The research programme at the University of Warwick, led by Andrew Pettigrew, has made a substantial contribution to UK work on change. The discussion included here is built on the assertion that much competitive success derives from the way in which firms manage change and in the attention they pay to changes in the business environment. Pettigrew and Whipp challenge the claim that there are any universal 'laws' of change, and instead offer a useful set of interrelated factors which, they argue, must all be considered and 'managed' during periods of change.

The Dopson and Stewart paper moves on to examine what is happening inside companies and institutions. They weigh up the evidence for and against the contribution of middle managers at a time when information technology continues to penetrate deeper into every corner of institutional life. Their own research is reported and compared to other findings, with the reassuring conclusion that middle managers have and will continue to have a key role as agents of change.

Ackoff writes both as an academic and as a successful consultant to many international organizations. His work in systems and cybernetics spans a broad area. He has thus had a profound influence on the field of organizational problem solving and his short essay brings into focus the questions of judgement and choice in change.

1

UNDERSTANDING THE ENVIRONMENT

Andrew Pettigrew and Richard Whipp

The major conclusion to be drawn from examining competition among the firms in the four sectors of automobile manufacture, book publishing, merchant banking and life assurance is that:

- there is an observable difference in the way the higher performing firms manage change from their lesser performing counterparts, and
- a pattern emerges, across the four sectors, from the actions taken by the higher performing organizations.

That pattern is represented in the five interrelated aspects of managing strategic and operational change shown in Figure 1.

Clearly these five factors require definition and elaboration. The task of this chapter therefore is to explore what the factors mean, how they are constituted and their relevance to the firms across the sectors concerned.

What will become clear is that each factor contains two main components:

1. the primary conditioning features which logically have to exist before
2. the secondary actions and mechanisms can have any meaningful effect.

Figure 2 provides a summary of the characteristics of each factor.

THE FIVE CENTRAL FACTORS FOR MANAGING CHANGE

Environmental assessment

The process of competition often begins from the understanding a firm develops of its environment. This research shows that it is not enough for firms to regard judgements of their external competitive world as only a technical procedure. On the contrary, the requirement is for organizations to

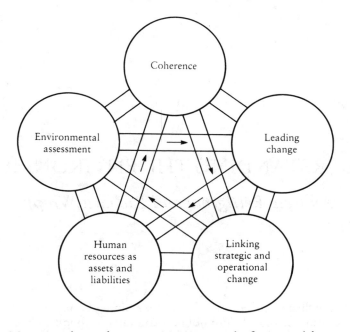

Figure 1 Managing change for competitive success: the five central factors

become open learning systems. In other words, the assessment of the competitive environment cannot be the responsibility of a specialist function. Nor does it happen through neat, separate acts. Strategy creation tends to emerge from the way a company, at all levels, processes information about its environment.

Leading change

The main conclusion with regard to leading change is that there are no universal rules. The opposite is true. Leadership is acutely sensitive to context. The choosing of a leader clearly is affected by those who make the choice and the circumstances in which they do so. The problems faced by the incoming leader are derived from the circumstances which the leader inherits. The areas of manoeuvre available to the new leader in deciding what to change and how to go about it are bounded by the environment within and outside the firm.

The critical leadership tasks in managing change are more incremental and often less spectacular than the prevailing business press images. Leading change involves linking action by people at all levels of the business. The primary conditioning features are critical. Early and bold actions can be counter-productive. More promising is the construction of a climate for change while at the same time laying out new directions, but prior to precise action being taken.

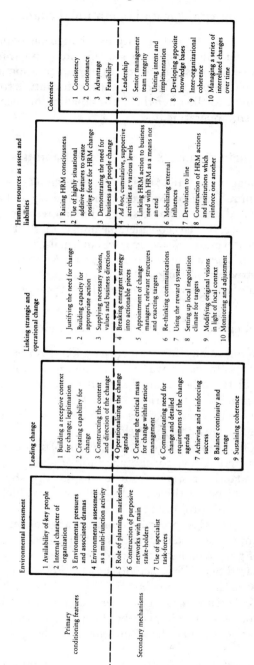

Figure 2 Managing change for competitive success: characteristics of the five central factors

Linking strategic and operational change

The process of linking strategic and operational change has both an intentional and emergent character. Intentions are implemented and transformed over time. The cumulative effect of separate acts of implementation may be immensely powerful. This may even supply a new context for future strategic choices. Strategies often amount to the after-the-event labelling of such unpredictable sequences of 'successful' operational acts.

Human resources as assets and liabilities

Human resource management (HRM) relates to the total set of knowledge, skills and attitudes that firms need to compete. The differing ability of the firms studied to recognize and carry out a version of human resource management is apparent. As we shall see, this has considerable impact on their relative competitive performance. However, the disparity is less unusual when one considers the time required to create such a fragile capacity. An HRM approach is not amenable to instant construction. A longer-term learning process is involved which requires the creation of successive positive spirals of development.

Coherence in the management of change

This factor in managing change for competitive success is the most complex of the five central factors. In many ways the requirements for coherence arise from the demands of the other four. As in all the other central factors the crucial need is in ensuring that the primary conditioning features are reinforced by a complementary set of mechanisms. It is worthwhile for this factor to consider these subsidiary features more closely.

The conditioning features relate to the formation of strategy. A given strategy should be characterized by: consistency (not present inconsistent goals); consonance (by an adaptive response to its environment); advantage (provide for the maintenance of competitive advantage); and feasibility (the strategy must not create unsolvable problems).

In order for these features to prevail requires a range of secondary, complementary management action to reinforce them. As Figure 2 indicates, there has to be a coherence of purpose among the senior management, even though individual emphases may differ. HRM activity has to produce a knowledge base which complements the strategic conditioning features. Similarly there must be interorganizational coherence across customers, suppliers, distributors and collaborators. The scope of activity implied by the preceding four factors puts the ability to manage a series of interrelated and emergent changes at a premium.

The subsequent chapters will demonstrate how the significance of the twin set of subsidiary features within each factor lies in their cumulative impact over time. The conditioning features and the secondary mechanisms derive their potency from not only complementarity but the way they interlock and their being applied in conjunction, with sustained effort and often repeated application. One of the central characteristics of the firms under study, therefore, is that the management of strategic and operational change for competitive success is an uncertain and emergent process. Managing that process places heavy requirements on the ability of companies to adapt in all five areas. Above all it calls into question a firm's ability to create and sustain a collection of 'intangible assets': difficult for the outsider to uncover but essential to the capacity to manage strategic change and competition.

ENVIRONMENTAL ASSESSMENT

The undoubted turbulence of the Western economies in the 1970s and 1980s has confirmed the importance of the way a firm understands its environment. Unfortunately for managers the volatile nature of that environment has made its assessment more difficult. And of course just when they were most needed, academic experts have fallen out over the optimum means of comprehending either the firm's environment or the way it might change.

Economic and business commentators, and in particular those associated with the computing and micro-electronics areas, are right to highlight the unique challenges posed by information technology. The ramifications of the use of the microchip are far-reaching and their collective impact has been rightly dubbed revolutionary. Computer-based, information technology looks set to recast the character of society in much the same way as the technologies associated with the agricultural and industrial transformations of previous centuries. Although computer technology has taken virtually the whole twentieth century to develop, its frightening potential became fully apparent during the 1980s.

The use of computer hardware and software has suggested truly epoch-making changes which have already altered the nature of industries and shifted the balance of whole economies. Yet beneath such over-arching movements at the level of society a formidable array of more specific problems have arisen from the baser rumblings of the business cycle, international trading relations or even consumers. There are truly novel aspects to the character of the environment which business has faced in the 1970s and 1980s. The machinations of politicians and their effects on industry and commerce have always been with us, yet the breaking of the post-war consensus in the 1980s is manifestly clear. In the economics sphere the conjunction of inflation and recession from the early 1970s was a phenomenon unknown to Keynesians and neo-liberals alike; it was even more baffling to those who had the responsibility of managing a business.

Beside the specific movements within sectors, all industries and services have experienced major dislocations. The traditional constellation of assumptions of industry boundaries, market mechanisms or commercial relations based on the post-war replacement demand or 1960s growth, have been shattered. In their place have appeared a new, less predictable firmament. This now includes: the management buy-out; the 'junk bond' financed acquisition used by the corporate raiders who stalk underperforming assets; Japanese producers with their own definitions of best practice confirmed by their market shares in Western countries; the penetration of marketing into organizations previously unconcerned with such instruments; and not least the unpredictable nature of international currencies and exchange rates.

Yet if this constellation has altered so dramatically, how are companies to produce accurate celestial maps? What devices are appropriate to assessing the movement of the commercial heavens? Above all, can one suggest means of strategic navigation which go beyond the sextant and the astrolabe? The first step to providing an answer is by inspecting the existing approaches to environmental assessment.

Industrial organization

The industrial organization (IO) economists have staked a strong claim to expert status in understanding a firm's environment. There now exist well-developed means of identifying competitive structures. These centre on the Porterian industry model, life cycle approaches and strategic group analysis (Porter 1980).

The hallmark of Porter is the way he addresses not only the 'established combatants in a particular industry', but also the potential entrants or substitutes and the bargaining force of buyers and suppliers. The strategist at company level can use the model to assess, for example, the threat of competition from outside the industry. This would include consideration of economies of scale, capital requirements, access to distribution channels, product differentiation, cost advantages derived from experience.

The model can be readily applied to the economic environment of the four sectors under study. In the car industry the enormous capital requirements of developing totally new models (around £2 billion in the late 1980s) is enough to exclude the new entrants to the ranks of the volume producers. In book publishing, desk top publishing systems have enabled the proliferation of small scale venture (10,000 were registered in 1989/90), yet their reliance on personal distribution severely limits their impact.

A firm can also locate itself within its environment according to the stage of its industry life cycle. Conditions will vary widely therefore between the early infant phase (with many entrants and products ill-defined) and maturity, with well-established products, saturated marketers and immense pressure on margins and market share.

Strategic group analysis has been developed in order to be more precise about the pattern of competitive relations in the view of the difficulty of defining the boundaries and participants of given industries. The approach has been developed in view of the upheavals of the 1970s and 1980s in particular. Applying a simple differentiation between domestic and international producers, or specialist and diversified, allows a more fine-grain map of the competitive environment to emerge. In merchant banking these criteria quickly distinguish those houses such as Warburg who attempt to offer a complete range of services both in the UK and abroad, versus those specializing in, say, corporate finance only within the City of London. Other means of creating such maps include the differences between organizations in size, pricing, ownership, technological leadership and product diversity.

It would be misleading to suggest that the powerful techniques of environmental assessment which have been developed within the IO tradition see the world through an entirely rational lens. Porter's work is often reconstructed around its central elements and simplifying themes – such as the value chain or generic strategies. Yet on closer inspection his work points to the complexities of understanding the environment and the range of possible action. As he stressed in 1987 (Porter 1987), in contrast to the Boston Consulting Group's emphasis on scale and market share leadership, 'there is an infinite number of possible strategies even within the same industry.' He also recognizes in passing how 'no tool can remove the need for creativity in selecting the right strategy. Great companies don't imitate competitors, they act differently . . . we do need to discover how the process of creativity takes place.'

Others who operate mainly within the bounds of IO and neo-classical economics have also come to recognize the limitations of the tools of their craft. Thomas and McGee (1985) in their paper 'Making sense of complex industries' (centred on the reprographics industry) acknowledge the key influence of the changes in industry and market composition in the long term. They highlight the importance of when and how firms enter an industry and the significance this may have subsequently for the way managers in those firms understand their environment. The natural logic of the industry life cycle advocates has shown them the immense difficulties of even conceiving of a firm's environment at certain points. The myriad technological possibilities contained within the period of infancy within a single industry has led them to place greater emphasis on the more subjective judgements of entrepeneurs (see, for example, Wheelwright 1987).

Planning

The first cousins of the industrial economists are the professional business planners. Their rise to prominence, notably in the USA, in the post-war years was founded on the conviction that the environment was amenable to rational observation and reasonably accurate forecasting. Business plans could be formulated accordingly. Company structures could be adjusted to complement those plans. The success of giant US corporations in Western mass markets down to the 1970s confirmed the view as well as providing a role model for some of the larger European companies (Marginson 1985).

The growth in the extent and depth of planning techniques over the post-war decades was prodigious. Attempts to categorize them agree on the breadth of the field. Pearce and Robinson (1985) distinguish between what they call the 'operating environment', specific to a firm, and the 'remote environment', which is common to most firms. The remote environment refers to national economic variables, social developments, technology, political and legal influences. It is interesting that they regard the marketing function as best-suited to collect and analyse data relating to the operating environment (made up of customers, markets, competitors and industries). A rather different picture will emerge from the evidence of our research companies below.

The major responsibility of the planner has been to link the result of this appraisal of the external environment with the internal abilities of the organization. The most well-known method for supplying that connection is through SWOT analysis. This requires, first, the identification and classification of opportunities and threats and second, the assessment of their relevance to the internal abilities (strengths and weaknesses) of the firm. The means of classifying and linking the two domains has become increasingly elaborate (for an overview see Greenley 1989). The rising popularity of marketing techniques – directed at exploiting the potential of both internal and external market relations – in the UK during the 1980s has added to the planners' SWOT armoury.

Indeed, the armoury is by now crammed full. If one takes the example of forecasting techniques applied to the environment the point is forcibly made. Higgins (1980) uses a three-fold classification embracing economic (e.g. regression analysis), technological (e.g. cross-impact analysis) and social and political (e.g. value profiles) forecasting techniques. His inventory runs to 26 major methods. Some of the methods by now have long pedigrees. Among the most prominent are the Delphi method and scenario analysis (Zenter 1982). The application of computer memory and processing power has added a new dimension to such techniques.

Just as some of the IO economists have found their weapons are not up to the onslaught presented by the 1980s, so this uncertainty has affected the planners. The major problem was that, in spite of this arsenal of forecasting and planning techniques, large parts of Western industry failed badly in the face of the barrage of environmental shifts in the 1980s (Zan 1987). The essential problem was two-fold. Many of the planning techniques assumed that they could (1) mount objective observations of the environment, and (2) plan accordingly.

It is noticeable that the more successful organizations have been much more self-critical of their planning. Above all they questioned its supposed objectivity. Shell International provides an excellent example. The group has made a series of alterations: from its 'comprehensive financial planning system' adopted in 1965, to its pioneering introduction of scenario planning in 1971, through to its total revamp of the system around internal 'strategy consultancy' in the 1980s. Perhaps the essence of their approach has been their refusal to rely on the techniques to supply adequate environmental assessment and planning. Shell instead has devoted enormous energy to discovering how their managers at all levels understand their environment, how that knowledge can be generalized and a 'common understanding' generated as the foundation for action.

Industry, culture and perception

Somewhat distant from the front line commercial battle of the planners, other analysts have developed a different way of understanding the environment. It does not constitute a school of thought. What unites these commentators is their willingness to tackle the imperfect and subjective way that managers perceive their environment.

One of the strongest brands of this thinking centres on the notion of industry culture. If an industry is a collective categorization of firms, then it is entirely logical for certain shared beliefs to emerge. Gregory (1982) shows how such a grid of values informed business relations in the development of the English woollen industry. Others have identified the changing pattern of these shared assumptions across the stages of sector life cycles (Shearman and Burrell 1987; Smith, Whipp and Willmott 1988; Huff 1982).

Researchers trying to explain the governance of the US economy have reached similar conclusions. They observe how governance is maintained via a range of mechanisms: markers, hierarchies, 'clan' and 'community' groupings. It appears that 'each of these mechanisms . . . operates according to different logics', where 'shared norms among different actors . . . are alternative mechanisms to markets and hierarchies for governing behaviour'. They conclude that 'non-market forces are far more important in the governance of the American economy than is usually recognised' (Hollingsworth and Lindberg 1985). Firms seldom collect 'clean' data on the environment; it has to be perceived, constructed. How that is done will be affected by the values of those concerned and the pre-existing norms which structures their thought.

Sound examples appear in the work of scholars from different countries. In the USA, Scott-Morton (1986) demonstrates the powerful impact of chief executives' world views on the way a company approaches, engages with and decodes information from its environment. Melin's (1985) study of the Scandinavian television industry in the 1970s and 1980s is equally instructive. The crisis in the industry in the 1970s arose from the demand for colour TV reaching saturation point, rapid changes in product and production technology, and the combination of over-capacity plus new entrants with unique advantages. Melin demonstrates that who was responsible for the unusual version of the environment held by the ailing Tandberg or Luxor companies was vital:

> The power structure, in both Luxor and Tandbergs, was centralised. In this autocratic milieu there was only one person who had the general view of the firm's activities and who monopolised the interpretation of the structural freedom of action for the firm. (Melin, 1985)

Understanding the environment: action and interpretation

The results of our research suggest that the way firms comprehend their environment, including the relevant bases of competition, cannot be encapsulated solely by the structures of the IO economists nor by reference to the tools of the planners alone. In order to appreciate how an organization reaches an understanding of its environment requires consideration of four related aspects:

1. how the process of understanding and assessment combines analysis, judgement and action
2. that the process is shaped jointly by the dominant logics of an industry and the internal features of the firm
3. recognition that environmental assessment occurs across the whole organization
4. above all, analysis, judgement and action seldom reflect the well-ordered progressions of the traditional planning manuals. The problems of recognition, acceptance and contest are legion.

The first point to appreciate about the way a firm assesses its environment is that it does not occur through a single act or at a given point. Instead it arises from a sequence of actions through time (cf. Gilbert and Strebel 1988: 79; Pettigrew 1985). That process is open to manifold influences. No matter how sophisticated the instruments which a firm uses, they have to be applied by someone. By themselves the techniques can do little. What matters is who uses them and how they are used. Computer networks in some sectors (e.g. travel, retailing – see Earl and Runge 1987) now supply unprecedented amounts of information: they do not tell the recipients what to do with it (Whipp, Pettigrew and Sparrow 1989).

The second key feature of the process of environmental assessment is its lack of innocence or isolation. Even in pure mathematics it is now recognized that the supposedly scientific laws and protocols of proof are not immune from the contexts in which they are produced. In management the link is even stronger. It is not simply that those who assess the firm's environment are influenced to a greater or lesser degree by their 'backgrounds' or personal values. This implies that there exists, external to the firm, an absolute, objective environment which awaits inspection. The problem is much deeper.

The individual or collective beliefs of managers fundamentally affect the way they conceive of the environment in the first place (Whipp 1984). Such beliefs are equally vital to the way they collect and evaluate what they see as relevant data (Grinyer and Spender 1979). By the very act of assessment and their subsequent behaviour, managers are in part creating their own environment. The major practical issue is that firms differ in the extent to which they recognize both the subjectivity of their understanding of their environment and the consequences of their actions.

In all of the organizations studied, the very attempt by someone to identify the critical components of the firm's competitive context implied judgement and choice between alternatives. Such choices were almost by definition controversial: they conflicted with the world view of certain functions or professional groups. The process of assessment, therefore, cannot be described simply as a technical exercise. In every case, as the process unfolded so it was open to influence. Acts of apparently clinical quantitative judgement (over the future size of the US book market, for example) triggered immense activity within firms; this concerned not only the accuracy of the forecasts but the implications for future resource allocation and power relations. Indeed it is the emphasis on the mode of analysis and the consequent neglect of its political significance which undermines the work of many planners.

The third and arguably the most evident common characteristic of the firms studied is that environmental assessment occurs across the organization, come what may. Each function of an organization engages with some aspect of its environment through its routine activities; distribution through customers or manufacturing with suppliers for example. A critical difference between firms is the extent to which this is realized, built upon and exploited. In other words, to assume that a single specialist planning or marketing function can by itself supply an adequate interpretation of a firm's environment is highly dangerous. In the case of Jaguar the realization was immensely valuable. Its whole turn-around rested on a new-found ability. To use the intelligence not only from its new product planning group from 1982 but also to combine it with the piercing insights which already existed elsewhere in the company. These included the views on product competition and demand from the service engineers or the movements in the industry from the purchasing department's relationships with their suppliers.

Evidence from other industries supports the point. A survey by Deloittes showed that there was no positive correlation between the performance of firms and whether they had a formal planning function (*The Economist* 1989). It is interesting also that major companies such as General Electric and IBM in the USA have drastically reduced their central planning or marketing functions in the last year and redistributed the staff to business unit level (Lorenz 1988). Conversely, the ability to absorb, process and act upon data from the environment systematically, at all levels of the firm, has of course been demonstrated in the most chilling fashion by certain Japanese companies such as Honda, Cannon or Fujitsu in the 1980s (Hamel and Prahalad 1989).

On the evidence of the firms we have studied, the process of environmental assessment concerns much more than just forecasting or the application of discrete planning techniques. It is an uncertain process, deeply conditioned by the industrial and organizational contexts from which it emerges, and can potentially relate to many parts of an organization. In order for this sort of process to work management has to take appropriate action. As Romme (1989) puts it, there is the problem of not only environmental 'sensing', but also of 'sense-making'. Sensing of a key threat may come from an individual or department. Sense-making is broader and requires a more collective impact. The threat has to be presented so that it makes sense to the company as a whole.

There are a number of ways in which sense-making can be achieved. The effect of task forces or specialist groups at J.C. Penney or Honeywell in the early 1980s was particularly strong (Kanter 1983). The keynote was that they were drawn deliberately from a variety of fields. No single function was given disproportionate power to define the focus of attention. Yet gaining acceptance of such threats or key changes in the environment may be especially difficult. This is particularly true where in-house recipe knowledge cannot decode new market information.

Some management have manufactured a drama or created a quasi-crisis to overcome such obstacles. Komatsu, for example, constructed a budget which deliberately created the problem of an overvalued yen (Hamel and Prahalad 1989: 67). Jaguar constructed a 'black museum' showing poor product quality to break open the complacency of its staff. There is a major need not only to open up but to update the cognitive maps of staff. Management can then monitor the extent to which the firm is (1) sensitive to environmental signals, but (2) can collectively make sense of those signals and act upon them. The huge upheaval in the 1980s caused by changes in demand and available technology has forced these issues to the fore in manufacturing. It is fitting then for a book (Hayes, Wheelwright & Clark 1988) which attempts to summarize these requirements in the production area alone to be entitled *Dynamic Manufacturing*. What is more interesting is the choice of sub-title: *Creating the Learning Organization*.

LIFE ASSURANCE

Evidence from the life assurance sector confirms the importance of the ability to mobilize new mechanisms of environmental assessment. At the same time Prudential drives home the point that such mechanisms can be diluted if attention is not paid to the deeper conditioning features already in existence.

The continued profitability of the Prudential across market cycles since the Second World War meant that the management had become disinclined to embrace major changes by the 1960s. The concern borne of the innately conservative actuarial mentality was with not losing the Prudential's leading position. At an operational level, the dual responsibility of field staff to generate business and administer premium collection further inhibited change.

None the less what distinguishes Prudential was the way critical aspects of its internal character were changed during the 1970s. These alterations enabled the Prudential to take a wholly different view of its sector's changing bases of competition, and in so doing lay the foundations for the competitive posture required in the 1980s.

The alterations in senior management, the creation of the Prudential corporation and the use of the investment management function to alert the Prudential to wider environmental changes in the 1970s went hand in hand. The appointment of Geoffrey Haslam as the first non-actuary to be general manager was a considerable breakthrough (sustained by the managerial approach of Brian Corby into the 1980s). He did not see the competitive relations by the conventional view of the actuarial risks involved. Quite the reverse: his work in the new group pensions business had provided him with an understanding of the possibilities of diversification. At the same time, Haslam's period in the organization and methods department convinced him that the Prudential needed to clarify its strategic planning as the activities of the Prudential expanded.

The way in which these alterations were mutually reinforcing is perfectly illustrated by the creation of the 'Prudential Corporation' in 1978. Incorporation meant a financial restructuring which gave Prudential access to both the debt and equity market for financing, the creation of a top level of management which could now divorce itself from the previous heavy operational responsibilities, and not least the opportunity to set up clear signals in-house and to the environment. As one executive concerned put it, 'creating the corporation was a more dramatic gesture to make people realize we were actually making changes, and to ram it home that this is the way we are going to manage' (interview).

Such changes, then, allowed the Prudential to consider the environment in different ways and to innovate accordingly. The role of investment management (not one of Prudential's traditional strengths) is a clear example of the way the new corporation was now opened up to what hitherto had been considered unthinkable. In the 1960s investment management had been traditionally kept separate from the rest of the organization. By the late 1970s it was apparent to the fund managers that investment performance was now growing as a measure of the firm's ability to attract funds in the sector. The previous restrictions on fund managers' decision making, with board members' agreement needed, were jettisoned. An aggressive stance was adopted with relevant performance data and a market rate salaries structure in order to retain a vital resource.

The success of the investment management operation in the 1980s is instructive. Above all it is indicative of the way the Prudential deployed a set of major internal restructurings which then released the full potential of more specialist mechanisms for understanding an environment which then became increasingly turbulent.

CONCLUSION

The starting point in the process of competition often derives from the understanding a firm develops of its environment. In general terms the research shows that it is insufficient for companies to regard the creation of knowledge and judgements of their external competitive world as simply a technique exercise. Rather the need is for organizations to become open learning systems. In other words, the assessment of the competitive environment does not remain the preserve of a single function nor the sole responsibility of one senior manager. Nor does it occur via isolated acts. Instead strategy creation is seen as emerging from the way a company, at various levels, acquires, interprets and processes information about its environment.

There are four conditioning features which help to explain the degree of openness of an organization to its environment and its receptiveness to the changes in its environment. These are:

1. the extent to which there are key actors within the firm who are prepared to champion assessment techniques which increase the openness of the organization
2. the structural and cultural characteristics of the company
3. the extent to which environmental pressures are recognized and their associated dramas develop, and

4. the degree to which assessment occurs as a multi-function activity which is not pursued as an end in itself but which is then linked to the central operation of the business.

However, even if this set of primary conditioning features existed within an enterprise then that would be no guarantee of the survival of its environmental assessment capacity. In order for it to endure, a set of secondary actions are required in order to stabilize and impel the assessment capacity forward. Incorporation of those responsible for planning and marketing is critical, as is the availability of purposive networks which link the firm with key stakeholders and interest groups. The use of specialist task forces or teams, beside their technical relevance, can often reinforce the importance attributed to the assessment process, especially if they are drawn from across functions.

At the start of this chapter we quoted Michael Porter's (1987) imperative 'to discover how the process of creativity takes place' in companies in order to understand the strategies they choose. The evidence from the sector considered here suggests that how management combines the range of possible activities within the process of environmental assessment accounts for a substantial part of the answer.

The material presented on the life assurance sector underlined the importance of mobilizing new mechanisms of environmental assessment, especially given their lack of development in that sector and elsewhere in the UK. However, Prudential confirms the point that even such sophisticated mechanisms can be rendered virtually useless if deeper conditioning features based on collective learning are ignored. The use of such learning ensures that the full implications of the firm's view of its environment are captured, understood and retained at all levels. This learning can then inform (1) subsequent actions over the long term, and (2) the way in which future shifts in the environment are approached. A large part of the task in leading change therefore becomes clear. Leaders have the responsibility not merely to ensure that the environment is understood; the vital need is to ensure that the organization can learn and act on such analysis over time.

REFERENCES

Earl, M. and Runge, D. (1987) Using telecommunications-based information systems for competitive advantage. Templeton College research paper 87/1.

The Economist (1989) The planned and the damned. 18 February, 80.

Gilbert, X. and Strebel, P. (1988) Developing competitive advantage. In: J.B. Quinn, H. Mintzberg and R.M. James (eds), *The Strategy Process: Concepts, Contexts and Cases*, Englewood Cliffs, NJ: Prentice Hall, 70–9.

Greenley, G. (1989) *Strategic Management.* Hemel Hempstead: Prentice-Hall.

Gregory, D. (1982) *Regional Transformation and Industrial Revolution.* London: Heinemann.

Grinyer, P. and Spender, J-C. (1979) *Turnaround: Managerial Recipes for Strategic Success.* London: Associated Business Press.

Hamel, G. and Prahalad, C.K. (1989) Strategic intent. *Harvard Business Review*, May/June, 63–76.

Hayes, R., Wheelwright, S. and Clark, K. (1988) *Dynamic Manufacturing: Creating the Learning Organization*. New York: Free Press.

Higgins, J. (1980) *Strategic and Operational Planning Systems*. London: Prentice-Hall.

Hollingsworth, J.R. and Lindberg, L. (1985) The governance of the American economy: the role of markets, clans, hierarchies and associate behaviour. IMM, Wissenschaftszentrum Berlin.

Huff, A. forthcoming: Mapping strategic thought. In A. Huff (ed.), *Mapping Strategic Thought*, Chichester: Wiley, chapter 1.

Kanter, R.M. (1983) *The Change Masters*. New York: Simon & Schuster.

Kanter, R.M. (1989) *When Giants Learn to Dance*. New York: Simon & Schuster.

Lorenz, C. (1988) Why strategy has been put in the hands of line managers. *Financial Times*, 18 May, 20.

Marginson, P. (1985) The multi-divisional firm and control over the work process. *International Journal of Industrial Organization*, 3, 37–56.

Melin, L. (1985) Strategies in managing turnaround. *Long Range Planning*, 18, 1, 80–6.

Pearce, J. and Robinson, R. (1985) *Strategic Management*, 2nd edn. Homewood, Illinois: Irwin.

Pettigrew, A.M. (1985) Examining change in the long-term context of culture and politics. In: J.M. Pennings (ed.), *Organizational Strategy and Changes*, San Francisco: Jossey-Bass, 269–318.

Porter, M. (1980) *Competitive Strategy*. New York: Free Press.

Porter, M. (1987) The man who put cash cows out to grass. *Financial Times*, 20 March, 18.

Romme, A.G. (1989) The dialects of closing and opening in strategy formation. Paper presented to the Workshop on Making History/Breaking History, European Institute for Advanced Studies in Management, Leuven, 28–9 September.

Scott-Morton, M. (1986) Strategy formulation methodologies. Sloan School, MIT, *Management in the 1990s* series.

Shearman, C. and Burrell, G. (1987) The structures of industrial development. *Journal of Management Studies*, 24, 4, July, 325–45.

Smith, C., Whipp, R. and Willmott, H. (1988) Case-study research: methodological breakthrough or ideological weapon. *Advances in Public Interest Accounting: A Research Annual*, New York: JAI Press, 95–120.

Thomas, H. and McGee, J. (1985) Making sense of complex industries. Mimeo, University of Illinois at Urbana-Champaign.

Wheelwright, S. (1987) Restoring competitiveness in US manufacturing. In D.J. Teece (ed.), *The Competitive Challenge: Strategies for Industrial Innovation and Renewal*, Cambridge, Mass.: Ballinger, 83–100.

Whipp, R. (1984) 'The art of good management': managerial control of work in the British pottery industry 1900–1925. *International Review of Social History*, XXIX, 3, 359–85.

Whipp, R., Pettigrew, A.M. and Sparrow, P. (1989) New technology, competition and the firm: a framework for research. *International Journal of Vehicle Design*, 10, 4, 453–69.

Zan, L. (1987) What's left for formal planning? *Economia Aziendale*, VI, 2, 187–204.

Zenter, R.D. (1982) Scenarios, past, present and future. *Long Range Planning*, 15, 3.

2

MANAGING 21st CENTURY NETWORK ORGANIZATIONS

Charles C. Snow, Raymond E. Miles and Henry J. Coleman, Jr.

What began, quietly, more than a decade ago, has become a revolution. In industry after industry, multilevel hierarchies have given way to clusters of business units coordinated by market mechanisms rather than by layers of middle-management planners and schedulers.

These market-guided entities are now commonly called 'network organizations,' and their displacement of centrally managed hierarchies has been relentless, though hardly painless – particularly to the million or so managers whose positions have been abolished. Our descriptions of emerging network structures in the late 1970s helped identify this organizational form. Since then, awareness and acceptance have spread rapidly throughout the business community, and recent authors have heralded the network as the organizational form of the future.

The widespread changeover is producing a new agenda for both managers and scholars. To this point, there is growing agreement about the basic characteristics of the network organization, the forces that have shaped it, and some of the arenas for which the network organization appears to be ideally suited, and in which it has achieved major success. What is much less clear, however, is how networks are designed and operated, and where their future applications lie. Most troublesome, perhaps, is the question of how the managers of tomorrow's network organizations should be selected and trained.

In this article, we first review the progress of the network form and the factors affecting its deployment across the developed and newly industrializing countries of the world. Next, we discuss the major varieties of the network organization, describing and illustrating three specific types of networks: stable, dynamic, and internal. Finally, we identify three managerial roles (architect, lead operator, and caretaker) critical to the success of every network, and we speculate on how the managers may be educated to carry out these roles.

NETWORK STRUCTURES – CAUSES AND EFFECTS

The large, vertically integrated companies that dominated the U.S. economy during the first three quarters of this century arose to serve a growing domestic market for efficiently produced goods. These companies then used their advantages of scale and experience to expand into overseas markets served by less efficient or war-damaged competitors.

Then, during the 1980s in particular, markets around the world changed dramatically, as did the technologies available to serve those markets. Today, competitive pressures demand both efficiency *and* effectiveness. Firms must adapt with increasing speed to market pressures and competitors' innovations, simultaneously controlling and even lowering product or service costs.

Confronted by these demands, the large enterprises designed for the business environment of the 1950s and 1960s – firms that typically sought scale economies through central planning and control mechanisms – understandably faltered. The declining effectiveness of traditionally organized firms produced a new business equation. Instead of advocating resource accumulation and control, this equation linked competitive success to doing fewer things better, with less. Specifically, managers who want their companies to be strong competitors in the 21st century are urged to:

- Search globally for opportunities and resources.
- Maximize returns on all the assets dedicated to a business – whether owned by the managers' firm or by other firms.
- Perform only those functions for which the company has, or can develop, expert skill.
- Outsource those activities that can be performed quicker, more effectively, or at lower cost, by others.

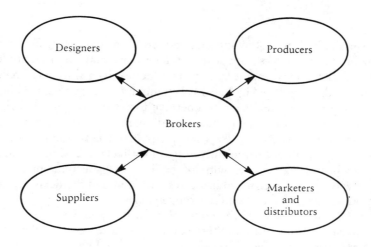

Figure 1 Network organization structure

Table 1 Organization responses to the new business environment

The new competitive reality	
Driving forces	**Interactive forces**
Globalization	Deregulation
Strong new payers at every stage of the value chain (upstream and downstream)	Legal and policy change produce uncertainty and increase competition
Competition has reduced all margins – no slack left in most economic systems	Public services are being privatized
	Changing workforce demographics
Technological change and technology transfer	Domestic workforce is becoming more mature, diverse, and less well trained and educated
Shorter product life cycles	Global workforce is becoming more mobile
Lower barriers to entry	
Economies of scope as well as scale	**Facilitating forces**
	CAD/CAM and other manufacturing advances
	Faster, lower cost communications and computer technologies
	More social and political freedom

Organizational imperatives	
Product and service demands	**Managerial requirements**
Focus on distinctive competence	Building smaller, better trained permanent workforces
Reduce costs and accelerate innovation	Develop and use links to part-time and temporary human resources
Hold only productive assets	Develop and use links to global technological resources
Reduce overall cycle time	

Not surprisingly, firms following these prescriptions frequently find themselves organizing into networks. One firm in the network may research and design a product, another may engineer and manufacture it, a third may handle distribution, and so on. (See Figure 1.) When numerous designers, producers, and distributors interact, they bring competitive forces to bear on each element of the product or service value chain, and market factors heavily influence resource-allocation decisions. By using a network structure, a firm can operate an ongoing business both efficiently and innovatively, focusing on those things it does well and contracting with other firms for the remaining resources. Alternatively, it can enter new businesses with minimal financial exposure and at an optimal size, given its unique competencies.

Table 1 summarizes both the competitive realities facing today's firms and the organizational imperatives these realities produce. The benefits of the network structure in meeting these imperatives, as well as some of the possible costs associated with networks, are discussed below.

Globalization and technological change

Globalization today is a compelling reality, with at least 70 to 85 percent of the U.S. economy feeling the impact of foreign competition. In growing strength and numbers, foreign competitors reduce profit margins on low-end goods to the barest minimum, and they innovate across high-end products and services at ever-increasing rates.

Moreover, foreign competitors are technologically sophisticated. Around the world, technology is changing at a faster rate than ever before. Perhaps more important, technological innovations are transferring from one industry to another and across international borders at increasing speed. Firms thus find it difficult to build barriers of either technology or location around their businesses.

As a response to increasing globalization and the ease of technology transfer, many U.S. firms are focusing on only those things they do especially well, outsourcing a growing roster of goods and services and ridding themselves of minimally productive assets. Such delayed companies are not only less costly to operate, they are also more agile. By limiting operations and performing them expertly, firms require less planning and coordination, and they can accelerate product and service innovations to keep pace with marketplace changes.

For these smaller, more adaptive companies, the global economy contains not only an increasing number of competitors but also more candidates for outsourcing and partnering relationships. Indeed, alliances of various kinds have given rise to the 'stateless' corporation in which people, assets, and transactions move freely across international borders. As the world economy continues to concentrate into three regional centers (Europe, North America, and the Pacific Rim), companies scramble for presence in each of these huge markets – something most cannot do single-handedly.

Thus, whether the objective is to extend distribution reach, increase manufacturing efficiency and adaptability, add design capability, or whatever, the global economy is full of opportunities for networking. Of course, the opportunities available to one firm are probably equally accessible to others, raising concern that the outsourcing firm may not find a manufacturer, supplier, distributor, or designer when one is needed. Further, there are oft-expressed concerns about quality assurance in geographically far-flung networks and worries that extensive outsourcing will increase the likelihood of innovative products being copied (and improved) as technological competence spreads.

Deregulation

Changing regulatory processes in the U.S. and abroad are a corollary of more sophisticated global competition. Financial deregulation, in particular, has caused an explosion of international profit-seeking activity. For example, the development of overseas capital markets has vaulted formerly minor functions, such as cash management, into the strategic limelight. Many U.S. companies now sweep excess cash from their accounts every afternoon and deposit the funds in overnight money market accounts somewhere in the world.

Frequently, firms find the rules of the game being rewritten after they have placed their bets. Cross-national differences and changes in tax laws, investment credits, and currency exchange rates force companies to constantly reevaluate how they report profits and invest excess cash.

Essentially, deregulation unleashes entrepreneurial behavior, which in turn raises the level of competition. Often deregulation creates new outsourcing opportunities – as seen, for example, in the increased privatization of public corporations and agencies in many countries. Most important, deregulation reduces margins, and this requires companies to maximize returns on all assets – those they control as well as those their vendors and partners control.

Work force demographics

Changes in the composition of the U.S. work force are also driving companies to abandon the old business equation. Our work force is becoming older, and its growth is slowing. Seventy-five percent of the people who will be in the work force in the year 2000 are already working. As the work force matures, human resource costs will rise, in part because older employees draw more heavily on their companies' health-care and pension benefits. Because older workers are less inclined to move or to be retrained, flexibility and mobility for this segment of the work force will decline. Rising costs and decreasing flexibility are stimulating U.S. companies to search globally for new human resources and to develop empowerment schemes that generate greater returns from their current stock of human capital. Increasingly, so-called minorities will become a larger majority. Women already form a sizable and growing segment of the work force. Immigration from non-English-speaking countries will likely continue (and perhaps expand), adding to training requirements at a time when U.S. public education is in a troubled state.

Given these demographic trends, the network structure and its operating mechanisms offer some distinct advantages. First, as older workers and some women with small children seek shorter working hours, firms already skilled in outsourcing will invent new means of accommodating these employees' requests for part-time and telecommuting work. Second, firms retain as small a permanent work force as possible, turning more frequently to consulting firms and other resources for temporary employees. Third, more and more firms will allow their employees to make their services available to other firms on a contractual basis.

Although the network form allows for a smaller permanent work force, it requires that work force to be highly trained. In fact, it is the ability of the various network components to apply their expertise to a wide range of related activities that provides the overall network with agility and cost efficiency. For their permanent employees, network firms must be prepared to make large and continuing investments in training and development. Most employees in these companies will need to know how to perform numerous operations, and demonstrate an in-depth understanding of the firm's technologies.

Communications and computer technologies

Network organizations cannot operate effectively unless member firms have the ability to communicate quickly, accurately, and over great distances. Advances in fiber optics, satellite communications, and facsimile machines have made it much easier for managers to communicate within international network organizations. In addition, microcomputers now offer managers and employees all the computational capacity they need, 24 hours a day. And the micros can follow their users wherever they go. Moreover, the cost of data transmission has been declining consistently since the early 1970s, and the decline shows no signs of slowing down. In short, information-processing capacity and geographic distance are no longer major constraints in designing an organization.

Even more important in the long run, computers are changing the traditional concept of product design and production. Today's computer-aided product engineer can quickly produce a multitude of designs or modifications, each complete with parts and components specifications. To evaluate the design of smaller components, an engineer can use stereo lithography, a computer-aided design/laser hookup that 'grows' a prototype in a vat, thus achieving a first stage of 'desktop manufacturing.' Moreover, computer-controlled, general-purpose plant equipment can manufacture directly from computer-stored specifications. Thus, a single manufacturing site can serve several product designers, using their instructions to guide expensive, but usually fully loaded, equipment. Organizationally speaking, we are at the point where capital investments in complex general-purpose machinery can provide a manufacturing component with the ability to serve numerous partners in a network arrangement.

To summarize, globalization and technological change, coupled with deregulation and changing work force demographics, have created a new competitive reality. Taken together, these forces are placing heavy demands on firms to be simultaneously efficient and adaptive. Global competition and deregulation have squeezed most of the slack out of the U.S. economy, and firms can afford to hold only fully employed, flexible resources. Fortunately, however, network structures permit both high utilization and flexibility. Relying on computer-aided communications, product design, and manufacturing, companies can now forge sophisticated linkages – quickly.

TYPES OF NETWORK ORGANIZATIONS

As firms turned to some form of network organization to meet competitive challenges, three types of structures became prominent: internal, stable, and dynamic. Though similar in purpose, each type is distinctly suited to a particular competitive environment. (See Figure 2.)

Internal network

An internal network typically arises to capture entrepreneurial and market benefits without having the company engage in much outsourcing. The

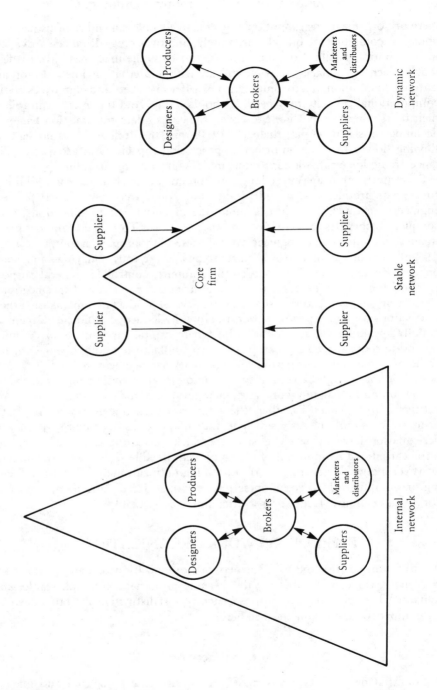

Figure 2   Common network types

internal-network firm owns most or all of the assets associated with a particular business. Managers who control these assets are encouraged (if not required) to expose them to the discipline of the market. The basic logic of the internal network is that if internal units have to operate with prices set by the market (instead of artificial transfer prices), then they will constantly seek innovations that improve their performance.

The General Motors' components business provides a good example of an internal network. Through a series of reorganizations and consolidations (mostly in the 1980s), GM reduced the number of its components divisions to eight. Each of the eight divisions pursues its own specialty; together, they create what has been called a 'specialization consortium.'

Turning GM's formerly rigid and inefficient components divisions into a group of coordinated and flexible subcontractors required two major actions. First, the parent corporation established clear performance measures for each of the divisions so that their behavior could be legitimately compared to that of external suppliers. Usually, this meant converting each components facility into a business unit that was encouraged to sell its products on the open market. Second, each division was assigned (or retained) an area of expertise related to a particular automotive system or subassembly. Each division was to be *the* expert at providing its product and to cooperate with other divisions in the consortium whenever appropriate.

To cite a specific example, the AC-Rochester Division was formed in 1988 by merging the former AC Spark Plugs Division and the Rochester Products Division. The combined division specializes in products that govern the flow of air and fluids into and out of the automobile (filters, fuel and exhaust systems, and so forth). The division is organized into several business units, each a specialist, just as AC-Rochester itself is a specialist within the consortium of components divisions. The various business units of AC-Rochester sell their products to GM, of course, but they also sell to Mitsubishi Motors (Japan), Daewoo (Korea), Opel (Europe), and other manufacturers.

If this organizational arrangement were to be extended throughout General Motors, then the parent corporation would eventually evolve toward the brokering function shown in Figure 1. That is, corporate headquarters would become a holding company that maintained an interest in a broad array of specialization consortia, each of which possessed the ability to compete favorably in international markets. It would seek, through subsidies, taxes, loans, and investments, to keep the 'internal economy' healthy, focused, and renewing.

Multinational resource-based companies also gravitate toward internal networks. For example, an international oil company would likely find it too costly to hold resources for exploration, extraction, refining, and distribution in every country in which it operates. Nor is deployment from a central location very practical. No matter where its resources were concentrated, the firm could not allocate them quickly and efficiently with a central planning mechanism. Instead, an internal network is constructed. For the network to operate properly, each of its nodes must interact regularly without outsiders – trading, buying, or selling products and raw materials to other firms in order to bring real prices to bear on internal transactions. Thus, inside the company, clusters of business units, grouped by region and product category, can be seen buying and selling from one another as well as from outside firms.

A well-conceived internal network can reduce resource redundancy and decrease response time to market opportunities. Such a network achieves total resource utilization. But there are pitfalls. Internal networks may sometimes fall victim to corporate politics. Instead of exchanging goods or services at verifiable market prices, divisions transfer goods at administered prices that do not reflect external realities – and bad decisions result.

Stable network

The stable network typically employs partial outsourcing and is a way of injecting flexibility into the overall value chain. In the stable network, assets are owned by several firms, but dedicated to a particular business. Often, a set of vendors is nestled around a large 'core' firm, either providing inputs to the firm or distributing its outputs. (Again, see Figure 2.)

BMW, for example, is organized as a stable network. In principle, any part of a BMW is a candidate for outsourcing, and somewhere between 55 and 75 percent of total production costs at BMW come from outsourced parts. As at GM, various internal BMW operating units are obligated to prove their competence according to market standards. Beyond this, however, BMW keeps pace with developments in a variety of relevant product and process technologies through its own subsidiaries, and by partnering with other firms. Three subsidiaries concentrate on technologically advanced forms of automobile development and production: BMW Motor Sports Group, Advanced Engineering Group, and the Motorcycle Group. Each of these subsidiaries, especially Motor Sports and Advanced Engineering, focuses on extending the boundaries of knowledge related to automobile engineering and design. The basic objective of these research groups is to understand enough about a particular technology to know who among potential outside vendors would be the best provider. Further, BMW engages in joint ventures and uses its own venture capital fund to participate financially in the operations of other firms. Currently, four areas are closely monitored: new product materials, new production technologies (e.g., with Cecigram in France), electronics (with Leowe Opta), and basic research in several related fields.

Thus, we can see different forms of network operating within the same industry. In its components business, GM is almost entirely an internal network, whereas BMW relies to a greater extent on outsourcing and partnering.

A stable network spreads asset ownership and risk across independent firms. In bad times, however, the 'parent' firm may have to protect the health of smaller 'family members.' The benefits of stability are the dependability of supply or distribution, as well as close cooperation on scheduling and quality requirements. The 'costs' of stability are mutual dependence and some loss of flexibility.

Dynamic network

In faster-paced or discontinuous competitive environments, some firms have pushed the network form to the apparent limits of its capabilities. Businesses such as fashion, toys, publishing, motion pictures, and biotechnology may require or allow firms to outsource extensively. (See Figure 2.) In such circumstances, the lead firm identifies and assembles assets owned largely (or entirely) by other companies. Lead firms typically rely on a core skill such as manufacturing (e.g., Motorola), R&D/design (e.g., Reebok), design/assembly (e.g., Dell Computer), or, in some cases, pure brokering.

An example of a broker-led dynamic network is Lewis Galoob Toys. Only a hundred or so employees run the entire operation. Independent inventors and entertainment companies conceive most of Galoob's products, while outside specialists do most of the design and engineering. Galoob contracts for manufacturing and packaging with a dozen or so vendors in Hong Kong, and they, in turn, pass on the most labor-intensive work to factories in China. When the toys arrive in the U.S., Galoob distributes through commissioned manufacturers' representatives. Galoob does not even collect its accounts. It sells its receivables to Commercial Credit Corporation, a factoring company that also sets Galoob's credit policy. In short, Galoob is the chief broker among all of these independent specialists.

Dynamic networks can provide both specialization and flexibility. Each network node practices its particular expertise, and, if brokers are able to package resources quickly, the company achieves maximum responsiveness. However, dynamic networks run the risk of quality variation across firms, of needed expertise being temporarily unavailable, and of possible exploitation of proprietary knowledge or technology. The dynamic network operates best in competitive situations where there are myriad players, each guided by market pressures to be reliable and to stay at the leading edge of its specialty. The dynamic network is also appropriate in settings where design and production cycles are short enough to prevent knockoffs or where proprietary rights can be protected by law or by outsourcing only standard parts and assemblies.

THE BROKER'S ROLE

In hierarchically organized firms, the fundamental role of management is to plan, organize, and control resources that are held in-house. In many network firms, however, certain key managers operate *across* rather than *within* hierarchies, creating and assembling resources controlled by outside parties. These managers, therefore, can be thought of as brokers. Three broker roles are especially important to the success of network organizations: architect, lead operator, and caretaker.

Architect

Managers who act as architects facilitate the emergence of specific operating networks. Entrepreneurial behavior of this sort has been going on for centuries. For example, beginning in the 13th century, some early network architects fueled the rapid growth of the European cottage textile industry by designing a 'putting out' system that organized an army of rural workers who spun thread and wove cloth in their homes. The architects of this system financed the network by providing workers with raw materials to be paid for when the finished goods were delivered. In some cases, brokers also supplied product designs and special equipment suitable for cottage production.

A network architect seldom has a clear or complete vision of all the specific operating networks that may ultimately emerge from his or her efforts. Frequently, the architect has in mind only a vague concept of the product and of the value chain required to offer it. This business concept is then brought into clearer focus as the broker seeks out firms with desirable expertise, takes an equity position in a firm to coax it into the value chain, helps create new groups that are needed in specialized support roles, and so on.

In designing an internal network, it may be relatively easy to identify the appropriate organizational units for each stage of the value chain. In the early years at General Motors, for example, Alfred Sloan envisioned an internal network of automotive suppliers, assemblers, producers, and distributors that could be assembled from among the various firms that William Durant had acquired. The internal network that GM uses today is the modern-day result of a similar process.

In both stable and dynamic networks, the architect's role is likely to be more complicated, because the resources that must be organized are not contained entirely within the firm. The managers who designed BMW's stable network, for example, had to identify several outside firms who would be suitable partners for long-term R&D relationships. When partners and relationships change frequently, as in dynamic networks, certain managers must devote ongoing effort to the architect's role.

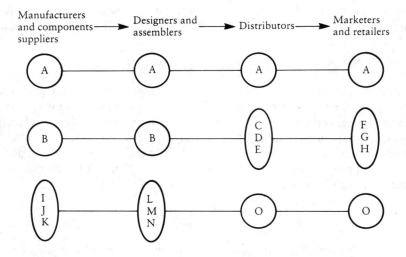

Figure 3   A value chain grid of firms and three operating networks

The overall result of the architect's efforts can be portrayed as a grid of firms and value-chain elements, such as that shown in Figure 3. A grid can be developed entirely within an industry, or it can cut across established industry boundaries. The critical factor is that all firms recognize that they are part of the grid and are at least minimally committed to supporting it. Under these conditions, a number of specific operating networks may emerge.

The personal computer business, for example, is organized in large part around three types of operating networks. One type, perhaps best represented by Tandy Corporation (Radio Shack) offers a product that is mostly designed, manufactured, and sold in-house. Thus, Tandy by itself performs all of the major functions along the value chain. A second network type, represented by Apple Computer, looks much like the Tandy network at the upstream (manufacturing) end, but it contains more distributors and retailers downstream. The third type of network, of which there are many examples, has as its center of gravity the distribution and retailing portion of the value chain. Here distributor-retailers buy off-the-shelf components from various manufacturers, then assemble and sell customized packages of computer hardware and software to specialized market segments.

Lead operator

As the grid of firms clustered around a particular business evolves, emphasis shifts from design to decisions about operation. Managers who act primarily as lead operators take advantage of the groundwork laid by manager-architects (although the two roles may overlap considerably and may be played by the same person or group). Essentially, this means that the lead operator formally connects specific firms together into an operating network. At Galoob Toys, for example, a handful of key executives perform this role. They select from a known set of potential partners those individuals and firms needed to design, manufacture, and sell children's toys. The firm outsources virtually every operating activity, choosing to perform only the brokering role in-house.

The lead-operator roles is often played by a firm positioned downstream in the value chain. Brokers in the lead firm rely on their negotiating and contracting skills to hook together firms into more-or-less permanent alliances. Nike, an R&D and marketing company, operates this way. However, the lead-operator role is not limited to downstream firms. For example, some large semiconductor manufacturers, such as Intel, have formed alliances with particular assemblers and distributors to promote the sale of new memory and operating chips. These firms advertise their new designs to potential end-users, and major exhibitions are staged to showcase the latest hardware and software developments.

Caretaker

Networks require continual enhancement if they are to operate smoothly and effectively. Thus, the process of network development is ongoing. Managers who focus on enhancement activity could be called caretakers. The caretaker role is multifaceted and may be just as important as the architect and lead-operator roles to the ultimate success of a network.

A caretaker may have to monitor a large number of relationships with respect to the specific operating network as well as to the larger grid of firms from which it came. In the operating network, this means sharing information among firms about how the network runs, as well as information on recent technological and marketing developments, schedules, and so on. Downstream firms in the value chain need to be kept abreast of new manufacturing capabilities, and upstream firms need an awareness and understanding of coming changes in the marketplace. Thus, the caretaker does more than help the network plan; managers who play this role also help the network learn.

With regard to the grid of potential network firms, the caretaker may engage in nurturing and disciplinary behavior. For example, a caretaker may notice that a particular firm appears to be falling behind technologically, or in some other way devaluing its usefulness to the grid. Appropriate actions could be taken to rectify the situation. An even more troublesome case occurs when a firm exploits its position in the grid – for example, by obtaining some short-run gain at the expense of its actual or potential partners. Here the caretaker's challenge is to point out the dysfunctional effects of such behavior on the overall system and teach the offending firm how to behave more appropriately for the common good.

IMPLICATIONS FOR BROKER SELECTION AND DEVELOPMENT

If, as seems likely, network organizations continue to spread, it is important to consider how managers with broker skills will be selected and developed. Positions labeled network architect, operator, or caretaker are not commonly found on organization charts, and no career paths are obvious. Nevertheless, it seems that many corporate experiences, and even some university courses, may be vehicles for developing needed skills. Some examples are discussed below.

Network design

Many business experiences have characteristics related to network design. For example, in consumer packaged goods firms, product and brand managers learn to build informal networks among the various designers, producers, distributors, and marketers involved in the offering of their product. Similarly, project managers in matrix organizations develop network-building skills as they work across the functional boundaries of their firms and with outside contractors.

Network designers are essentially entrepreneurs, not only pulling together the skills and equipment needed to produce a new product or service, but also, on occasion, arranging the financing. Indeed, many of the network organizations found today in the personal computer, biotechnology, fashion, and entertainment businesses are the joint product of numerous entrepreneurs who originally created a piece of the overall value-chain grid.

However, in most corporations only a limited number of managers are individuals with direct entrepreneurial experience that can be drawn on as a resource. Therefore, firms like 3M and Texas Instruments practice 'intrapreneuring' – rewarding their employees for turning ideas into prototype products or services, frequently with limited resources. In fact, one Swedish consulting firm (the Foresight Group) helps firms select and develop intrapreneurs. Interestingly, these consultants accept only volunteers, and they require them to work on their chosen projects while carrying out their regular duties (some limited financial support is also provided). Volunteers are encouraged to 'scrounge' for needed resources – both inside and outside the organization. This process has developed many new products, complete with their own internal or external network already in place. The characteristics of intrapreneuring – individual initiative, cross-functional team building, resource acquisition, and so on – are very consistent with the development of successful networks.

Many business schools now offer courses or workshops in entrepreneurship, and most of these cover product and project management, intrapreneuring, and the writing of business plans. While coursework is not a direct substitute for hands-on experience, these courses, often relying on guest lecturers, give students opportunity to explore many aspects of network design and operation.

Network operation

The task of putting a network into operation by linking all the value-chain components needed for a given product or service involves not only conceptual and organizational skills but also the skill to negotiate mutually beneficial returns for the contributions of all participants. Here one might look to purchasing or sales as a likely breeding ground for negotiations knowledge and skill. However, experience in such arenas as construction or engineering management may be even more relevant, in that the process of subcontracting is closely akin to network operation. 'Partnering' is now common in the construction industry, a process whereby the various parties involved in a project meet in a team-building session to uncover mutual interests and to create the mechanisms and build the trust necessary for resolving the inevitable disputes and inequities.

Again, many business schools now offer courses in negotiation strategies and skills, with emphasis on collaboration and ethical behavior. Understanding the processes of (and the responsibilities involved in) collaborative negotiation is an essential characteristic of the lead operator. The quest is not for an airtight legal contract guaranteeing one's own rights, but for an objective, clearly understood relationship that protects all parties' interests.

Increasingly, as networks extend across international borders, both the network architect and lead operator will require extensive international knowledge and experience. Architects must keep abreast of available skills and resources around the world, and operators must understand how cross-cultural relationships are forged and maintained. It seems likely that courses exploring general international similarities and differences will be helpful, as will courses focused on specific skills, such as those involved in countertrade. Japanese companies are noted for both their ability to build lasting relationships and for their extensive programs for assuring that managers gain hands-on experience across their organizations and various operating regions. Few U.S. firms appear to be as dedicated to such cross-training and experience, and few are as adept at building effective internal and external relationships.

Network caretaking

In some ways, the function of caretaking – maintaining and enhancing an existing network – is both the least understood and the most challenging of the three broker roles. One aspect of caretaking is simply taking care of one's self – for example, by being an active member of a trade association. A more important purpose of the caretaking function is to develop a sense of community among the members of a network. Networks operate effectively when member firms voluntarily behave as if they are all part of a broader organization sharing common objectives and rewards. This sense of community may be easier to instill in an internal network, where assets are held by a single firm, than in a dynamic network, where assets are spread across changeable combinations of designers, manufacturers, suppliers, and so on. Nevertheless, in either case, the network somehow must create an organization 'culture' that transcends ownership and national borders.

Clearly, brokers involved in the task of nurturing networks will benefit from team-building skills. General Electric's Workout Program, for example, is designed in part to bring GE's managers, customers, and vendors together to form effective working relationships. Once more, business school courses may be helpful in this area, but theory lags.practice. That is, courses in organization development and change contain many useful concepts, but most are oriented toward developing the single firm, not the set of firms that constitutes a network.

In sum, the job of broker, with its attendant roles of architect, lead operator, and caretaker, is unlikely to be filled by managers from any particular part of today's corporation. Individuals from product management, sales, and purchasing may possess some of the knowledge and skills required by the effective network broker. However, none of these functions appears to be the sole source of future brokers. Further, the broker's job is far too complex to lend itself to the use of any available selection instruments. Consequently, as is often the case, a manager's track record may be the best selection and placement device. In any case, however they are chosen, managers must be found for an increasing number of broker positions in the next century.

3

WHAT *IS* HAPPENING TO MIDDLE MANAGEMENT?

Sue Dopson and Rosemary Stewart

Few people have anything encouraging to say about middle management: past, present or future. The picture of middle management that comes from many articles and from the business press is predominantly a gloomy one. Most writers portray the middle manager as a frustrated, disillusioned individual caught in the middle of a hierarchy, impotent and with no real hope of career progression. The work is dreary, the careers are frustrating and information technology, some writers argue, will make the role yet more routine, uninteresting and unimportant. The numbers and the role of middle managers will, therefore, decline. Our recent study suggests a different picture of middle management today, so do a few other studies. This article will compare and discuss the two views.

THE GLOOMY VIEW

Reasons for middle managers' dissatisfaction

1. Being in the middle of a long hierarchy

This is perhaps the most common reason underlying many of the most pessimistic writings on middle management. John Dickson (1977) for example, gave a very gloomy picture of the role of the middle manager in a large nationalized industrial complex. He suggests that:

> . . . What remains to them – the management of procedure and reaction to company strategy – is both dispiriting and demotivating. They feel that they lack influence on decisions . . .

An additional problem for middle management is that they may be bypassed by top management. Schlesinger and Oshry (1984) argue from their experience of the impact of quality of working life initiatives in over 25 organizations in the USA, that managers find themselves by-passed by top management efforts to increase employee involvement.

2. *Having to cope with conflicting expectations*

There are the conflicting expectations of those above and below in the hierarchy, as Kanter (1986) put it:

> The squeeze between the demands of strategies they do not influence and ambitions of increasingly independent-minded employees.

Middle managers are also, as Keys and Bell (1982) pointed out:

> frequently caught in the cross fires between internal departments and outside customers and suppliers.

3. *Loss of technical expertise*

Torrington and Weightman (1982) suggest that dissatisfaction amongst middle managers is greatest amongst those with technical qualifications. They argue that evidence from extensive interviews with ten middle managers suggest that British organizations encourage those with proven technical expertise to abandon it in favour of administrative tasks. One consequence of this is that technical managers compensate for their gradual loss of technical expertise and growing insecurity by asserting a more hierarchical management style.

4. *Career disillusionment*

Some writers emphasize the career disillusionment amongst middle managers in explaining their low morale and suggest that the unsatisfactory nature of the jobs has meant that careers have become more important. Hunt (1986) discussed four research areas: burn out, professional suicide, learned helplessness and mid-career crisis. He concluded that these labels described 'extremely similar conditions' and attributed these reactions amongst middle managers to rejection and career failure arising from large employers cutting staff at all levels in response to increased competition. The result was a breaking of middle management expectations of life-time careers.

Hunt argued that another cause of the problem of career disillusionment amongst middle managers was that the post war baby boom had arrived at that career stage. Indeed he argued:

> There is a major sociological and psychological problem we cannot ignore – the post war baby boom has nowhere to go.

Some writers believe that even for those who remain, the prospect of promotion in an expanding organization has disappeared. Torrington and Weightman (1987) argue that this leads to:

Career-seeking sycophancy . . . producing all too many unwillingly plateaued managers who will make no progress beyond their present job, leading to resentment, disillusionment and frustration.

Goffee and Scase (1986), in one of the more comprehensive attempts to obtain data on male middle managers' attitudes to their jobs and careers, reiterate the theme of a growing sense of frustration and powerlessness amongst middle managers. Their data was derived from a questionnaire based on a survey of 323 male managers, the majority of whom were middle managers, within six large scale UK based organizations covering the public and private sector. In-depth loosely structured interviews were subsequently conducted with one in five of these respondents. They found that managers feel they have to make greater efforts in their jobs but perceive the rewards to be diminishing. Career progress is seen as an important job reward, but opportunities for achieving this are seen as limited and managers are dissatisfied with their salaries. They highlight four major influences on managerial jobs that have shaped these attitudes:

1. a decline in organizational growth that has led to shorter, less predictable career paths;
2. organizational restructuring leading to organic, flatter structures, where managers are expected to behave as risk-taking entrepreneurs and to measure performance, increasingly in terms of economy, efficiency and effectiveness;
3. technological change that has affected the skill requirements of managerial jobs; and
4. socio-economic changes that have undermined the authority of traditional forms of management. The spread of unionism amongst administrative and clerical employees has led to a questioning of managerial prerogatives and a rejection of more autocratic leadership styles.

This changing work context, argue Goffee and Scase, has meant the development of a new form of psychological contract between managers and their employing organization, which replaces 'total commitment' and 'emotional immersion' with 'detachment' and 'instrumentalism'. High levels of managerial commitment will only be achieved they argue if managers are convinced that the rewards are worth the effort.

Predictions about the future of middle management

Leavitt and Whistler (1958) gave the earliest, and much quoted, prediction, arguing that a combination of management science and information technology would cause middle management to shrink, top management to take on more creative functions and large organizations to centralize again. Furthermore, they argued, the work experience of many middle managers in the middle 1980s, would be programmed, routine, structured, requiring less experience, judgement and creativity and would receive less status and reward in return.

This negative prediction of the future role of middle management was followed in 1960 by Herbert Simon who argues that middle management decisions can be made at least as well by computers since the majority of decisions made by middle managers he regarded as repetitive and required 'little of the flexibilities that constitute man's principal comparative advantage over machine'.

A number of later writers reiterate the argument that information technology would have a negative impact on the future of middle management. Hicks (1971) argues that as a result of the application of systems management through the utilization of the computer, we will see the middle manager gradually disappear from the corporate scene. For Hicks, middle management jobs from the 1970s onwards will evolve into 'super' clerical positions, highly programmed, technically oriented jobs and the top manager of the future will assume the middle manager's line function. He also predicts that formal training will become more important in organizations as the middle management training ground disappears.

Neumann (1978) argues that developments in automated manufacturing, data processing and telecommunications, have enabled senior managers to widen their potential span of control. They can also monitor the work of staff more directly and over greater distances. The computer provides most of the information flow to top management that once was provided by middle management and can accomplish this task with greater speed, accuracy and selectivity. Robbed of this information role, he says the future of middle management is dismal.

Some writers argue that information technology has strengthened the position of first line managers at the expense of the middle manager. Polozynski (1983), for example, states that information technology allows the market place and manufacturing decisions to be made more easily by first line managers, thus shrinking the numbers and influence of middle managers.

Most recently, Drucker (1988) predicts that information-based organizations will threaten the status and opportunities of middle management because:

> Whole layers of management neither make decisions nor lead . . . instead their main, if only function, is to serve as relays, human boosters for the faint, unfocused signals that pass for communication in the traditional, pre-information organizations.

Drucker believes the success of information-based organizations to be in the hands of specialists 'who do different work and direct themselves'. He sees the traditional sequence of research, development, manufacturing and marketing as being replaced by 'synchrony: specialists from these functions work as a team from the inception of research to a product establishment in the market.'

A number of writers argue that reduction in organizational levels indicates a decline in middle management, for example Neumann (1978), Polozynski (1983), Tomkin (1987), Business Week Survey (1983) and International Management Journal Survey (1982). Unfortunately such claims are rarely accompanied by credible figures showing the claimed decline in numbers. A survey carried out by A.T. Kearney, management consultants of New York is often cited. The survey estimated that middle management positions around the world would decline by 15 per cent between 1979 and 1982. Another well used source of evidence is a 1982 Harris poll of 1,200 American companies which found that 40 per cent had cut their middle management positions. To say that organizations that have slimmed down have cut the numbers of levels of middle management is different from saying that middle management is declining. For that assertion to be true, there needs to be a disproportionate decline in the numbers of middle management positions in large organizations and an overall decline in the numbers of middle management jobs.

A MORE OPTIMISTIC VIEW

A number of studies on the impact of information technology have found a different picture from that given in the gloomy predictions. Polakoff (1987), Nonaka (1988), Buchanan and McCalman (1988), Weiss (1988), Millman and Hartwick (1987) and Kanter (1982), argue from their research that information technology has led to a reshaping of the middle management role, rather than to its decline.

Polakoff (1987) suggests that new manufacturing technologies will release middle managers from their traditional coordinating functions to take on new challenges. In doing so, they must acquire new skills, such as specifying information requirements and judgement in the use of information and will address new and sophisticated challenges.

Nonaka (1988) cites a case study of the Honda City car production as showing that the intensity of market conditions and the need for speedy information has led to 'compressive management', that is top management creates the vision, middle management creates and implements concrete concepts to solve and transcend the contradictions arising from gaps between what exists at the moment and what top management hopes to create. He argues that middle managers are the agents for changing the organization's 'self-renewal process' because they are able to eliminate the 'noise fluctuation and chaos within an organization' by serving as the starting point for action.

Buchanan and McCalman (1988) in a study of a hotel computing system, argue that the original predictions made by Leavitt and Whistler and Herbert Simon, underestimated the ill-structured problem that face management in the volatile market in the late 20th century. In particular they note that Leavitt and Whistler overestimated the extent to which senior managers want to exercise detailed control over business operations. They believe that middle managers can now use the computer systems to remove the uncertainty associated with their decisions, and this enhances their positions.

Weiss (1988) suggests that technologies will increase the complexity of an organization's operations thus heightening the middle managers' coordination role.

Millman and Hartwick's (1987) study of office automation describes the resulting changes in middle managers' work. Their work is more demanding, there is more of it, their personal autonomy has increased as has feedback, and greater skill and accuracy are required. Almost without exception, these changes were seen by the middle managers they interviewed as making their jobs and work more enriching and satisfying. Their sample perceived a greater opportunity for advancement and, for some, in job security. They felt their own effectiveness and that of the organization had improved.

Kanter (1982) is perhaps the strongest advocate of the need to recognize the increased importance of middle management when she states that a company's productivity will increasingly depend on the degree to which it allows its middle managers to be innovative and to combine ideas with action.

Studies of the middle managers' role in strategy also suggest that they play more of a role than the pessimists describe. Schilit (1987) in a study of 60 middle managers representing 57 organizations found that middle managers frequently participate in strategic decisions and are more influential in low risk decisions. Such 'upward influence' is more frequent in the private sector than in the public sector. Guth and Macmillan (1986) note that their sample of 60 middle managers, who were working for a part time business degree, were more prepared to intervene in strategic issues when their self-interest was at stake even when such decisions had an impact beyond their own department, and felt frequently successful in their intervention attempts.

The main factors identified by writers as affecting the future of middle management are as follows.

1. The bulk of predictions are negative. Middle management is portrayed as declining primarily because information technology can provide routine information more quickly and reliably than middle managers, and because the need for organizations to rationalize has meant a reduction in the numbers of middle management jobs. This picture of the whittling away of middle management is reinforced by a number of journalistic articles which appear at intervals in many well-known management journals.

2. The evidence on the decline in the numbers of middle management is sparse, yet writers seem untroubled by this in their predictions.

3. Most of the more pessimistic writers draw on their experience in consultancy and the teaching of management in discussing the decline of middle management. They rarely draw on existing studies of middle management work, such as they are, nor do they attempt to give any evidence to support their predictions. Predictions, therefore, become assertions. In part this can be explained by the scarcity of studies examining the nature of middle management and the role of the middle manager. As Torrington and Weightman (1987) say, the role of the middle manager in the public and private sector has received little serious attention from academic researchers. There is, therefore, no comprehensive body of theoretical or empirical knowledge on the role, function and responsibilities of the middle manager.

4. Those writers making predictions, who have carried out research on middle management work, put forward a more positive picture of the future of the middle management role.
5. Predictions and assessments of the effects of change on middle management are usually discussed in terms of a particular change, for example information technology or increased competition.
6. The predictions are about middle management in general. There is no attempt to differentiate between the future of middle management in different organizational contexts. It may well be that the work and situation of the middle manager in the public sector is very different from that of the middle manager working in a traditional industry or a fast-growing computer company. These differences are important, and if researched, may well provide a less homogeneous picture of the middle managers' situation.
7. A major methodological inadequacy of the existing studies of middle management is that very few studies attempt to examine empirically the relationship between the processes of change in the wider environment and changes within management itself. Goffee and Scase are a notable exception. Most studies of middle management are snapshots of complex changes affecting the middle managers' role and situation. This is not to decry the importance and utility of such snapshots, but merely to point out that claims for findings need to be balanced by recognition that middle management work is a moving, complex picture.

Our own study

Our recent study also does not support the dismal picture of middle management. In this its findings resemble those of studies quoted earlier of the impact of information technology. We have been participating in a six-country Western European study, initiated and partially funded by the European Foundation for Living and Working Conditions, which has been examining the nature of the changes affecting middle management jobs and careers and middle managers' reactions to such changes. The definition of middle management takes in all those below top management and in large companies, the divisional board.

This was a relatively small-scale study despite its broad scope. It relied on literature searches in the UK, eight broad case studies in a diversity of organizations including two from the public sector and three more detailed studies of a traditional manufacturing company, a new public sector agency and a distributor of autoparts. In this article we restrict ourselves to the UK research and in particular, to that made possible by a grant from the Leverhulme Trust which allowed us to carry out the second phase of the research, an intensive literature search and three more detailed case studies.

We sought to understand the complexity of the changes affecting different types of organizations, and the organizations' responses to these changes. In each of the eight general case studies, we interviewed a senior personnel had seen the most radical restructuring. As one middle-aged production manager who had spent his working life in the car industry put it:

> I know that if there was a better person for the job he would have it.

This is an example of the confidence some middle managers had gained from surviving the radical changes in the organization, and also in his case, from having been through the company's assessment centre.

The career disillusionment and frustration emphasized by several writers did not emerge in our study. Neither did the more instrumental orientation to work found by Goffee and Scase. This may partly be explained by the more general focus of our research. There were, however, concerns about future career paths now that the management hierarchy had been reduced but for most managers, particularly from the private sector, the increased responsibilities and accountability had, in part at least, compensated for uncertain career paths and had made their work more rewarding in itself.

Some writers seem to assume that many managers will necessarily be frustrated if they do not get promotion beyond middle management and see no hope of doing so: 'only a few will make it' as Hunt (1986) puts it, and Torrington and Weightman (1987) 'To be a middle manager is the ambition of hardly anyone. It is regarded as a time of transition, after the escape from routine or technical specialization and before promotion to the halcyon realms of senior management or even top management'.

In our experience, both as researchers and teachers, middle managers may not want to go to top management. The older ones, particularly those who are not graduates – like so many British managers – may have got further than they expected and look where they have come from rather than lament at not getting to the top. There are others who increasingly recognize that top management is not 'halcyon', but often involves even harder work, more risk and, in some companies, more travelling.

There were of course some negative comments about the ways in which the changes had affected their jobs. There were general complaints about the coping with the additional pressures and the increased workload in expanded jobs. Some managers felt more insecure fearing further changes. Others complained that the refocusing of tasks meant they lost aspects of their job that they enjoyed. There were also problems of having to adapt to changes, particularly when they were unexpected and when they were not fully consulted about those changes.

There seems to be more resistance to changes in middle management jobs in the public than in the private sector. From our research, we hypothesize that whether the middle managers see changes as positive or negative seems to depend on:

1. How clear is the need for change within the organization, competitive threat provides a more acceptable reason for change than politicians' decisions.
2. The extent to which change is seen as normal, which is probably a major distinction between traditional organizations and those in new industries.

3. What is done to try and help managers think positively and adapt to change, for example, incentives, management training, communication about the rationale for change and the example set by top management.
4. Whether the managers see themselves primarily as professionals, as many do in the public sector, or primarily as managers.

There are, of course, other factors such as age, personality, including whether the individual enjoys wider responsibility and accountability, or prefers a more secure and less challenging job, that are likely to influence individual reactions, as well as job experience and the organizational culture. The complexity of the intervening variables affecting the reactions of managers to change is given cursory treatment by some writers in this area.

CONCLUSIONS

So what is happening to middle management? The evidence is not clear because the research is too limited to support firm conclusions and because the figures about the changes in the numbers of middle managers are neither comprehensive nor easily accessible. Our limited evidence suggests that the gloomy predictions are at least an exaggeration as they do not apply to some middle managers in some organizations. We found that a slimmer middle management in a time of rapid change has a more important role to play than before. Yet we, like other, writers, need to be cautious about generalizing when the changes are complex and the situations within which middle managers work are so diverse, as are their own backgrounds and attitudes – hence our cautious 'some managers in some organizations'. If writing in this area is to amount to anything more than armchair theorizing, it is crucial that more empirical work be done. Failure to do so may lead to yet more sweeping assertions about the future of middle management.

REFERENCES

Buchanan, D. and McCalman, J. (1988) Confidence, visibility and pressure: the effects of shared information in computer aided hotel management. *New Technology Work and Employment*, 3, 38–46.
Business Week (1983) A new era for management. *Business Week* No. 2787, 50–53.
Clutterbuck, D. (1982) The whittling away of middle management. November, *International Management*. 10–16.
Dickson, J. (1977) Plight of the middle manager. *Management Today*, December, 66–69.
Drucker, P.F. (1988) The coming of the new organization. *Harvard Business Review*, 45–53.
Goffee, R. and Scase, R. (1986) Are the rewards worth the effort? Changing managerial values in the 1980s. *Personnel Review*, 15, 3–6.
Guth, W.D. and Macmillan, I.C. (1986) Strategic implementation versus middle management self-interest. *Strategic Management Journal*, 7, 313–327.
Hicks, R.L. (1971) Developing the top management group in a total systems organization. *Personnel Journal*, 50, 675–682.
Hunt, J. (1986) Alienation among managers – the new epidemic or the social scientists' invention? *Personnel Review*, 15, 21–25.

exclusively or allow it to play a decisive role. They incorporate its outputs into the pool of judgment that is dominated by qualitative experience. The research they carry out or use tends to be based on surveys of opinions, attitudes, or characteristics of people. Tests, questionnaires, and interviews are the principal instruments used.

Most managers are problem resolvers. They defend their approach to problems by citing the lack of information and time required to do anything else. Clinicians also argue that real problems are so messy as to render alternative approaches either inapplicable or inappropriate. Furthermore, they claim their approach minimizes risk and therefore maximizes the likelihood of survival.

SOLVING

To *solve* a problem is to select a course of action that is believed to yield the *best possible* outcome, that *optimizes*. We call this the *research* approach because it is largely based on scientific methods, techniques, and tools. It makes extensive use of mathematical models and real or simulated experimentation; therefore, it relies heavily on observation and measurements and aspires to complete objectivity (Ackoff, 1979). The research approach is used mostly by Management Scientists and technologically oriented managers whose organizational objective tends to be the *thrival* rather than mere survival; they are growth seekers.

The researcher, and particularly the decision maker who uses the output of research, often resorts to clinical treatment of those aspects of a problem that cannot be treated quantitatively, hence cannot be included in mathematical models. Researchers, more than managers, tend to resist the dilution of optimal solutions with qualitative considerations and often prefer an optimal solution of an incompletely formulated problem to a less-than-optimal solution of a completely formulated problem.

DISSOLVING

To *dissolve* a problem is to change the nature, and/or the environment, of the entity in which it is imbedded so as to remove the problem. Problem dissolvers *idealize* rather than satisfice or optimize because their objective is to change the system involved or its environment in such a way as to bring it closer to an ultimately desired state, one in which the problem cannot or does not arise. We call this the *design* approach. The designer makes use of the methods, techniques, and tools of both the clinician and researcher, and much more; but he uses them synthetically rather than analytically. He tries to dissolve problems by changing the characteristics of the larger system containing the problem. He looks for dissolutions in the containing whole rather than solutions in the contained parts.

The design approach is used by that minority of managers and management scientists whose principal organizational objective is *development* rather than growth or survival, and who know the difference. To develop is to increase one's ability and desire to improve one's own quality of life and that of others. Development and growth are not the same thing and are not even necessarily related. Either can take place without the other; a trash heap can grow without developing, and a person can develop without growing.

AN EXAMPLE

An example may help to clarify the differences between the three approaches to problems. A large machine-tool manufacturing company was confronted with abrupt changes in the demand for its products. Reactions to these fluctuations were both disruptive and costly. Among other things, the company seemed to alternate continually between hiring and firing personnel, many of whom were highly skilled. This made for low morale, and low morale made for low productivity, not to mention hostility between labor and management.

The company's management periodically resolved its problem by drawing on past experience, using 'good sound judgment' and common sense. This approach came to be regarded as inadequate because the problem kept reappearing and it tended to get worse over time. (It is not unusual for problems that are treated clinically to reappear and get worse. This failing has plagued psychotherapy and sociotherapy since their inception. The treatments of alcoholism now in vogue are cases in point.)

Out of desperation management decided to give Operations Research and optimization a try. The researchers who were called in to do the job formulated the problem as one of production smoothing, the solution to which depended critically on the accuracy of demand in the forecast. Unfortunately, good forecasts could not be obtained. Therefore, the solutions obtained by optimizing the model of the problem were only marginally better than those previously obtained by problem resolving.

An attack using design was then made on the problem. First, the problem was reformulated to one requiring the reduction of fluctuations of demand rather than response to existing demand. The business of the company was redesigned to reduce these fluctuations. A product line was added the demand for which was counter-cyclical relative to that for machine tools, but with production requiring the same technology, and some of the same parts and sub-assemblies used in machine-tool manufacture. The new product line, road building equipment, could also employ virtually the same distribution and marketing system as machine tools. Subsequent fluctuations of combined demand for the two types of product were about 7% of the fluctuations for machine tools alone.

The dissolution of the problem by redesign of the business moved the company closer to at least one of its ideals, stable employment. It also significantly improved the company's earning stream and reduced its cash-flow and labor-management problems.

Improvements obtained by resolving problems tend to have shorter lives than dissolutions. Few if any problems, however, are ever permanently resolved, solved, or dissolved; every treatment of a problem generates new

Formulating the mess. This is done in such a way as to capture and highlight the essential systemic properties of the mess, not by listing independently formulated threats and opportunities, but by projecting the future that the system would have if it, and its environment, were to continue unchanged. It is the future that a system currently 'is in.'

Ends planning. This involves selecting the ideals, objectives, and goals to be pursued by preparing an idealized redesign of the system planned for, a design with which the relevant stakeholders would replace the existing system today if they were free to do so. (The differences between this most desired design and the description developed in the first phase define the gaps to be filled by the remainder of the planning process.)

Means planning. Here the ways of filling the gaps are selected. (These are more likely to require invention than discovery.) They can take the form of policies, programs, projects, procedures, practices, or individual courses of action.

Resource planning. A determination is made of how much of each type of resource – people, facilities and equipment, materials and energy, money, information, knowledge, and understanding – will be required by the means selected, and when these requirements will arise. Then it is necessary to determine whether, and how, these requirements can be met. If they are found to be infeasible, the previously formulated ends or means will have to be modified and the cycle repeated.

Design of implementation and control. Decisions are made as to who is to do what, where, and when, and how their behavior and its effects are to be monitored and modified when necessary.

These phases of design-oriented planning are carried out as participatively as possible, ideally providing all stakeholders – not just their representatives – with an opportunity to take part. They are organized into small planning teams and these teams are so organized and managed as to assure coordination of their efforts the outputs of which can then be integrated into a comprehensive plan (Ackoff, 1970). The planning process is also designed to facilitate continuous improvement of plans and continuous organizational and individual learning, adaptation, and development.

Both the clinical and research approaches to planning are incorporated into the design approach. Clinical methods are used heavily in each phase of the process, but ideas – that is, information, knowledge, and understanding – derived from research are continually fed into the participative process by professional planners. Moreover, whenever there is collective doubt, or the professional planners doubt collective judgment and it is possible to remove such doubt by research, it is used.

Research is also heavily used in inventing, elaborating, and evaluating new ideas generated by the design process, by providing the designers with the information, knowledge, and understanding they require for effective design. The professionals have responsibility not only for revealing the potential uses of the output of research, and for designing and conducting research to provide useful output, but also for revealing its limitations and showing where and how judgment is required to supplement it.

The participation of the stakeholders is structured to the extent necessary to carry through each of the five phases of planning. Moreover, the participants are coached by the professionals in the methodology of planning, how to design and conduct research, and how to organize and operate productive teams. Thus the design-oriented planner has responsibility for continuous education of the participants and for developing both the form and content of such education. In addition, he has responsibility for removing the principal obstruction between stakeholders and the future they most desire: self-imposed constraints. He must convince them that many of the constraints that they believe are imposed on them from without either lie within themselves or are imaginary.

SUMMARY

The design-oriented planner, in effect, has a major responsibility for providing inputs to the planning process, in organizing and guiding it, in educating those involved in it, in specifying the nature of the output that is required, in providing criteria by which the output can be evaluated, and in facilitating such evaluation. The design-oriented planner must be competent in the use of the methods, techniques, and tools of both the clinician and the researcher. He need not be as skilled in the use of their instruments as they are, but he must know them well enough to be able to use those who have these skills effectively. He must do more than this: he must know how to design and invent, and he must be able to encourage and facilitate the efforts of others to do so. He must be a generalist who is familiar with the capabilities and limitations of relevant specialists; he must be a humanist as well as a scientist; and he must be as much at home with art as he is with technology. Finally, he must be as concerned with the qualities of life as he is with its quantities.

None of us in S³ pretend to be all these things, but collaboratively we are trying to produce professionals who are. We believe that doing so requires new forms and content of education. We must redesign the educational process. (See Ackoff, 1979). The focus on design of those of us in academia leaves us with more than the need to develop a new kind of education; it leaves us with the need to develop an adequate *methodology of design,* a *logic of creativity.* This must be very different from the conventional logic of classes because it must be a logic of uniqueness, of individuality. It cannot be an inductive or deductive logic such as is adequate for clinical judgment or scientific inference. It must be a logic of intuition from which creativity springs.

This sounds like a contradiction because we have traditionally taken intuition to be immune to logic, to be the antithesis of it. Therefore, we must generalize the concept of logic itself. What an exciting challenge this is! It is at least as exciting as Aristotle's effort to harness reason in logic, and the efforts of John Stuart Mill (1862) and R.A. Fisher (1949) to harness experience in experiment.

PART 2:
PROCESS OF CHANGE

Perhaps the most important 'change in change thinking' over the last few years has been the gradual diminution in the strength of arguments for formalized, top-down, directive styles of change management. In their place we are seeing highly participative approaches with an emphasis on 'process'. The selection of five papers presented here give meaning and force to the observable transition. They explain in part the social, cultural and political changes which we have experienced in Europe and in the UK in particular. The nature of the work, coupled with concerns such as the equality of opportunity, have brought about subtle changes in the social grouping which we label as the 'organization'; now more than ever the multiple goals of all the actors have to be harnessed to create a successful enterprise. Johnson, Quinn and Pugh, in particular, bring out this argument. Beer's paper has proved popular with students as a means of unravelling the frequent failures of overambitious top-down change.

Gerry Johnson's work on strategy and change is critical of 'rationalistic' models; instead he argues for a greater appreciation of incremental approaches and the importance of cultural and cognitive factors. Writing from his background in social anthropology, Johnson is well placed to comment on the changes in political alliances which he sees as a precursor of change actions. Indeed, if we extend his argument, we may even suggest that these changes in attitude and perception are the key elements of change, without contradicting the reasoning advanced by Pettigrew and Whipp.

The Quinn and Nadler papers are both substantial pieces of work in their own right, with the Quinn argument fast becoming a 'classic' in this field in advocating 'incrementalism' as a route to identifying the elements of a pieceful, but nonetheless carefully structured, process of change. Using examples from Xerox, GM and IBM, this second US perspective is one of the papers which signalled a new direction for work on change during the last decade. Nadler's

INCREMENTALISM

There are discernible patterns of strategic development in organizations. Typically, for example, organizations go through long periods when strategies appear to be developed incrementally (Mintzberg, 1978), that is, strategic decisions build one upon another, in small steps, following a path in which history appears to play an important role in shaping future strategy. Again, there occurs infrequently in organizations, more fundamental shifts in strategy as more major readjustment of the strategic direction of the firm takes place. Some writers, notably Quinn (1980), and Lindblom (1958), have argued that such incremental development in organizations is not only inevitable, but also logical. Managers consciously pursue an incremental approach to the management of complexity: they are aware that it is not possible to 'know' about all the influences that could inconceivably affect the future of the organization. Moreover they are aware that the organization is a political entity in which trade-offs between different groups is inevitable; it is therefore not possible to arrive at an optimal goal or an optimal strategy; strategies must be compromises which allow the organization go to forward. To cope with this uncertainty and such compromise, strategies must be developed in stages, carrying the members of the organization with them, and by trying out new ideas and experiments to see which are likely to be effective and to induce commitment within the organization through continual, but low scale change. This is what has become known as 'logical incrementalism'.

There is no denial here that an incremental pattern of strategy is discernible in many organizations. However, there are other explanations as to how such patterns of strategic development come about. Indeed, the whole idea of 'logical incrementalism' can be seen as a rationalization interpretation of processes which can be accounted for in quite different ways.

We need to be careful about building too much upon what managers espouse: because they espouse the idea of logical incrementalism does not necessarily mean they behave in such ways. Still less does it mean that we can build normative models of management upon such espousal. Explanations of management, and such lessons as can be drawn, must, rather, build on the empirical investigation of practice in the political, cultural and cognitive arena we call the organization.

A CULTURAL AND COGNITIVE PERSPECTIVE

The study upon which this paper is based (Johnson, 1987) examined strategic change processes longitudinally and contextually (Pettigrew 1985a), focussing on the cultural political and cognitive aspects of management. If the management process is viewed in such a way, what emerges is that the complexity that managers face cannot be objectively analysed continually within the managerial task. So much has been well enough established by other researchers (e.g. Weick, 1979; Schon, 1983).

Managers hold to a set of core beliefs and assumptions, specific and relevant to the organization in which they work. Whilst individual managers may hold quite varying sets of beliefs about many different aspects of that organizational world, there is likely to exist at some level a core set of beliefs and assumptions held relatively commonly by the managers. This has variously been called ideational culture, myths (Hedberg and Jonsson, 1977), interpretative schemes (Bartunek, 1984), or the term used here, paradigms (also Pfeffer, 1981; Sheldon, 1980). This set of beliefs, which evolves over time, might embrace assumptions about the nature of the organizational environment, the managerial style in the organization, the nature of its leaders, and the operational routines seen as important to ensure the success of the organization.

The paradigm is essentially cultural; that is, it is held relatively commonly, taken for granted and not problematic. It may be more easily perceived by those outside the organization than those inside the organization to whom its constructs may be self evident. It is this paradigm which, in many organizations, creates a relatively homogeneous approach to the interpretation of the complexity that the organization faces. The various and often confusing signals that the organization faces are made sense of, are filtered, in terms of this paradigm. Moreover, since it evolves over time and is reinforced through the history and success of the organization, it also provides a repertoire of actions and responses to the interpretation of signals, which are experienced by managers and seen by them as demonstrably relevant. It is at one and the same time, a device for interpretation and a formula for action. The strategies organizations follow, grow out of this paradigm.

Managers may therefore recognize changes going on around them, within or without the organization: but this does not necessarily mean that they see such changes as directly relevant to their organization. It is quite likely, for example that an observer from outside the organization could perceive competitive actions as impinging on or threatening the organization, when managers internally, whilst knowing about such activity, do not see it as relevant to their organization. Relevance is determined, not by the competitive activity, but by the constructs of the paradigm; if such stimuli can be explained within that paradigm then, that becomes 'the reality' for organizational action.

The paradigm is hedged about and protected by a web of cultural artefacts – symbols, myths and rituals which legitimize its constructs; organizational routines and systems which programme the way organizational members respond to given situations, delineate 'the way we do things around here' (Deal and Kennedy, 1982), and may even be capitalized in hardware such as computer systems. Moreover, it is likely that those with the greatest power in organizations derive that power from, amongst other things, their association with the constructs of that paradigm; their association with its complexity and uncertainty reducing mechanisms, enhances their status and links them to the perceived success of the organization (Hickson et al. 1971; Hambrick, 1981). It would therefore be a mistake to conceive of the paradigm as merely a set of beliefs removed from organizational action. It lies within a cultural web which bonds it to the action of organizational life.

SUMMARY

Traditionally strategic management has been conceived of in the literature as an analytical, rational exercise, most commonly thought of in terms of strategic planning. This paper, on the other hand, has argued that strategic management is essentially a cultural and cognitive phenomenon – that strategies in organizations are configured and persist in terms of the cultural history and cognitive dimensions within which managers work. The result, over time, is likely to be strategic drift and, eventually, the need for major strategic reorientation. The paper argued that the processes of strategic change also need to be understood in cultural and cognitive terms. The implication is that, the traditional planning approaches to the management of strategic change, though necessary, are in themselves insufficient and potentially dangerous. Unless the processes of strategic change are underway, analytical challenging of the status quo can result in a resistance, rather than a willingness, to change strategies.

REFERENCES

Bartunek, J.M. (1984) Changing interpretive schemes and organisational restructuring: the examples of a religious order. *Administrative Science Quarterly*, 29, 355–372.

Dandridge, T.C., Mitroff, I., and Joyce, W.F. (1980) Organisational symbolism: a topic to expand organisational analysis. *Academy of Management Review*, 5, 77–82.

Deal, T., and Kennedy, A. (1982) *Corporate Cultures: The Rites and Rituals of Corporate Life*. Addison Wesley.

Hambrick, D.W. (1981) Environment, strategy and power within top management teams. *Administrative Science Quarterly*, 26, 253–276.

Hedberg, C. and Jonsson, S. (1977) Strategy making as a discontinuous process. *International Studies of Management and Organisation*, VII, 88–109.

Hickson, D.J., Hinings, G.P., Lee, C.A., Schneck, P.E., and Dennings, J.M. (1971). A Strategic contingencies theory of intraorganisational power. *Administrative Science Quarterly*, 16, No. 2, 216–229.

Johnson, G. (1987) *Strategic Change and the Management Process*. Blackwell.

Kanter, M. (1984) *The Change Masters: Innovation for Productivity in the American Corporation*. Simon and Schuster.

Lindblom, C.E. (1958) The science of muddling through. *Public Administration Review*, 19, Spring, 79–88.

Mintzberg, H. (1978) Patterns in strategy formation. *Management Science*, May, 934–948.

Pettigrew, A.M. (1973) *The Politics of Organisational Decision Making*. Tavistock.

Pettigrew, A.M. (1985a) Examining change in the long term context of culture and politics. In: J.M. Pennings (ed.) *Organizational Strategy and Change*, pp. 269–318, Jossey-Bass.

Pettigrew, A.M. (1985b) *The Awakening Giant*. Basil Blackwell.

Pfeffer, J. (1981) Management as symbolic action: the creation and maintenance of organisational paradigms. In: L.L. Cummings and B.M. Staw (eds.) *Research in Organizational Behavior*, JAI Press, Vol. 3, pp. 1–15.

Quinn, J.B. (1980) *Strategies for Change*. Irwin.

Schon, D. (1983) *The Reflective Practitioner*. Basic Books.

Sheldon, A. (1980) Organisational paradigms: a theory of organisational change. *Organisational Dynamics*, 8, No. 3, 61–71.

Weick, K.E. (1979) *The Social Psychology of Organizing*, Addison Wesley.

Wilkins, A.L. (1983) Organizational stories as symbols which control the organization. In: L.R. Pondy, P.J. Frost, G. Morgan, T.C. Dandridges (eds.) *Organizational Symbolism*, JAI Press.

6

MANAGING STRATEGIC CHANGE

James Brian Quinn

Previous articles have tried to demonstrate why executives managing strategic change in large organizations should not – and do not – follow highly formalized textbook approaches in long-range planning, goal-generation and strategy formulation. Instead, they artfully blend formal analysis, behavioural techniques and power politics to bring about cohesive, step-by-step movement towards ends which initially are broadly conceived, but which are than constantly refined and reshaped as new information appears. Their integrating methodology can best be described as 'logical incrementalism'.

But is this truly a process in itself, capable of being managed? Or does it simply amount to applied intuition? Are there some conceptual structures, principles or paradigms that are generally useful? Wrapp, Normann, Braybrooke, Lindblom and Bennis provide some macrostructures incorporating many important elements they have observed in strategic change situations. These studies offer important insights into the management of change in large organizations. But my data suggest that top managers in such enterprises develop their major strategies through processes which neither these studies nor formal approaches to planning adequately explain. Managers *consciously* and *proactively* move forward *incrementally*:

- To improve the quality of information utilized in corporate strategic decisions
- To cope with the varying lead times, pacing parameters and sequencing needs of the 'subsystems' through which such decisions tend to be made
- To deal with the personal resistance and political pressures any important strategic change encounters
- To build the organizational awareness, understanding and psychological commitment needed for effective implementation

- To decrease the uncertainty surrounding such decisions by allowing for interactive learning between the enterprise and its various impinging environments
- To improve the quality of the strategic decisions themselves by: systematically involving those with most specific knowledge; obtaining the participation of those who must carry out the decisions; and avoiding premature momenta or closure which could lead the decision in improper directions

How does one manage the complex incremental processes which can achieve these goals? The following is perhaps the most articulate short statement on how executives proactively manage incrementalism in the development of corporate strategies:

> Typically you start with general concerns, vaguely felt. Next you roll an issue around in your mind till you think you have a conclusion that makes sense for the company. You then go out and sort of post the idea without being too wedded to its details. You then start hearing the arguments pro and con, and some very good refinements of the idea usually emerge. Then you pull the idea in and put some resources together to study it so it can be put forward as more of a formal presentation. You wait for 'stimuli occurrences' or 'crises', and launch pieces of the idea to help in these situations. But they lead toward your ultimate aim. You know where you want to get. You'd like to get there in six months. But it may take three years, or you may not get there. And when you do get there, you don't know whether it was originally your own idea – or somebody else had reached the same conclusion before you and just got you on board for it. You never know. The president would follow the same basic process, but he could drive it much faster than an executive lower in the organization.[1]

Because of differences in organizational form, management style or the content of the individual decisions, no single paradigm can hold for all strategic decisions. However, very complex strategic decisions in my sample of large organizations tended to evoke certain kinds of broad process steps. These are briefly outlined. While these process steps occur generally in the order presented, stages are by no means orderly or discrete. Executives do consciously manage individual steps proactively, but it is doubtful that any one person guides a major strategic change sequentially through all the steps. Developing most strategies requires numerous loops back to earlier stages as unexpected issues or new data dictate. Or decision times can become compressed and require short-circuiting leaps forward as crises occur. Nevertheless, certain patterns are clearly dominant in the successful management of strategic change in large organizations.

CREATING AWARENESS AND COMMITMENT –
INCREMENTALLY

Although many of the sample companies had elaborate formal environmental scanning procedures, most major strategic issues first emerged in vague or undefined terms, such as 'organizational overlap', 'product proliferation', 'excessive exposure in one market' or 'lack of focus and motivation'. Some appeared as 'inconsistencies' in internal action patterns of 'anomalies' between the enterprise's current posture and some perception of its future environment. Early signals may come from anywhere and may be difficult to distinguish from the background 'noise' or ordinary communications. Crises, of course, announce themselves with strident urgency in operations-control systems. But, if organizations wait until signals reach amplitude high enough to be sensed by formal measurement systems, smooth, efficient transitions may be impossible.

Need-sensing: leading the formal information system

Effective change managers actively develop informal networks to get objective information – from other staff and line executives, workers, customers, board members, suppliers, politicians, technologists, educators, outside profession-als, government groups and so on – to sense possible needs for change. They purposely use these networks to short-circuit all the careful screens their or-ganizations build up to 'tell the top only what it wants to hear'. For example:

> Peter McColough, chairman and CEO of Xerox, was active in many high-level political and charitable activities – from treasurer of the Democratic National Committee to chairman of the Urban League. In addition, he said, 'I've tried to decentralize decision-making. If something bothers me, I don't rely on reports or what other executives may want to tell me. I'll go down very deep into the organization, to certain issues and people, so I'll have a feeling for what they think.' He refused to let his life be run by letters and memos. 'Because I came up by that route, I know what a salesman can say. I also know that before I see . . . [memos] they go through fifteen hands, and I know what that can do to them.[2]

To avoid undercutting intermediate managers, such bypassing has to be lim-ited to information-gathering, with no implication that orders or approvals are given to lower levels. Properly handled, this practice actually improves formal communications and motivational systems as well. Line managers are less tempted to screen information and lower levels are flattered to be able 'to talk about the very top'. Since people sift signals about threats and opportunities through perceptual screens defined by their own values, careful executives make sure their sensing networks include people who look at the world very differently than do those in the enterprise's dominating culture. Effective ex-ecutives consciously seek options and threat signals beyond the *status quo*. 'If I'm not two to three years ahead of my organization, I'm not doing my job' was a common comment of such executives in the sample.

Amplifying understanding and awareness

In some cases executives quickly perceive the broad dimensions of needed change. But they still may seek amplifying data, wider executive understanding of issues or greater organizational support before initiating action. Far from accepting the first satisfactory (satisfying) solution – as some have suggested they do – successful managers seem consciously to generate and consider a broad array of alternatives. Why? They want to stimulate and choose from the most creative solutions offered by the best minds in their organizations. They wish to have colleagues knowledgeable enough about issues to help them think through all the ramifications. They seek data and arguments sufficiently strong to dislodge preconceived ideas or blindly followed past practices. They do not want to be the prime supporters of losing ideas or to have their organizations slavishly adopted 'the boss's solution'. Nor do they want – through announcing decisions too early – to threaten prematurely existing power centres which could kill any changes aborning.

Even when executives do not have in mind specific solutions to emerging problems, they can still proactively guide actions in intuitively desired directions – by defining what issues staffs should investigate, by selecting principal investigators and by controlling reporting processes. They can selectively 'tap the collective wit' of their organizations, generating more awareness of critical issues and forcing initial thinking down to lower levels to achieve greater involvement. Yet they can also avoid irreconcilable opposition, emotional overcommitment or organizational momenta beyond their control by regarding all proposals as 'strictly advisory' at this early stage.

As issues are clarified and options are narrowed, executives may systematically alert ever wider audiences. They must first 'shop' key ideas among trusted colleagues to test responses. Then they may commission a few studies to illuminate emerging alternatives, contingencies or opportunities. But key players might still not be ready to change their past action patterns or even be able to investigate options creatively. Only when persuasive data are in hand and enough people are alerted and 'on board' to make a particular solution work, might key executives finally commit themselves to it. Building awareness, concern and interest to attention-getting levels is often a vital – and slowly achieved – step in the process of managing basic changes. For example:

In the early 1970s there was still a glut in world oil supplies. Nevertheless, analysts in the General Motors Chief Economist's Office began to project a developing US dependency on foreign oil and the likelihood of higher future oil prices. These concerns led the board in 1972 to create an ad hoc energy task force headed by David C. Collier, then treasurer, later head of GM of Canada and then of the Buick Division. Collier's group included people from manufacturing, research, design, finance, industry-government relations, and the economics staff. After six months of research, in May of 1973 the task force went to the board with three conclusions: (1) there was a developing energy problem, (2) the government had no particular plan to deal with it, (3) energy costs would have a profound effect on GM's business. Collier's report created a good deal of discussion around the company in the ensuing months. 'We were trying to get other people to think about the issue,' said Richard C. Gerstenberg, then chairman of GM.[3]

Changing symbols: building credibility

As awareness of the need for change grows, managers often want to signal the organization that certain types of change are coming, even if specific solutions are not in hand. Knowing they cannot communicate directly with the thousands who would carry out the strategy, some executives purposely undertake highly visible actions which wordlessly convey complex messages that could never be communicated as well – or as credibly – in verbal terms. Some use symbolic moves to preview or verify intended changes in direction. At other times, such moves confirm the intention of top management to back a thrust already partially begun – as Mr. McColough's relocation of Xerox headquarters to Connecticut (away from the company's Rochester reprographics base) underscored that company's developing commitment to product diversification, organizational decentralization and international operations. Organizations often need such symbolic moves – or decisions they regard as symbolic – to build credibility behind a new strategy. Without such actions even forceful verbiage might be interpreted as mere rhetoric. For example:

In GM's downsizing engineers said that one of top management's early decisions affected the credibility of the whole weight-reduction program. 'Initially, we proposed a program using a lot of aluminium and substitute materials to meet the new "mass" targets. But this would have meant a very high cost, and would have strained the suppliers' aluminium capacity. However, when we presented this program to management, they said, "Okay, if necessary, we'll do it." They didn't back down. We began to understand then that they were dead serious. Feeling that the company would spend the money was critical to the success of the entire mass reduction effort.

Legitimizing new viewpoints

Often before reaching specific strategic decisions, it is necessary to legitimize new options which have been acknowledged as possibilities, but which still entail an undue aura of uncertainty or concern. Because of their familiarity, older options are usually perceived as having lower risks (or potential costs) than newer alternatives. Therefore, top managers seeking change often consciously create forums and allow slack time for their organizations to talk through threatening issues, work out the implications of new solutions, or gain an improved information base that will permit new options to be evaluated objectively in comparison with more familiar alternatives. In many cases, strategic concepts which are at first strongly resisted gain acceptance and support simply by the passage of time, if executives do not exacerbate hostility by pushing them too fast from the top. For example:

When Joe Wilson thought Haloid Corporation should change its name to include Xerox, he first submitted a memorandum asking colleagues what they thought of the idea. They rejected it. Wilson then explained his concerns more fully, and his executives rejected the idea again. Finally

Wilson formed a committee headed by Sol Linowitz, who had thought a separate Xerox subsidiary might be the best solution. As this committee deliberated, negotiations were under way with the Rank Organizations and the term Rank-Xerox was commonly heard and Haloid-Xerox no longer seemed so strange. 'And so,' according to John Dessauer, 'a six-month delay having diluted most opposition, we of the committee agreed that the change to Haloid-Xerox might in the long run produce sound advantages.'[4]

Many top executives consciously plan for such 'gestation periods' and often find that the strategic concept itself is made more effective by the resulting feedback.

Tactical shifts and partial solutions

At this stage in the process, guiding executives might share a fairly clear vision of the general directions for movement. But rarely does a total, new corporate posture emerge full-grown – like Minerva from the brow of Jupiter – from any one source. Instead, early resolutions are likely to be partial, tentative or experimental. Beginning moves often appear as mere tactical adjustments in the enterprise's existing posture. As such, they encounter little opposition, yet each partial solution adds momentum in new directions. Guiding executives try carefully to maintain the enterprise's ongoing strengths while shifting its total posture incrementally – at the margin – towards new needs. Such executives themselves might not yet perceive the full nature of the strategic shifts they have begun. They can still experiment with partial, new approaches and learn without risking the viability of the total enterprise. Their broad early step can still legitimately lead to a variety of different success scenarios. Yet logic might dictate that they wait before committing themselves to a total new strategy. As events unfurl, solutions to several interrelated problems might well flow together in a not-yet-perceived synthesis. For example:

> In the early 1970s at General Motors there was a distinct awareness of a developing fuel economy ethic. General Motors executives said, 'Our conclusions were really at the conversational level – that the big car trend was at an end. But we were not at all sure sufficient numbers of large car buyers were ready to move to dramatically lighter cars.' Nevertheless, GM did start concept studies that resulted in the Cadillac Seville.
>
> When the oil crisis hit in fall 1973, the company responded in further increments, at first merely increasing production of its existing small-car lines. Then as the crisis deepened, it added another partial solution, the subcompact 'T car' – the Chevette – and accelerated the Seville's development cycle. Next, as fuel economy appeared more saleable, executives set an initial target of removing 400 pounds from B-C bodies by 1977. As fuel economy pressures persisted and engineering feasibilities offered greater confidence, this target was increased to 800–1000 pounds (three mpg). No step by itself shifted the company's total strategic posture until the full downsizing of all lines was announced. But each partial solution built confidence and commitment toward a new direction.[5]

Broadening political support

Often these broad, emerging, strategic thrusts need expanded political support and understanding to achieve sufficient momentum to survive. Committees, task forces, and retreats tend to be favoured mechanisms for accomplishing this. If carefully managed, these do not become the 'garbage cans' of emerging ideas, as some observers have noted. By selecting the committee's chairman, membership, timing and agenda, guiding executives can largely influence and predict a desired outcome, and can force other executives towards a consensus. Such groups can be balanced to educate, evaluate, neutralize or overwhelm opponents. They can be used to legitimize new options or to generate broad cohesion among diverse thrusts, or they can be narrowly focused to build momentum. Guiding executives can constantly maintain complete control over these 'advisory processes' through their various influences and veto potentials. For example:

> IBM's Chairman Watson and Executive Vice President Learson had become concerned over what to do about: third generation computer technology, a proliferation of designs from various divisions, increasing costs of developing software, internal competition among their lines, and the needed breadth of line for the new computer applications they began to foresee. Step by step, they oversaw the killing of the company's huge Stretch computer line (uneconomic), a proposed 8000 series of computers (incompatible software), and the prototype English Scamp Computer (duplicative). They then initiated a series of 'strategic dialogues' with divisional executives to define a new strategy. But none came into place because of the parochial nature of divisional viewpoints.
>
> Learson, therefore, set up the SPREAD Committee, representing every major segment of the company. Its twelve members included the most likely opponent of an integrated line (Haanstra), the people who had earlier suggested the 8000 and Scamp designs, and Learson's handpicked lieutenant (Evans). When progress became 'hellishly slow', Haanstra was removed as chairman and Evans took over. Eventually the committee came forth with an integrating proposal for a single, compatible line of computers to blanket and open up the market for both scientific and business applications, with 'standard interface' for peripheral equipment. At an all-day meeting of the fifty top executives of the company, the report was not received with enthusiasm, but there were no compelling objections. So Learson blessed the silence as consensus saying, 'OK, we'll do it – i.e., go ahead with a major development program.'[6]

In addition to facilitating smooth implementation, many managers reported that interactive consensus building processes also improves the quality of the strategic decisions themselves and help achieve positive and innovative assistance when things otherwise could go wrong.

Overcoming opposition: 'zones of indifference' and 'no lose' situations

Executives of basically healthy companies in the sample realized that any attempt to introduce a new strategy would have to deal with the support its predecessor had. Barring a major crisis, a frontal attack on an old strategy could be regarded as an attack on those who espoused it – perhaps properly – and brought the enterprise to its present levels of success. There often exists a variety of legitimate views on what could and should be done in the new circumstances that a company faces. And wise executives do not want to alienate people who would otherwise be supporters. Consequently, they try to get key people behind their concepts whenever possible, to coopt or neutralize serious opposition, if necessary, or to find 'zones of indifference' where the propositions would not be disastrously opposed.[7] Most of all they seek 'no lose' situations which will motivate all the important players toward a common goal. For example:

> When James McFarland took over at General Mills from his power base in the Grocery Products Division, another serious contender for the top spot had been Louis B. 'Bo' Polk, a very bright, aggressive young man who headed the corporation's acquisition-diversification program. Both traditional lines and acquisitions groups wanted support for their activities and had high-level supporters. McFarland's corporate-wide 'goodness to greatness' conferences . . . first obtained broad agreement on growth goals and criteria for all areas.
>
> Out of this and the related acquisition proposal process came two thrusts: (1) to expand – internally and through acquisition – in food-related sectors and (2) to acquire new growth centers based on General Mills' marketing skills. Although there was no formal statement, there was a strong feeling that the majority of resources should be used in food-related areas. But neither group was foreclosed, and no one could suggest the new management was vindictive. As it turned out, over the next five years about $450 million was invested in new businesses, and the majority were not closely related to foods.

But such tactics do not always work. Successful executives surveyed tended to honour legitimate differences in viewpoints and noted that initial opponents often shaped new strategies in more effective directions and became supporters as new information became available. But strong-minded executives sometimes disagreed to the point where they had to be moved or stimulated to leave; timing could dictate very firm top-level decisions at key junctions. Barring crises, however, disciplinary steps usually occurred incrementally as individual executives' attitudes and competencies emerged vis-à-vis a new strategy.

Structuring flexibility: buffers, slacks and activists

Typically there are too many uncertainties in the total environment for managers to programme or control all the events involved in effecting a major change in strategic direction. Logic dictates, therefore, that managers purposely design flexibility into their organizations and have resources ready to develop incrementally as events demand. Planned flexibility requires: proactive horizon scanning to identify the general nature and potential impact of opportunities and threats the firm is most likely to encounter; creating sufficient resource buffers – or slacks – to respond effectively as events actually unfurl; developing and positioning 'credible activists' with a psychological commitment to move quickly and flexibly to exploit specific opportunities as they occur; and shortening decision lines from such people (and key operating managers) to the top for the most rapid system response. These – rather than precapsuled (and shelved) programmes to respond to stimuli which never quite occur as expected – are the keys to real contingency planning.

The concept of resource buffers requires special amplification. Quick access to resources is needed to cushion the impact of random events, to offset opponents' sudden attacks, or to build momentum for new strategic shifts. Some examples will indicate the form these buffers may take.

> For critical purchased items, General Motors maintained at least three suppliers, each with sufficient capacity to expand production should one of the others encounter a catastrophe. Thus, the company had expandable capacity with no fixed investment. Exxon set up its Exploration Group to purposely undertake the higher risks and longer-term investments necessary to search for oil in new areas, and thus to reduce the potential impact on Exxon if there were sudden unpredictable changes in the availability of Middle East oil. Instead of hoarding cash, Pillsbury and General Mills sold off unprofitable businesses and cleaned up their financial statements to improve their access to external capital sources for acquisitions. Such access in essence provided the protection of a cash buffer without its investment. IBM's large R&D facility and its project team approach to development assured that it had a pool of people it could quickly shift among various projects to exploit interesting new technologies.[8]

When such flexible response patterns are designed into the enterprise's strategy, it is proactively ready to move on those thrusts – acquisitions, innovations or resource explorations – which require incrementalism.

Systematic waiting and trial concepts

The prepared strategist may have to wait for events, as Roosevelt awaited a trauma like Pearl Harbor. The availability of desired acquisitions or real estate might depend on a death, divorce, fiscal crisis, management change or an erratic stock market break. Technological advances may have to await new knowledge, inventions or lucky accidents. Despite otherwise complete preparations, a planned market entry might not be wise until new legislation, trade agreements, or competitive shake-outs occur. Organizational moves have to be timed to retirements, promotions, management failures and so on. Very often the specific strategy adopted depends on the timing or sequence of such random events. For example:

> Although Continental Group's top executives had thoroughly discussed and investigated energy, natural resources, and insurance as possible 'fourth legs' for the company, the major acquisition possibilities were so different that the strategic choice depended on the fit of particular candidates – e.g., Peabody Coal or Richmond Insurance – within these possible

industries. The choice of one industry would have precluded the others. The sequence in which firms became available affected the final choice, and that choice itself greatly influenced the whole strategic posture of the company.

In many of the cases studied, strategies proactively launched trial concepts – Mr McColough's 'architecture of information' (Xerox), Mr Spoor's 'Super Box' (Pillsbury) – in order to generate options and concrete proposals. Usually these 'trial balloons' were phrased in very broad terms. Without making a commitment to any specific solution, the executive can activate the organization's creative abilities. This approach keeps the manager's own options open until substantive alternatives can be evaluated against each other and against concrete current realities. It prevents practical line managers from rejecting a strategic shift, as they might if forced to compare a 'paper option' against well-defined current needs. Such trial concepts give cohesion to the new strategy while enabling the company to take maximum advantage of the psychological and informational benefits of incrementalism.

SOLIDIFYING PROGRESS – INCREMENTALLY

As events move forward, executives can more clearly perceive the specific directions in which their organizations should – and realistically can – move. They can seek more aggressive movement and commitment to their new perceptions, without undermining important ongoing activities or creating unnecessary reactions to their purposes. Until this point, new strategic goals might remain broad, relatively unrefined, or even unstated except as philosophic concepts. More specific dimensions might be incrementally announced as key pieces of information fall into place, specific unanswered issues approach resolution, or significant resources have to be formally committed.

Creating pockets of commitment

Early in this stage, guiding executives may need actively to implant support in the organizations for new thrusts. They may encourage an array of exploratory projects for each of several possible options. Initial projects can be kept small, partial or ad hoc, neither forming a comprehensive programme nor seeming to be integrated into a cohesive strategy. Executives often provide stimulating goals, a proper climate for imaginative proposals and flexible resource support, rather than being personally identified with specific projects. In this way they can achieve organizational involvement and early commitment without focusing attention on any one solution too soon or losing personal credibility if it fails.

Once under way, project teams on the more successful programme in the sample became ever more committed to their particular areas of exploration. They became pockets of support for new strategies deep within the organization. Yet, if necessary, top managers could delay until the last moment their final decisions blending individual projects into a total strategy. Thus, they were able to obtain the best possible match among the company's technical abilities, its psychological commitments, and its changing market needs. By making final choices more effectively – as late as possible with better data, more conscientiously investigated options and the expert critiques competitive projects allowed – these executives actually increased technical and market efficiencies of their enterprises, despite the apparent added costs of parallel efforts.

In order to maintain their own objectivity and future flexibility, some executives choose to keep their own political profiles low as they build a new consensus. If they seem committed to a strategy too soon, they might discourage others from pursuing key issues which should be raised. By stimulating detailed investigations several levels down, top executives can seem detached yet still shape both progress and ultimate outcomes – by reviewing interim results and specifying the timing, format and forums for the release of data. When reports come forward, these executives can stand above the battle and review proposals objectively, without being personally on the defensive for having committed themselves to a particular solution too soon. From this position they can more easily orchestrate a high-level consensus on a new strategic thrust. As an added benefit, negative decisions on proposals often come from a group consensus that top executives can simply confirm to lower levels, thereby preserving their personal veto for more crucial moments. In many well-made decisions people at all levels contribute to the generation, amplification and interpretation of options and information to the extent that it is often difficult to say who really makes the decision.

Focusing the organization

In spite of their apparent detachment, top executives do focus their organizations on developing strategies at critical points in the process. While adhering to the rhetoric of specific goal-setting, most executives are careful *not* to state new goals in concrete terms before they have built a consensus among key players. They fear that they will prematurely centralize the organization, preempt interesting options, provide a common focus for otherwise fragmented opposition or cause the organization to act prematurely to carry out a specified commitment. Guiding executives may quietly shape the many alternatives flowing upward by using what Wrapp refers to as a 'hidden hand'. Through their information networks they can encourage concepts they favour, let weakly supported options die through inaction and establish hurdles or tests for strongly supported ideals with which they do not agree but which they do not wish to oppose openly.

Since opportunities for such focusing generally develop unexpectedly, the timing of key moves is often unpredictable. A crisis, a rash of reassignments, a reorganization or a key appointment may allow an executive to focus attention on particular thrusts, add momentum to some and, perhaps, quietly phase out others. Most managers surveyed seemed well aware of the notion that 'if there are no other options, mine wins'. Without being Machiavellian, they did not want misdirected option to gain strong political momentum and later have to be terminated in an open bloodbath. They also did not want to send false signals that simulated other segments of their organizations to make proposals in undesirable directions. They sensed very clearly that the patterns in which proposals are approved or denied will inevitably be perceived by lower echelons as precedents for developing future goals or policies.

Managing coalitions

Power interactions among key players are important at this stage of solidifying progress. Each player has a different level of power determined by his or her information base, organizational position and personal credibility. Executives legitimately perceive problems or opportunities differently because of their particular values, experiences and vantage points. They will promote the solutions they perceive as the best compromise for the total enterprise, for themselves, and for their particular units. In an organization with dispersed power, the key figure is the one who can manage coalitions. Since no one player has all the power, regardless of that individual's skill or position, the action that occurs over time might differ greatly from the intentions of any of the players. Top executives try to sense whether support exists among important parties for specific aspects of an issue and try to get partial decisions and momenta going for those aspects. As 'comfort levels' or political pressures within the top group rise in favour of specific decisions, the guiding executive might, within his or her concept of a more complete solution, seek – among the various features of different proposals – a balance that the most influential and credible parties can actively support. The result tends to be a stream of partial decisions on limited strategic issues made by constantly changing coalitions of the critical power centres. These decisions steadily evolve toward a broader consensus, acceptable to both the top executive and some 'dominant coalition' among these centres.

As a partial consensus emerges, top executives might crystallize issues by stating some broad goals in more specific terms for internal consumption. Finally, when sufficient general acceptance exists and the timing is right, the goals may begin to appear in more public announcements. For example:

> As General Mills divested several of its major divisions in the early 1960s, its annual reports began to refer to these as deliberate moves 'to concentrate on the company's strengths' and 'to intensify General Mills' efforts in the convenience foods field'. Such statements could not have been made until many of the actual divestitures were completed, and a sufficient consensus existed among the top executives to support the new corporate concept.

Formalizing commitment by empowering champions

As each major strategic thrust comes into focus, top executives try to ensure that some individual or group feels responsible for its goals. If the thrust will project the enterprise in entirely new directions, executives often want more than mere accountability for its success – they want real commitment. A significantly new major thrust, concept, product or problem solution frequently needs the nurturing hand of someone who genuinely identifies with it and whose future depends on its success. For example:

> Once the divestiture program at General Mills was sufficiently under way, General Rawlings selected young 'Bo' Polk to head up an acquisition program to use the cash generated. In this role Polk had nothing to lose. With strong senior management in the remaining consumer products divisions, the ambitious Polk would have had a long road to the top there. In acquisitions, he provided a small political target, only a $50 000 budget in a $500 million company. Yet he had high visibility and could build his own power base, if he were successful. With direct access to and the support of Rawlings, he would be protected through his early ventures. All he had to do was make sure his first few acquisitions were successful. As subsequent acquisitions succeeded, his power base could feed on itself – satisfying both Polk's ego needs and the company's strategic goals.

In some cases, top executives have to wait for champions to appear before committing resources to risky new strategies. They may immediately assign accountability for less dramatic plans by converting them into new missions for ongoing groups.

From this point on, the strategy-process is familiar. The organization's formal structure has to be adjusted to support the strategy. Commitment to the most important new thrusts has to be confirmed in formal plans. Detailed budgets, programmes, controls and reward-systems have to reflect all planned strategic thrusts. Finally, the guiding executive has to see that recruiting and staffing plans are aligned with the new goals and that – when the situation permits – supporters and persistent opponents of intended new thrusts are assigned to appropriate positions.

Continuing the dynamics by eroding consensus

The major strategic changes studied tended to take many years to accomplish. The process was continuous, often without any clear beginning or end. The decision-process constantly moulded and modified management's concerns and concepts. Radical crusades became the new conventional wisdom and over time totally new issues emerged. Participants or observers were often not aware of exactly when a particular decision had been made or when a subsequent consensus was created to supersede or modify it; the process of strategic change was continuous and dynamic. Several GM executives described the frequently imperceptible way in which many strategic decisions evolved:

> We use an iterative process to make a series of tentative decisions on the way we think the market will go. As we get more data we modify these continuously. It is often difficult to say who decided something and when – or even who originated a decision. . . . Strategy really evolves as a series

of incremental steps. . . . I frequently don't know when a decision is made in General Motors. I don't remember being in a committee meeting when things came to a vote. Usually someone will simply summarize a developing position. Everyone else either nods or states his particular terms of consensus.

A major strategic change in Xerox was characterized this way:

How was the overall organization decision made? I've often heard it said that after talking with a lot of people and having trouble with a number of decisions which were pending, Archie McCardell really reached his own conclusion and got Peter McColough's backing on it. But it really didn't happen quite that way. It was an absolutely evolutionary approach. It was a growing feeling. A number of people felt we ought to be moving toward some kind of matrix organization. We have always been a pretty democratic type of organization. In our culture you can't come down with mandates or ultimatums from the top on major changes like this. You almost have to work these things through and let them grow and evolve, keep them on the table so people are thinking about them and talking about them.

Once the organization arrives at its new consensus, the guiding executive has to move immediately to ensure that this new position does not become inflexible. In trying to build commitment to a new concept, individual executives often surround themselves with people who see the world in the same way. Such people can rapidly become systematic screens against other views. Effective executives therefore purposely continue the change process, constantly introducing new faces and stimuli at the top. They consciously begin to erode the very strategic thrusts they may have just created – a very difficult, but essential, psychological task.

INTEGRATION OF PROCESSES AND OF INTERESTS

In the large enterprises observed, strategy formulation was a continuously evolving analytical-political consensus process with neither a finite beginning nor a definite end. It generally followed the sequence described. Yet the total process was anything but linear. It was a grouping, cyclical process that often circled back on itself, with frequent interruptions and delays. Pfiffner aptly describes the process of strategy formation as being 'like fermentation in biochemistry, rather than an industrial assembly line'.[9]

Such incremental management processes are not abrogations of good management practice. Nor are they Machiavellian or consciously manipulative manoeuvres. Instead, they represent an adaptation to the practical psychological and informational problems of getting a constantly changing group of people with diverse talents and interests to move together effectively in a continually dynamic environment. Much of the impelling force behind logical incrementalism comes from a desire to tap the talents and psychological drives of the whole organization, to create cohesion and to generate identity with the emerging strategy. The remainder of that force results from the interactive nature of the random factors and lead times affecting the independent sub-systems that compose any total strategy.

An incremental – not piecemeal – process

The total pattern of action, though highly incremental, is not piecemeal in well-managed organizations. It requires constant, conscious reassessment of the total organizations, its capacities and its needs as related to surrounding environments. It requires continual attempts by top managers to integrate these actions into an understandable, cohesive whole. How do top managers themselves describe the process? Mr Estes, president of General Motors, said:

> We try to give them the broad concepts we are trying to achieve. We operate through questioning and fact gathering. Strategy is a state of mind you go through. When you think about a little problem, your mind begins to think how it will affect all the different elements in the total situation. Once you have had all the jobs you need to quality for this position, you can see the problem from a variety of viewpoints. But you don't try to ram your conclusions down people's throats. You try to persuade people what has to be done and provide confidence and leadership for them.

Formal-analytical techniques

At each stage of strategy development, effective executives constantly try to visualize the new patterns that might exist among the emerging strategies of various subsystems. As each subsystem strategy becomes more apparent, both its executive team and top-level groups try to project its implications for the total enterprise and to stimulate queries, support and feedback from those involved in related strategies. Perceptive top executives see that the various teams generating subsystem strategies have overlapping members. They require periodic updates and reviews before higher echelon groups that can bring a total corporate view to bear. They use formal planning processes to interrelate and evaluate the resources required, benefits sought, and risks undertaken vis-à-vis other elements of the enterprise's overall strategy. Some use scenario-techniques to help visualize potential impacts and relationships. Others utilize complex forecasting models to understand better the basic interactions among subsystems, the total enterprise and the environments. Still others use specialized staffs, 'devil's advocates', or 'contention teams' to make sure that all important aspects of their strategies receive a thorough evaluation.

Power-behavioural aspects: coalition management

All of the formal methodologies help, but the real integration of all the components in an enterprise's total strategy eventually takes place only in the minds of high-level executives. Each executive may legitimately perceive the intended balance of goals and thrusts differently. Some of these differences may be openly expressed as issues to be resolved when new information becomes available. Some differences may remain unstated – hidden agenda to

emerge at later dates. Others may be masked by accepting so broad a statement of intention that many different views are included in a seeming consensus, when a more specific statement might be divisive. Nevertheless, effective
strategies do achieve a level of understanding and consensus sufficient to
focus action.

Top executives deliberately manage the incremental processes within each
subsystem to create the basis for consensus. They also manage the coalitions
that lie at the heart of most controlled strategy developments.[10] They recognize that they are at the confluence of innumerable pressures – from stock-
holders, environmentalists, government bodies, customers, suppliers,
distributors, producing units, marketing groups, technologists, unions, special issue activists, individual employees, ambitious executives and so on –
and that knowledgeable people of good will can easily disagree on proper
actions. In response to changing pressures and coalitions among these
groups, the top management team constantly forms and reforms its own
coalitions on various decisions.[11]

Most major strategic moves tend to assist some interests – and executives'
careers – at the expense of others. Consequently, each set of interests serves as
a check on the others and thus helps maintain the breadth and balance of
strategy.[12] To avoid significant errors some managers try to ensure that all
important groups have representation at or access to the top.[13] The guiding
executive group may continuously adjust the number, power or proximity of
such access points in order to maintain a desired balance and focus.[14] These
delicate adjustments require constant negotiations and implied bargains within
the leadership group. Balancing the focuses that different interests exert on key
decisions is perhaps the ultimate control top executives have in guiding and
coordinating the formulation of their companies' strategies.[15]

Establishing, measuring and rewarding key thrusts

Few executives or management teams can keep all the dimensions of a complex
evolving strategy in mind as they deal with the continuous flux of urgent issues.
Consequently, effective strategic managers seek to identify a few central
themes that can help to draw diverse efforts together in a common cause.[16]
Once identified, these themes help to maintain focus and consistency in the
strategy. They make it easier to discuss and monitor proposed strategic thrusts.
Ideally, these themes can be developed into a matrix of programmes and goals,
cutting across formal divisional lines and dominating the selection and ranking
of projects within divisions. This matrix can, in turn, serve as the basis for
performance measurement, control and reward systems that ensure the intended strategy is properly implemented.

Unfortunately, few companies in the sample were able to implement such a
complex planning and control system without creating undue rigidities. But all
did utilize logical incrementalism to bring cohesion to the formal-analytical
and power-behavioural processes needed to create effective strategies. Most
used some approximation of the process sequence previously described to form

their strategies at both subsystem and overall corporate levels. A final summary example demonstrates how deliberate incrementalism can integrate the key elements in more traditional approaches to strategy formulation.

In the late 1970s a major nation's largest bank named as its new president and CEO a man with a long and successful career, largely in domestic operating positions. The bank's chairman had been a familiar figure on the international stage and was due to retire in three to five years. The new CEO, with the help of a few trusted colleagues, his chief planner, and a consultant, first tried to answer the questions: 'If I look ahead seven to eight years to my retirement as CEO, what should I like to leave behind as the hallmarks of my leadership? What accomplishments would define my era as having been successful?' He chose the following goals:

1. To be the country's number one bank in profitability and size without sacrificing the quality of its assets or liabilities;
2. To be recognized as a major international bank;
3. To improve substantially the public image and employee perceptions of the bank;
4. To maintain progressive policies that prevent unionization;
5. To be viewed as a professional, well-managed bank with strong, planned management continuity;
6. To be clearly identified as the country's most professional corporate finance bank, with a strong base within the country but with foreign and domestic operations growing in balance;
7. To have women in top management and to achieve full utilization of the bank's female employees;
8. To have a tighter, smaller headquarters and a more rationalized, decentralized corporate structure.

The CEO brought back to the corporate offices the head of his overseas divisions to be COO and to be a member of the executive committee, which ran the company's affairs. The CEO discussed his personal views concerning the bank's future with this committee and also with several of his group VPs. Then, to arrive at a cohesive set of corporate goals, the executive committee investigated the bank's existing strengths and weaknesses (again with the assistance of consultants) and extrapolated its existing growth trends seven to eight years into the future. According to the results of this exercise, the bank's foreseeable growth would require that:

1. The bank's whole structure be reoriented to make it a much stronger force in international banking;
2. The bank decentralize operations much more than it ever had;
3. The bank find or develop at least 100 new top-level specialists and general managers within a few years;
4. The bank reorganize around a 'four-bank' principle (international, commercial, investment and retail banks) with entirely new linkages forged among these units;

5. These linkages and much of the bank's new international thrust be built on its expertise in certain industries, which were the primary basis of its parent country's international trade;

6. The bank's profitability be improved across the board, especially in its diverse retail banking units.

To develop more detailed data for specific actions and to further develop consensus around needed moves, the CEO commissioned two consulting studies: one on the future of the bank's home country and the other on changing trade patterns and relationships worldwide. As these studies became available, the CEO allowed an ever wider circle of top executives to do a critique on the studies' findings and to share their insights. Finally, the CEO and the executive committee were willing to draw up and agree to a statement of 10 broad goals (parallel to the CEO's original goals but enriched in flavour and detail). By then, some steps were already under way to implement specific goals (for example, the four-bank concept). But the CEO wanted further participation of his line officers in the formulation of the goals and in the strategic thrusts they represented across the whole bank. By now 18 months had gone by, but there was widespread consensus within the top management group on major goals and directions.

The CEO then organized an international conference of some 40 top officers of the bank and had a background document prepared for this meeting containing: the broad goals agreed upon; the 10 major thrusts that the executive committee thought were necessary to meet these goals; the key elements needed to back up each thrust; and a summary of the national and economic analyses the thrusts were based upon. The 40 executives had two full days to do a critique, question, improve and clarify the ideas in this document. Small work groups of line executives reported their findings and concerns directly to the executive committee. At the end of the meeting, the executive committee tabled one of the major thrusts for further study, agreed to refined wording for some of the bank's broad goals and modified details of the major thrusts in line with expressed concerns.

The CEO announced that within three months each line officer would be expected to submit his/her own statement of how his/her unit would contribute to the major goals and thrusts agreed on. Once these unit goals were discussed and negotiated with the appropriate top executive group, the line officers would develop specific budgetary and nonbudgetary programmes showing precisely how their units would carry out each of the major thrusts in the strategy. The CEO was asked to develop measures both for all key elements of each unit's fiscal performance and for performance against each agreed upon strategic thrust within each unit. As these plans came into place, it became clear that the old organization had to be aligned behind these new thrusts. The CEO had to substantially redefine the CEO's job, deal with some crucial internal political pressures, and place the next generation of top managers in the line positions supporting each major thrust. The total process from concept formulation to implementation of the control system was to span three to four years, with new goals and thrusts emerging flexibly as external events and opportunities developed.

CONCLUSIONS

In recent years, there has been an increasingly loud chorus of discontent about corporate strategic planning. Many managers are concerned that despite elaborate strategic planning systems, costly staffs for planning and major commitments of their own time, their most elaborately analysed strategies never get implemented. These executives and their companies generally have fallen into the trap of thinking about strategy formulation and implementation as separate, sequential processes. They rely on the awesome rationality of their formally derived strategies and the inherent power of their positions to cause their organizations to respond. When this does not occur, they become bewildered, if not frustrated and angry. Instead, successful managers in the companies observed acted logically and incrementally to improve the quality of information used in key decisions; to overcome the personal and political pressures resisting change; to deal with the varying lead times and sequencing problems in critical decisions; and to build the organizational awareness, understanding and psychological commitment essential to effective strategies. By the time the strategies began to crystallize, pieces of them were already being implemented. Through the very processes they used to formulate their strategies, these executives had built sufficient organizational momentum and identity with the strategies to make them flow toward flexible and successful implementation.

REFERENCES

1. See J.B. Quinn (1979) Xerox Corporation (B) (copyrighted case, Amos Tuck School of Business Administration, Dartmouth College, Hanover, NH)
2. Quinn (1979) *op. cit.*
3. See J.B. Quinn (1978) General Motors Corporation: the downsizing decision (copyrighted case, Amos Tuck School of Business Administration, Dartmouth College, Hanover, NH)
4. See J.H. Dessauer (1971) *My Years with Xerox: the billions nobody wanted,* Doubleday, Garden City, NY
5. Quinn (1979) *op. cit.*
6. See T.A. Wise (1966) I.B.M.'s $5 billion gamble, *Fortune,* September, pp. 118–24; T.A. Wise (1966), The rocky road to the marketplace (Part II: I.B.M.'s $5 billion gamble), *Fortune,* October, pp. 138–52
7. For an excellent overview of the processes of co-optation and neutralization, see Sayles (1964). For perhaps the first reference to the concept of the 'zone of indifference,' see C.I. Barnard (1938) *The Functions of the Executive,* Harvard University Press, Cambridge, MA. The following two sources note the need of executives for coalition behaviour to reduce the organizational conflict resulting from differing interests and goal preferences in large organizations: Cyert and March (1963); J.G. March (1964) *Business Decision Making,* In H.J. Leavitt and L.R. Pondy (Eds) *Readings in Managerial Psychology,* University of Chicago Press, Chicago
8. Quinn (1979) *op. cit.*

9. See J.M. Pfiffner (1960) Administrative rationality, *Public Administration Review,* Summer, pp. 125–32.
10. See R. James (1978) *Corporate Strategy and Change – The Management of People,* monograph, The University of Chicago. The author does an excellent job of pulling together the threads of coalition management at top organizational levels
11. See Cyert and March (1963), p 115
12. Lindblom (Spring 1959) notes that every interest has a 'watchdog' and that purposely allowing these watchdogs to participate in and influence decisions creates consensus decisions that all can live with. Similar conscious access to the top for different interests can now be found in corporate structures
13. See Zaleznik (May–June 1970)
14. For an excellent view of the bargaining processes involved in coalition management, see Sayles (1964), pp. 207–17
15. For suggestions on why the central power figure in decentralized organizations must be the person who manages its dominant coalition, the size of which will depend on the issues involved, and the number of areas in which the organizations must rely on judgemental decisions, see Thompson (1967)
16. Wrapp (September–October 1967) notes the futility of a top manager trying to push a full package of goals

7

CONCEPTS FOR THE MANAGEMENT OF ORGANIZATIONAL CHANGE

David A. Nadler

Bringing about major change in a large and complex organization is a difficult task. Policies, procedures, and structures need to be altered. Individuals and groups have to be motivated to continue to perform in the face of major turbulence. People are presented with the fact that the 'old ways,' which include familiar tasks, jobs, procedures, and structures are no longer applicable. Political behavior frequently becomes more active and more intense. It is not surprising, therefore, that the process of effectively implementing organizational change has long been a topic that both managers and researchers have pondered. While there is still much that is not understood about change in complex organizations, the experiences and research of recent years do provide some guidance to those concerned with implementing major changes in organizations.

This paper is designed to provide some useful concepts to aid in understanding the dynamics of change and to help in the planning and managing of major organizational changes. The paper is organized into several sections. We will start with a brief discussion of a model of organizational behavior. This discussion is necessary since it is difficult to think about changing organizations without some notion of why they work the way they do in the first place. Second, we will define what we mean by organizational change and identify criteria for the effective management of change. Third, we will discuss some of the basic problems of implementing change. In the last section, we will list some specific methods and tools for effective implementation of organizational changes.

A VIEW OF ORGANIZATIONS

There are many different ways of thinking about organizations and the patterns of behavior that occur within them. During the past two decades, there has emerged a view of organizations as complex open social systems (Katz & Kahn, 1966), mechanisms which take input from the larger environment and subject that input to various transformation processes that result in output.

As systems, organizations are seen as composed of interdependent parts. Change in one element of the system will result in changes in other parts of the system. Similarly, organizations have the property of equilibrium; the system will generate energy to move towards a state of balance. Finally, as open systems, organizations need to maintain favorable transactions of input and output with the environment in order to survive over time.

While the systems perspective is useful, systems theory by itself may be too abstract a concept to be a usable tool for managers. Thus, a number of organizational theorists have attempted to develop more pragmatic theories or models based on the system paradigm. There are a number of such models currently in use. One of these will be employed here.

The particular approach, called a *Congruence Model of Organizational Behavior* (Nadler & Tushman, 1977; 1979) is based on the general systems model. In this framework, the major inputs to the system of organizational behavior are the *environment* which provides constraints, demands and opportunities, the *resources* available to the organization, and the *history* of the organization. A fourth input, and perhaps the most crucial, is the organization's *strategy*. Strategy is the set of key decisions about the match of the organization's resources to the opportunities, constraints, and demands in the environment within the context of history.

The output of the system is, in general, the effectiveness of the organization's performance, consistent with the goals of strategy. Specifically, the output includes *organizational performance*, as well as *group performance* and *individual behavior and affect* which, of course, contribute to organizational performance.

The basic framework thus views the organization as being the mechanism that takes inputs (strategy and resources in the context of history and environment) and transforms them into outputs (patterns of individual, group, and organizational behavior). This view is portrayed in Figure 1.

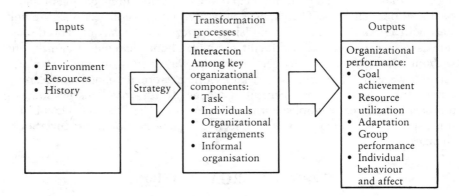

Figure 1   The systems model applied to organizational behavior

The major focus of organizational analysis is therefore the transformation process. The model conceives of the organization as being composed of four major components. The first component is the task of the organization, or the work to be done and its crucial characteristics. The second component is composed of the *individuals* who are to perform organizational tasks. The third component includes all of the *formal organizational arrangements*, including various structures, processes, systems, etc. which are designed to motivate and facilitate individuals in the performance of organizational tasks. Finally, there is a set of *informal organizational arrangements*, which are usually neither planned nor written, but which tend to emerge over time. These include patterns of communication, power and influence, values and norms, etc. which characterize how an organization actually functions.

How do these four components (task, individuals, organizational arrangements, and the informal organization) relate to one another? The relationship among components is the basic dynamic of the model. Each component can be thought of as having a relationship with each other component. Between each pair, then, we think of a relative degree of consistency, congruence, or 'fit.' For example, if we look at the type of work to be done (task) and the nature of the people available to do the work (individuals) we could make a statement about the congruence between the two by seeing whether the demands of the work are consistent with the skills and abilities of the individuals. At the same time we would compare the rewards that the work provides to the needs and desires of the individuals. By looking at these factors, we would be able to assess how congruent the nature of the task was with the nature of the individuals in the system. In fact, we could look at the

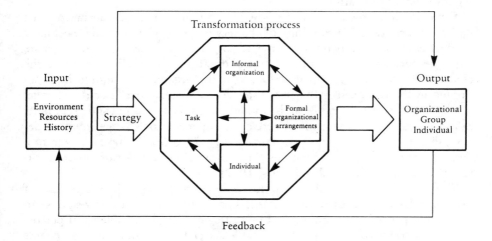

Figure 2 A congruence model of organizational behavior (source: Nadler D.A. and Tushman M.L. (1979) A congruence model for diagnosing organizational behavior. In: D. Kolb, I. Rubin and J. McIntyre (eds) *Organizational Psychology: A Book of Readings* (3rd edn). Englewood Cliffs, NJ: Prentice-Hall)

question of congruence among all the components, or in terms of all six of the possible relationships among them (see Figure 2). The basic hypothesis of the model is therefore that *organizations will be most effective when their major components are congruent with each other.* To the extent that organizations face problems of effectiveness due to management and organizational factors, these problems will stem from poor fit, or lack of congruence, among organizational components.

This approach to organization is thus a contingency approach. There is not one best organization design, or style of management, or method of working. Rather, different patterns of organization and management will be most appropriate in different situations. The model recognizes the fact that individuals, tasks, strategies, and environments may differ greatly from organization to organization.

THE TASK OF IMPLEMENTING CHANGE

Having briefly presented some concepts that underlie our thinking about organizations, the question of change can now be addressed. Managers are frequently concerned about implementing organizational changes. Often changes in the environment necessitate organizational change. For example, factors related to competition, technology, or regulation, shift and thus necessitate changes in organizational strategy. If a new strategy is to be executed, then the organization and its various subunits (departments, groups, divisions, etc.) must perform tasks that may be different from those previously performed. Building on the organizational model presented above, this means that modification may need to be made in organizational arrangements, individuals and the informal organization.

Typically, implementing a change involves moving an organization to some desired future state. We can think of changes in terms of transitions (Beckhard & Harris, 1977). At any point in time, the organization exists in a current state (A). The current state describes how the organization functions prior to the change. The future state (B) describes how the organization should be functioning in the future. It is the state that ideally would exist after the change. The period between A and B can be thought of as the transition state (C). In its most general terms, then, the effective managements of change involves developing an understanding of the current state (A), developing an image of a desired future state (B), and moving the organization from A through a transition period to B (Beckhard & Harris, 1977).

Major transitions usually occur in response to changes in the nature of organizational inputs or outputs. Most significant changes are in response to or in anticipation of environmental or strategic shifts, or problems of performance. In terms of the congruence model, a change occurs when managers determine that the configuration of the components in the current state is not effective and the organization must be reshaped. Often this means a rethinking and redefining of the organization's task followed by changes in other components to support that new task (see Figure 3).

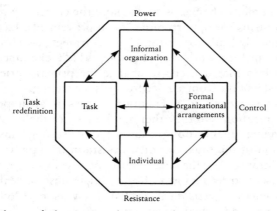

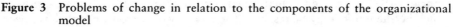

Figure 3 Problems of change in relation to the components of the organizational model

What constitutes effective management of these changes? There are several criteria to consider. Building on the transition framework presented above, organizational change is effectively managed when:

1. The organization is moved from the current state to the future state.
2. The functioning of the organization in the future state meets expectations; i.e. it works as planned.
3. The transition is accomplished without undue cost to the organization.
4. The transition is accomplished without undue cost to individual organizational members.

Of course, not every organizational change can be expected to meet these criteria, but such standards provide a target for planning change. The question is how to manage the way in which the change is implemented so as to maximize the chances that the change will be effective. Experience has shown that the way that a change is implemented can influence the effectiveness of the transition as much as the content of that change.

PROBLEMS IN IMPLEMENTING CHANGE

Experience and research have shown that the process of creating change is more difficult than it might seem. It is tempting to think of an organization as a large machine where parts can be replaced at will. On the contrary, the task of changing the behavior of organizations, groups and individuals has turned out to be a difficult and often frustrating endeavor.

Using the organizational model presented above, we can envision how organizations, as systems, are resistant to change. The forces of equilibrium tend to work to cancel out many changes. Changing one component of an organization may reduce its congruence with other components. As this happens, energy develops in the organization to limit, encapsulate, or revise the change.

The first issue in many changes is to diagnose the current system to identify the source of problems (or opportunities for improvement). In a large organization, this frequently leads to a rethinking of strategy, and a redefinition of the organization's task or work. For example, AT&T examines the environment and determines that it needs to change the primary orientation of its strategy, and thus, its task from service towards marketing.

The analysis of strategy and redefinition of task is an important step in changing an organization. On the other hand, many of the most troublesome problems of changing organizations occur not in the strategic/task shift, but in the implementation of the organizational transition to support the change in the nature of the strategy and the work. More specifically, any major organizational change presents three major problems which must be dealt with.

First is the problem of *resistance* to change (Watson, 1969; Zaltman & Duncan, 1977). Any individual faced with a change in the organization in which he/she works may be resistant for a variety of reasons. People have need for a certain degree of stability or security; change presents unknowns which cause anxiety. In addition, a change that is imposed on an individual reduces his/her sense of autonomy or self-control. Furthermore, people typically develop patterns for coping with or managing the current structure and situation. Change means that they will have to find new ways of managing their own environments – ways that might not be as successful as those currently used. In addition, those who have power in the current situation may resist change because it threatens that power. They have a vested interest in the status quo. Finally, individuals may resist change for ideological reasons; they truly believe that the way things are done currently is better than the proposed change. Whatever the source, individual resistance to change must be overcome for implementation of a change to be successful.

A second problem is that of organizational *control*. Change disrupts the normal course of events within an organization. It thus disrupts and undermines existing systems of management control, particularly those developed as part of the formal organizational arrangements. Change may make those systems irrelevant and/or inappropriate. As a result, during a change, it may become easy to lose control of the organization. As goals, structures, and people shift, it becomes difficult to monitor performance and make corrections as in normal control processes.

A related problem is that most formal organizational arrangements are designed for stable states, not transition states. Managers become fixated on the future state (B) and assume that all that is needed is to design the most effective organizational arrangements for the future. They think of change from A to B as simply a mechanical or procedural detail. The problems created by the lack of concern for the transition state are compounded by the inherent uniqueness of it. In most situations, the management systems and structures developed to manage A or B are simply not appropriate or adequate for the management of C. They are steady state management systems, designed to run organizations already in place, rather than transitional management systems.

A third problem is *power*. Any organization is a political system made up of different individuals, groups, and coalitions competing for power (Tushman, 1977; Salancik & Pfeffer, 1977).

Political behavior is thus a natural and expected feature of organizations. This occurs in both states A and B. In state C (transition), however, these dynamics become even more intense as the old order is dismantled and a new order emerges. This happens because any significant change poses the possibility of upsetting or modifying the balance of power among groups. The uncertainty created by change creates ambiguity, which in turn tends to increase the probability of political activity (Thompson & Tuden, 1959). Individuals and groups may take action based on their perception of how the change will affect their relative power position in the organization. They will try to influence where they will sit in the organization that emerges from the transition, and will be concerned about how the conflict of the transition period will affect the balance of power in the future state. Finally, individuals and groups may engage in political action because of their ideological position on the change – it may be inconsistent with their shared values or image of the organization (Pettigrew, 1972).

In some sense, each of these problems is related primarily to one of the components of the organization (see Figure 3). Resistance relates to the individual component, getting people to change their behavior. Control concerns the design of appropriate organization arrangements for the transition period. Power relates to the reactions of the informal organization to change. Therefore, if a change is to be effective, all three problems – resistance, control, and power – must be addressed.

GUIDELINES FOR IMPLEMENTING CHANGE

The three basic problems that are inherent in change each lead to a general implication for the management of change (see Figure 4).

The implication of the resistance problem is the need to *motivate* changes in behavior by individuals. This involves overcoming the natural resistance to change that emerges, and getting individuals to behave in ways consistent with both the short-run goals of change and the long-run organizational strategy.

The implication of the control problem is the need to *manage the transition*. Organizational arrangements must be designed and used to ensure that control is maintained during and after the transition. They must be specifically appropriate to the transition period rather than to the current or future state.

Finally, the implication of the power issue is the need to *shape the political dynamics* of change so that power centers develop that support the change, rather than block it (Pettigrew, 1975).

Each of these general implications suggests specific actions that can be taken to improve the chances of achieving an effective change. A number of action steps can be identified for each of the three implications.

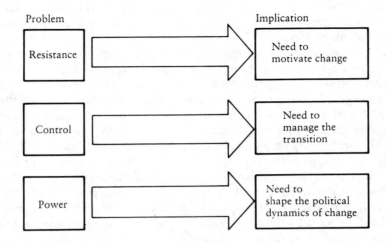

Figure 4   Problems of change and implications for change management

Action steps to motivate change

The first action step is to *identify and surface dissatisfaction with the current state*. As long as people are satisfied with the current state, they will not be motivated to change; people need to be 'unfrozen' out of their inertia in order to be receptive to change (Lewin, 1947; Bennis et al. 1973). The greater the pain and dissatisfaction with the current state, the greater the motivation to change and the less the resistance to change. As a consequence, the management of change may require the creation of pain and dissatisfaction with the status quo. Dissatisfaction most commonly results from information concerning some aspect of organizational performance which is different from either desired or expected performance. Discrepancies can therefore be used to create dissatisfaction. As a result, data can be an important tool to initiate a process of change (Nadler, 1977).

The second action step is to build in *participation* in the change. One of the most consistent findings in the research on change is that participation in the change tends to reduce resistance, build ownerships of the change, and thus motivate people to make the change work (Coch & French, 1948; Vroom, 1964; Kotter & Schlesinger, 1979). Participation also facilitates the communication of information about what the change will be and why it has come about. Participation may also lead to obtaining new information from those participating, information that may enhance the effectiveness of the change or the future state.

On the other hand, participation has costs since it involves relinquishing control, takes time, and may create conflict. For each situation, different degrees of participation may be most effective (Vroom & Yetton, 1973). Participation may involve work on diagnosing the present situation, in planning change, in implementing change, or in combinations of the above. Participation may also vary in the specific devices that are used, ranging from large-scale data collection to sensing groups, to questionnaires, to cross unit committees, etc.

A third action step is to build in *rewards* for the behavior that is desired both during the transition state and in the future state. Our understanding of motivation and behavior in organizations suggests that people will tend to be motivated to behave in ways that they perceive as leading to desired outcomes (Vroom, 1964; Lawler, 1973). This implies that both formal and informal rewards must be identified and tied to the behavior that is needed, both for the transition and for the future state. The most frequent problem is that organizations expect individuals to behave in certain ways (particularly in a transition) while rewarding them for other conflicting behaviors (Kerr, 1975). In particular, rewards such as bonuses, pay systems, promotion, recognition, job assignment, and status symbols all need to be carefully examined during major organizational changes and restructured to support the direction of the transition.

Finally, people need to be provided with the *time and opportunity to disengage from the present state*. Change frequently creates feelings of loss, not unlike a death. People need to mourn for the old system or familiar way of doing things. This frequently is manifested in the emergence of stories or myths about the 'good old days,' even when those days weren't so good. The process of dealing with a loss and going through mourning takes time, and those managing change should take this into account. This factor underscores the need to provide information about the problems of the status quo and also to plan for enough time in advance of a change to allow people to deal with the loss and prepare for it.

Action steps to manage the transition

One of the first and most critical steps for managing the transition state is to *develop and communicate a clear image of the future* (Beckhard & Harris, 1977). Resistance and confusion frequently develop during an organizational change because people are unclear about what the future state will be like. Thus the goals and purposes of the change become blurred, and individual expectancies get formed on the basis of information that is frequently erroneous. In the absence of a clear image of the future, rumors develop, people design their own fantasies, and they act on them. Therefore, as clear an image as possible of the future state should be developed to serve as a guideline, target, or goal. In particular, a written statement or description of the future state may be of value in clarifying the image. Similarly, it is important to communicate information to those involved in the change, including what the future state will be like, how the transition will come about, why the change is being implemented, and how individuals will be affected by the change. This communication can be accomplished in a variety of ways, ranging from written communications to small group meetings, large briefing sessions, videotaped presentations, etc.

A second action step for managing the transition involves the use of *multiple and consistent leverage points*. If, building on the model presented above, an organization is made up of components which are interdependent, then the successful alteration of organizational behavior patterns must involve the use of multiple leverage points, or modifications in the larger set of components which shape the behavior of the organization and the people in it (Nadler & Tichy, 1980). Structural change, task change, change in the social environment, as well as changes in individuals themselves are all needed to bring about significant and lasting changes in the patterns of organizational behavior. Changes that are targeted at individuals and social relations (such as training, group interventions, etc.) tend to fade out quickly with few lasting effects when done in isolation (Porter, Lawler & Hackman, 1975). On the other hand, task and structural changes alone, while powerful and enduring, frequently produce unintended and dysfunctional consequences (see, for example, literature on control systems; e.g., Lawler & Rhode, 1976). Change which is in the direction intended and which is lasting therefore requires the use of multiple leverage points to modify more than a single component. Similarly, the changes have to be structured so that they are consistent; the training of individuals, for example, should dovetail with new job descriptions, rewards systems, or reporting relationships. In the absence of consistency, changes run the risk of creating new 'poor fits' among organizational components. The result is either an abortive change, or decreases in organizational performance.

The third action steps involves a number of different activities. *Organizational arrangements for the transition* need to be explicitly considered, designed, and used. As mentioned earlier, the organizational arrangements that function in either the present or future state are typically steady state designs, rather than designs for use in managing the transition state. The whole issue of developing structures to manage the transition has been discussed in depth elsewhere (see Beckhard & Harris, 1977), but a number of the most important elements should be mentioned here. In particular, the following organizational arrangements are important for managing the change.

A. A transition manager

Someone should be designated as the manager of the organization for the transition state. This person may be a member of management, a chief executive, or someone else, but frequently it is difficult for one person to manage the current state, prepare to manage the future state, and simultaneously manage the transition. This person should have the power and authority needed to make the transition happen, and should be appropriately linked to the steady state managers, particularly the future state manager.

B. Resources for the transition

Major transitions involve potentially large risks for organizations. Given this, they are worth doing well and it is worth providing the needed resources to make them happen effectively. Resources such as personnel, dollars, training expertise, consultative expertise, etc. must be provided for the transition manager.

C. Transition plan

A transition is a movement from one state to another. To have that occur effectively, and to measure and control performance, a plan is needed with benchmarks, standards of performance, and similar features. Implicit in such a plan is a specification of the responsibilities of key individuals and groups.

D. Transition management structures

Frequently it is difficult for a hierarchy to manage the process of change itself. As a result, it may be necessary to develop other structures or use other devices outside the regular organizational structure during the transition management period. Special task forces, pilot projects, experimental units, etc. need to be designed and employed for this period (see again Beckhard & Harris, 1977 for a discussion of these different devices).

The final action step for transition management involves developing *feedback mechanisms* to provide transition managers with information on the effectiveness of the transition and provide data on areas which require additional attention or action. There is a huge amount of anecdotal data about senior managers ordering changes and assuming those changes were made, only to find out to their horror that the change never occurred. Such a situation develops because managers lack feedback devices to tell them whether actions have been effective or not. During stable periods, effective managers tend to develop various ways of eliciting feedback. During the transition state, however, these mechanisms often break down due to the turbulence of the change, or because of the natural inclination not to provide 'bad news.' Thus, it becomes important for transition managers to develop multiple, redundant, and sensitive mechanisms for generating feedback about the transition. Devices such as surveys, sensing groups, consultant interviews, etc. as well as informal communication channels need to be developed and used during this period.

Action steps for shaping the political dynamics of change

If an organization is a political system composed of different groups competing for power, then the most obvious action step involves *ensuring or developing the support of key power groups*. For a change to occur successfully, a critical mass of power groups has to be assembled and mobilized in support of the change. Those groups that may oppose the change have to in some way be compensated for or have their effects neutralized. Not all power groups have to be intimately involved in the change. Some may support the change on ideological grounds, while others may support the change because it enhances their own power position. With other groups, they will have to be included in the planning of the change so that their participation will motivate them, or co-opt them (Selznick, 1949). Still others may have to be dealt with by bargaining or negotiations. The main point is that the key groups who may be affected by the change need to be identified, and strategies for building support among a necessary portion of those groups need to be developed and carried out (Sayles, 1979).

A major factor affecting the political terrain of an organization is the behavior of key and powerful leaders. Thus a second major action step involves *using leader behavior to generate energy in support of the change.* Leaders can mobilize groups, generate energy, provide models, manipulate major rewards, and do many other things which can affect the dynamics of the informal organization. Sets of leaders working in coordination can have a tremendously powerful impact on the informal organization. Thus leaders need to think about using their own behavior to generate energy (see House, 1976 on charismatic leadership) as well as to build on the support and behavior of other leaders (both formal and informal) within the organization.

The third action step involves *using symbols and language to create energy* (Peters, 1978; Pfeffer, 1980). By providing a language to describe the change and symbols that have emotional impact, it is possible to create new power centers or to bring together power centers under a common banner. Language is also important in defining an ambiguous reality. If, for example, a change is declared a success then it may become a success in the perception of others.

Finally, there is the need to *build in stability.* Organizations and individuals can only stand so much uncertainty and turbulence. An overload of uncertainty may create dysfunctional effects, as people may begin to panic, engage in extreme defensive behavior, and become irrationally resistant to any new change proposed. The increase of anxiety created by constant change thus has its costs. One way of dealing with this is to provide some sources of stability (structures, people, physical locations, etc. that stay the same) that serve as 'anchors' for people to hold onto and provide a means for definition of the self in the midst of turbulence. While too many anchors can encourage resistance, it is important to provide some stability. More importantly, it is necessary to communicate the stability. People may not take comfort from something that is stable if they are unsure of its stability. Thus those aspects of the organization that will not change during a transition period need to be identified and communicated to organization members.

SUMMARY

This paper has attempted to identify some of the problems and issues of bringing about changes in complex organizations. At the same time, a number of general and specific action steps have been suggested. To understand how to change organizational behavior, we need a tool to understand how it occurs in the first place. The model used here (Nadler & Tushman, 1977; 1979) suggests that any change will encounter three general problems: resistance, control, and power. The general implication is the need to motivate change, manage the transition, and shape the political dynamics of change. For each of these three general implications, a number of specific action steps have been identified (see Figure 5).

Obviously, each of these action steps will be more or less critical (and more or less feasible) in different situations. Thus students of organization and

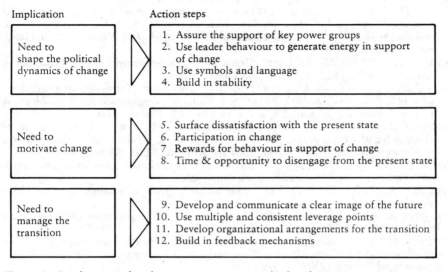

Implication   Action steps

| Need to shape the political dynamics of change | 1. Assure the support of key power groups
2. Use leader behaviour to generate energy in support of change
3. Use symbols and language
4. Build in stability |

| Need to motivate change | 5. Surface dissatisfaction with the present state
6. Participation in change
7 Rewards for behaviour in support of change
8. Time & opportunity to disengage from the present state |

| Need to manage the transition | 9. Develop and communicate a clear image of the future
10. Use multiple and consistent leverage points
11. Develop organizational arrangements for the transition
12. Build in feedback mechanisms |

Figure 5 Implications for change management and related action steps

managers alike need to be diagnostic in their approach to the problems of managing change. Each situation, while reflecting general patterns, has unique characteristics, based on its own differences of individuals, history, and situations. Thus specific variants of the action steps need to be developed for specific situations. To do this, managers need diagnostic models to understand problems, as well as guidelines for implementing changes, as presented here. Together, these two types of tools can be powerful aids in building and maintaining effective organizations.

REFERENCES

Beckhard, R. & Harris, R. (1977) *Organizational Transitions*. Reading, Massachusetts: Addison-Wesley.

Bennis, W.G., Berlew, D.E., Schein, E.H. & Steele, F.I. (1973) *Interpersonal Dynamics: Essays and Readings on Human Interaction*. Homewood, Ill.: Dorsey Press.

Coch, L. & French, J.R.P., Jr. (1948) Overcoming resistance to change. *Human Relations*, 11, 512–532.

House, Robert, J. (1976) A 1976 theory of charismatic leadership (mimeo). Faculty of Management Studies, University of Toronto.

Katz, D. & Kahn, R.L. (1966) *The Social Psychology of Organizations*. New York: John Wiley & Sons.

Kerr, S. (1975) On the folly of rewarding A while hoping for B. *Academy of Management Journal*, December, 769–783.

Kotter, J.P. & Schlesinger, L.A. (1979) Choosing strategies for change. *Harvard Business Review*, (March–April), 106–114.

Lawler, E.E. (1973) *Motivation in Work Organizations*. Belmont, California: Wadsworth Publishing Co.

Lawler, E.E. & Rhode, J.G. (1976) *Information and Control in Organizations*. Santa Monica, California: Goodyear.

Lewin, K. (1947). Frontiers in group dynamics. *Human Relations*, 1, 5–41.

Nadler, D.A. & Tushman, M.L. (1981) A congruence to model for diagnosing organizational behavior. In: D.A. Nadler, M.L. Tushman & N.G. Hatvany (eds.). *Approaches to Managing Organizational Behavior: Models, Readings, and Cases.* Boston: Little, Brown.

Nadler, D.A. (1977) *Feedback and Organization Development: Using Data Based Methods.* Reading, Massachusetts: Addison-Wesley.

Nadler, D.A. & Tushman, M.L. (1979) A congruence model for diagnosing organizational behavior. In: D. Kolb, I. Rubin, & J. McIntyre. *Organizational Psychology: A Book of Readings.* (3rd edn). Englewood Cliffs, N.J.: Prentice-Hall.

Nadler, D.A. & Tichy, N.M. (1980) The limitations of traditional intervention technology in health care organizations. In: N. Margulies & J. Adams (eds.) *Organization Development in Health Care Organizations.* Reading, Mass: Addison-Wesley.

Peters, T.J. (1978) Symbols, patterns, and settings: an optimistic case for getting things done. *Organizational Dynamics.* (Autumn), 3–23.

Pettigrew, A. (1972) *The Politics of Organizational Decision-making.* London: Tavistock Press.

Pettigrew, A. (1978) Towards a political theory of organizational intervention. *Human Relations,* 28, 191–208.

Pfeffer, J. (1980) Management as symbolic action: the creation and maintenance of organizational paradigms. In: L.L. Cummings & B.M. Staw (eds.) *Research in Organizational Behavior* (Vol. 3), JAI Press.

Porter, L.W., Lawler, E.E. & Hackman, J.R. (1975) *Behavior in Organizations.* New York: McGraw-Hill.

Salancik, G.R. & Pfeffer, J. (1977) Who gets power and how they hold on to it: a strategic-contingency model of power. *Organizational Dynamics.* (Winter), 3–21.

Sayles, L.R. (1979) *Leadership: What Effective Managers Really Do and How They Do It.* McGraw-Hill.

Selznick, P. (1949) *TVA and the Grass Roots.* Berkley: University of California Press.

Thompson, J.D. & Tuden, A. (1959) Strategies, structures and processes of organizational decision. In: J.D. Thompson et al. (eds.). *Comparative Studies in Administration.* Pittsburgh: University of Pittsburgh Press.

Tushman, M.L. (1977) A political approach to organizations: a review and rationale. *Academy of Management Review,* 2, 206–216.

Vroom, V.H. (1964) *Work and Motivation.* New York: Wiley.

Vroom, V.H. and Yetton, P.W. (1973) Leadership and decision making. Pittsburgh: University of Pittsburgh Press.

Watson, G. (1969) Resistance to change. In: W.G. Bennis, K.F. Benne & R. Chin (eds.) *The Planning of Change.* New York: Holt, Rinehart, Winston.

Zaltman, G. & Duncan, R. (1977) *Strategies for Planned Change.* New York: John Wiley.

8

WHY CHANGE PROGRAMS DON'T PRODUCE CHANGE

Michael Beer, Russell A. Eisenstat and Bert Spector

(This material has been excerpted from the original.)

Most change programs don't work because they are guided by a theory of change that is fundamentally flawed. The common belief is that the place to begin is with the knowledge and attitudes of individuals. Changes in attitudes, the theory goes, lead to changes in individual behavior. And changes in individual behavior, repeated by many people, will result in organizational change. According to this model, change is like a conversion experience. Once people 'get religion,' changes in their behavior will surely follow.

This theory gets the change process exactly backward. In fact, individual behavior is powerfully shaped by the organizational roles that people play. The most effective way to change behavior, therefore, is to put people into a new organizational context, which imposes new roles, responsibilities, and relationships on them. This creates a situation that, in a sense, 'forces' new attitudes and behaviors on people. (See Table 1.)

One way to think about this challenge is in terms of three interrelated factors required for corporate revitalization. *Coordination* or teamwork is especially important if an organization is to discover and act on cost, quality, and product development opportunities. The production and sale of innovative, high-quality, low-cost products (or services) depend on close coordination among marketing, product design, and manufacturing departments, as well as between labor and management. High levels of *commitment* are essential for the effort, initiative, and cooperation that coordinated action demands. New *competencies* such as knowledge of the business as a whole, analytical skills, and interpersonal skills are necessary if people are to identify and solve problems as a team. If any of these elements are missing, the change process will break down.

The problem with most companywide change programs is that they address only one or, at best, two of these factors. Just because a company issues a

Table 1   Contrasting assumptions about change

Programmatic Change	Task Alignment
Problems in behavior are a function of individual knowledge, attitudes, and beliefs.	Individual knowledge, attitudes, and beliefs are shaped by recurring patterns of behavioral interactions.
The primary target of renewal should be the content of attitudes and ideas; actual behavior should be secondary.	The primary target of renewal should be behavior; attitudes and ideas should be secondary.
Behavior can be isolated and changed individually.	Problems in behavior come from a circular pattern, but the effects of the organizational system on the individual are greater than those of the individual on the system.
The target for renewal should be at the individual level.	The target for renewal should be at the level of roles, responsibilities, and relationships.

philosophy statement about teamwork doesn't mean its employees necessarily know what teams to form or how to function within them to improve coordination. A corporate reorganization may change the boxes on a formal organization chart but not provide the necessary attitudes and skills to make the new structure work. A pay-for-performance system may force managers to differentiate better performers from poorer ones, but it doesn't help them internalize new standards by which to judge subordinates' performances. Nor does it teach them how to deal effectively with performance problems. Such programs cannot provide the cultural context (role models from whom to learn) that people need to develop new competencies, so ultimately they fail to create organizational change.

Similarly, training programs may target competence, but rarely do they change a company's patterns of coordination. Indeed, the excitement engendered in a good corporate training program frequently leads to increased frustration when employees get back on the job only to see their new skills go unused in an organization in which nothing else has changed. People end up seeing training as a waste of time, which undermines whatever commitment to change a program may have roused in the first place.

When one program doesn't work, senior managers often try another, instituting a rapid progression of programs. But this only exacerbates the problem. Because they are designed to cover everyone and everything, programs end up covering nobody and nothing particularly well. They are so general and standardized that they don't speak to the day-to-day realities of particular units. Buzzwords like 'quality,' 'participation,' 'excellence,' 'empowerment,' and 'leadership' become a substitute for a detailed understanding of the business.

And all these change programs also undermine the credibility of the change effort. Even when managers accept the potential value of a particular program for others – quality circles, for example, to solve a manufacturing problem – they may be confronted with another, more pressing business problem such as new product development. One-size-fits-all change programs take energy *away* from efforts to solve key business problems – which explains why so many general managers don't support programs, even when they acknowledge that their underlying principles may be useful.

This is not to state that training, changes in pay systems or organizational structure, or a new corporate philosophy are always inappropriate. All can play valuable roles in supporting an integrated change effort. The problems come when such programs are used in isolation as a kind of 'magic bullet' to spread organizational change rapidly through the entire corporation. At their best, change programs of this sort are irrelevant. At their worst, they actually inhibit change. By promoting skepticism and cynicism, programmatic change can inoculate companies against the real thing.

SIX STEPS TO EFFECTIVE CHANGE

Companies avoid the shortcomings of programmatic change by concentrating on 'task alignment' – reorganizing employee roles, responsibilities, and relationships to solve specific business problems. Task alignment is easiest in small units – a plant, department, or business unit – where goals and tasks are clearly defined. Thus the chief problem for corporate change is how to promote task-aligned change across many diverse units.

We saw that general managers at the business unit or plant level can achieve task alignment through a sequence of six overlapping but distinctive steps, which we call the *critical path*. This path develops a self-reinforcing cycle of commitment, coordination, and competence. The sequence of steps is important because activities appropriate at one time are often counterproductive if started too early. Timing is everything in the management of change.

1. Mobilize commitment to change through joint diagnosis of business problems

As the term task alignment suggests, the starting point of any effective change effort is a clearly defined business problem. By helping people develop a shared diagnosis of what is wrong in an organization and what can and must be improved, a general manager mobilizes the initial commitment that is necessary to begin the change process.

Consider the case of a division we call Navigation Devices, a business unit of about 600 people set up by a large corporation to commercialize a product originally designed for the military market. When the new general manager took over, the division had been in operation for several years without ever making a profit. It had never been able to design and produce a high-quality, cost-competitive product. This was due largely to an organization in which decisions were made at the top, without proper involvement of or coordination with other functions.

The first step the new general manager took was to initiate a broad review of the business. Where the previous general manager had set strategy with the unit's marketing director alone, the new general manager included his entire management team. He also brought in outside consultants to help him and his managers function more effectively as a group.

Next, he formed a 20-person task force representing all the stakeholders in the organization – managers, engineers, production workers, and union officials. The group visited a number of successful manufacturing organizations in an attempt to identify what Navigation Devices might do to organize more effectively. One high-performance manufacturing plant in the task force's own company made a particularly strong impression. Not only did it highlight the problems at Navigation Devices but it also offered an alternative organizational model, based on teams, that captured the group's imagination. Seeing a different way of working helped strengthen the group's commitment to change.

The Navigation Devices task force didn't learn new facts from this process of joint diagnosis; everyone already knew the unit was losing money. But the group came to see clearly the organizational roots of the unit's inability to compete and, even more important, came to share a common understanding of the problem. The group also identified a potential organizational solution: to redesign the way it worked, using ad hoc teams to integrate the organization around the competitive task.

2. Develop a shared vision of how to organize and manage for competitiveness

Once a core group of people is committed to a particular analysis of the problem, the general manager can lead employees toward a task-aligned vision of the organization that defines new roles and responsibilities. These new arrangements will coordinate the flow of information and work across interdependent functions at all levels of the organization. But since they do not change formal structures and systems like titles or compensation, they encounter less resistance.

At Navigation Devices, the 20-person task force became the vehicle for this second stage. The group came up with a model of the organization in which cross-functional teams would accomplish all work, particularly new product development. A business-management team composed of the general manager and his staff would set the unit's strategic direction and review the work of lower level teams. Business-area teams would develop plans for specific markets. Product-development teams would manage new products from initial design to production. Production-process teams composed of engineers and production workers would identify and solve quality and cost problems in the plant. Finally, engineering-process teams would examine engineering methods and equipment. The teams got to the root of the unit's problems – functional and hierarchical barriers to sharing information and solving problems.

To create a consensus around the new vision, the general manager commissioned a still larger task force of about 90 employees from different levels and functions, including union and management, to refine the vision and obtain everyone's commitment to it. On a retreat away from the workplace, the group further refined the new organizational model and drafted a values statement, which it presented later to the entire Navigation Devices workforce. The vision and the values statement made sense to Navigation Devices employees in a way many corporate mission statements never do – because it grew out of the organization's own analysis of real business problems. And it was built on a model for solving those problems that key stakeholders believed would work.

3. Foster consensus for the new vision, competence to enact it, and cohesion to move it along

Simply letting employees help develop a new vision is not enough to overcome resistance to change – or to foster the skills needed to make the new organization work. Not everyone can help in the design, and even those who do participate often do not fully appreciate what renewal will require until the new organization is actually in place. This is when strong leadership from the general manager is crucial. Commitment to change is always uneven. Some managers are enthusiastic; others are neutral or even antagonistic. At Navigation Devices, the general manager used what his subordinates termed the 'velvet glove.' He made it clear that the division was going to encourage employee involvement and the team approach. To managers who wanted to help him, he offered support. To those who did not, he offered outplacement and counseling.

Once an organization has defined new roles and responsibilities, people need to develop the competencies to make the new setup work. Actually, the very existence of the teams with their new goals and accountabilities will force learning. The changes in roles, responsibilities, and relationships foster new skills and attitudes. Changed patterns of coordination will also increase employee participation, collaboration, and information sharing.

But management also has to provide the right supports. At Navigation Devices, six resource people – three from the unit's human resource department and three from corporate headquarters – worked on the change project. Each team was assigned one internal consultant, who attended every meeting, to help people be effective team members. Once employees could see exactly what kinds of new skills they needed, they asked for formal training programs to develop those skills further. Since these courses grew directly out of the employees' own experiences, they were far more focused and useful than traditional training programmes.

4. Spread revitalization to all departments without pushing it from the top

With the new ad hoc organization for the unit in place, it is time to turn to the functional and staff departments that must interact with it. Members of teams cannot be effective unless the department from which they come is organized and managed in a way that supports their roles as full-fledged participants in team decisions. What this often means is that these departments will have to rethink their roles and authority in the organization.

At Navigation Devices, this process was seen most clearly in the engineering department. Production department managers were the most enthusiastic about the change effort; engineering managers were more hesitant. Engineering had always been king at Navigation Devices; engineers designed products to the military's specifications without much concern about whether manufacturing could easily build them or not. Once the new team structure was in place, however, engineers had to participate on product-development teams with production workers. This required them to reexamine their roles and rethink their approaches to organizing and managing their own department.

The impulse of many general managers faced with such a situation would be to force the issue – to announce, for example, that now all parts of the organization must manage by teams. The temptation to force newfound insights on the rest of the organization can be great, particularly when rapid change is needed, but it would be the same mistake that senior managers make when they try to push programmatic change throughout a company. It short-circuits the change process.

It's better to let each department 'reinvent the wheel' – that is, to find its own way to the new organization. At Navigation Devices, each department was allowed to take the general concepts of coordination and teamwork and apply them to its particular situation. Engineering spent nearly a year agonizing over how to implement the team concept. The department conducted two surveys, held off-site meetings, and proposed, rejected, then accepted a matrix management structure before it finally got on board. Engineering's decision to move to matrix management was not surprising, but because it was its own choice, people committed themselves to learning the necessary new skills and attitudes.

5. Institutionalize revitalization through formal policies, systems, and structures

There comes a point where general managers have to consider how to institutionalize change so that the process continues even after they've moved on to other responsibilities. Step five is the time: the new approach has become entrenched, the right people are in place, and the team organization is up and running. Enacting changes in structures and systems any earlier tends to backfire. Take information systems. Creating a team structure means new information requirements. Why not have the MIS department create new systems that cut across traditional functional and departmental lines early in the change process? The problem is that without a well-developed understanding of information requirements, which can best be obtained by placing people on task-aligned teams, managers are likely to resist new systems as an imposition by the MIS department. Newly formed teams can often pull together enough information to get their work done without fancy new systems. It's better to hold off until everyone understands what the team's information needs are.

What's true for information systems is even more true for other formal structures and systems. Any formal system is going to have some disadvantages; none is perfect. These imperfections can be minimized, however, once people have worked in ad hoc team structure and learned what interdependencies are necessary. Then employees will commit to them too.

Again, Navigation Devices is a good example. The revitalization of the unit was highly successful. Employees changed how they saw their roles and responsibilities and became convinced that change could actually make a difference. As a result, there were dramatic improvements in value added per employee, scrap reduction, quality, customer service, gross inventory per employee, and profits. And all this happened with almost no formal changes in reporting relationships, information systems, evaluation procedures, compensation, or control systems.

When the opportunity arose, the general manager eventually did make some changes in the formal organization. For example, when he moved the vice president of operations out of the organization, he eliminated the position altogether. Engineering and manufacturing reported directly to him from that point on. For the most part, however, the changes in performance at Navigation Devices were sustained by the general manager's expectations and the new norms for behavior.

6. Monitor and adjust strategies in response to problems in the revitalization process

The purpose of change is to create an asset that did not exist before – a learning organization capable of adapting to a changing competitive environment. The organization has to know how to continually monitor its behavior – in effect, to learn how to learn.

Some might say that this is the general manager's responsibility. But monitoring the change process needs to be shared, just as analyzing the organization's key business problem does.

At Navigation Devices, the general manager introduced several mechanisms to allow key constituents to help monitor the revitalization. An oversight team – composed of some crucial managers, a union leader, a secretary, an engineer, and an analyst from finance – kept continual watch over the process. Regular employee attitude surveys monitored behavior patterns. Planning teams were formed and reformed in response to new challenges. All these mechanisms created a long-term capacity for continual adaptation and learning.

The six-step process provides a way to elicit renewal without imposing it. When stakeholders become committed to a vision, they are willing to accept a new pattern of management – here the ad hoc team structure – that demands changes in their behavior. And as the employees discover that the new approach is more effective (which will happen only if the vision aligns with the core task), they have to grapple with personal and organizational changes they might otherwise resist. Finally, as improved coordination helps solve relevant problems, it will reinforce team behavior and produce a desire to learn new skills. This learning enhances effectiveness even further and results in an even stronger commitment to change. This mutually reinforcing cycle of improvements in commitment, coordination, and competence creates a growing sense of efficacy. It can continue as long as the ad hoc team structure is allowed to expand its role in running the business.

THE ROLE OF TOP MANAGEMENT

To change an entire corporation, the change process we have described must be applied over and over again in many plants, branches, departments, and divisions. Orchestrating this companywide change process is the first responsibility of senior management. Doing so successfully requires a delicate balance. Without explicit efforts by top management to promote conditions for change in individual units, only a few plants or divisions will attempt change, and those that do will remain isolated. The best senior manager leaders we studied held their subordinates responsible for starting a change process without specifying a particular approach.

Create a market for change

The most effective approach is to set demanding standards for all operations and then hold managers accountable to them. At our best-practice company, which we call General Products, senior managers developed ambitious product and operating standards. General managers unable to meet these product standards by a certain date had to scrap their products and take a sharp hit to their bottom lines. As long as managers understand that high standards are not arbitrary but are dictated by competitive forces, standards can generate enormous pressure for better performance, a key ingredient in mobilizing energy for change.

Use successfully revitalized units as organizational models for the entire company

Another important strategy is to focus the company's attention on plants and divisions that have already begun experimenting with management innovations. These units become developmental laboratories for further innovation.

There are two ground rules for identifying such models. First, innovative units need support. They need the best managers to lead them, and they need adequate resources – for instance, skilled human resource people and external consultants. In the most successful companies that we studied, senior managers saw it as their responsibility to make resources available to leading-edge units. They did not leave it to the human resource function.

Second, because resources are always limited and the costs of failure high, it is crucial to identify those units with the likeliest chance of success. Successful management innovations can appear to be failures when the bottom line is devastated by environmental factors beyond the unit's control. The best models are in healthy markets.

Develop career paths that encourage leadership development

Without strong leaders, units cannot make the necessary organizational changes, yet the scarcest resource available for revitalizing corporations is leadership. Corporate renewal depends as much on developing effective change leaders as it does on developing effective organizations. The personal learning associated with leadership development – or the realization by higher management that a manager does not have this capacity – cannot occur in the classroom. It only happens in an organization where the teamwork, high commitment, and competencies we have discussed are already the norm.

The only way to develop the kind of leaders a changing organization needs is to make the leadership an important criterion for promotion, and then manage people's careers to develop it. At our best-practice companies, managers were moved from job to job and from organization to organization based on their learning needs, not on their position in the hierarchy. Successful leaders were assigned to units that had been targeted for change. People who needed to sharpen their leadership skills were moved into the company's model units where those skills would be demanded and therefore learned. In effect, top management used leading-edge units as hothouses to develop revitalization leaders.

At this point, senior managers must make an effort to adopt the team behavior, attitudes, and skills that they have demanded of others in earlier phases of change. Their struggle with behavior change will help sustain corporate renewal in three ways. It will promote the attitudes and behavior needed to coordinate diverse activities in the company; it will lend credibility to top management's continued espousal of change; and it will help the CEO identify and develop a successor who is capable of learning the new behaviors. Only such a manager can lead a corporation that can renew itself continually as competitive forces change.

Companies need a particular mind-set for managing change: one that emphasizes process over specific content, recognizes organization change as a unit-by-unit learning process rather than a series of programs, and acknowledges the payoffs that result from persistence over a long period of time as opposed to quick fixes. This mind-set is difficult to maintain in an environment that presses for quarterly earnings, but we believe it is the only approach that will bring about successful renewal.

9

UNDERSTANDING AND MANAGING ORGANIZATIONAL CHANGE

Derek Pugh

It is a paradox of organizational life that situations and problems which cry out most strongly for change are often the very ones which resist change most stubbornly.

On *logical* grounds, this is most difficult to understand. If, in economic terms, firms are rational, resource-allocating mechanisms for optional performance, then proposals for increasing output or efficiency by changing methods, procedures or organization should be easily discussed and adopted. And this should be particularly so in situations where performance is far from optimal.

Yet, as anyone who has tried it knows, this does not happen. The most likely response to a change proposal is a series of outraged objections, some relevant (for no proposer of change can have thought out all the implications), some irrelevant (just waiting for an opportunity to surface and using this one).

The most likely results are: nothing happens; if the proposer has sufficient persuasiveness, there is a cosmetic change but the underlying situation remains unaltered or soon reverts to what it was before; if the proposer has sufficient power, the change is pushed through but at the cost of conflict, resentment and reduced motivation which results in negative consequences which were not intended and which may be greater than the benefits.

As a behavioural scientist, I get involved in situations, for example, where a traditional administrative constultant's 'rationalization' has been railroaded through by top management, and where the indignations and resentments still fester among the management and staff affected, two or three years after the event.

On *psychological* grounds, which are not necessarily the same as logical ones, these results are easier to understand. Most individuals react to threats and unknown dangers by going rigid (which is why the 007s of this world have to undertake considerable and rigorous training to maintain their flexibility in conditions of danger).

The most usual reaction of a manager or department which is failing or under pressure is to go for 'more of the same'; to carry on doing harder what was done before, even if this is manifestly seen – by others – to be inadequate. As the frustration increases so the people will become aggressive – but aggressively rigid. Try suggesting a change in this situation, but be ready to duck, since in the extreme the aggression will not be limited to words. Clearly this is not the time for a rational discussion of change.

On *organizational* grounds too, resistance to change can be understood when it is realized that from the behavioural point of view, organizations are coalitions of interest groups in tension. Management vs workers, production vs sales, accounting vs R and D, Union A vs Union B, Head Office vs production location, the groupings and the accompanying tensions are legion. The resultant organization is a particular balance of forces which had been hammered out over a period of time and which is continually subject to minor modifications through hierarchically initiated adjustments and cross-group negotiations.

A real change proposal, that will almost inevitably change the current balance, is thus likely to encounter resistance. And when this is compounded by psychological resistance from rigid people under threat, it is not surprising that managing change is difficult.

It is for this reason that one of the most basic characteristics of organizations is that they are what is called *ultrastable*. They find it difficult to change, not because of inertia but because they run like mad to stay in the same place. It is not that unusual for me to be told by directors, managers and shop stewards in a firm that personally they would like to see change made, but it cannot be done.

So real organizational change often comes about: much too late, in situations of considerable failure (orders lost, profits down, budgets out of control, morale low, resentment high); with little time for thought and only scant consideration of alternatives because of the need to cope with the emergency; and paying the price of considerable frustration, conflict and dislocation in order to live to fight another day.

An effective manager, on the other hand: *anticipates* the need for change as opposed to reacting after the event to the emergency; *diagnoses* the nature of the change that is required and carefully considers a number of alternatives that might improve organizational functioning, as opposed to taking the fastest way to escape the problem; and *manages* the change process over a period of time so that it is effective and accepted as opposed to lurching from crisis to crisis.

Here are four principles for understanding organizational change.

Principle One: Organizations are organisms. They are not mechanisms which can be taken apart and reassembled differently as required. They can be changed, but the change must be approached carefully with the implications for the various groupings thought out and the participants convinced of the worthwhileness from their point of view. They must be given time to understand the change proposals, and to 'digest' the changes after they have been made. Do not make changes too frequently. They are too hard to digest and will become disfunctional or cosmetic.

Principle Two: Organizations are occupational and political systems as well as rational resource-allocation ones. Every reaction to a change proposal must be interpreted not only in terms of the rational arguments of what is best for the firm (which are the ones actually used). The reactions must also be understood in relation to the occupational system (how will it affect the ways of working, number of jobs, career prospects, motivation, of the particular person or group whose arguments are being heard) and the political system (how will it affect the power, status, prestige of the group?).

Principle Three: All members of an organization operate simultaneously in all three systems – the rational, the occupational and the political ones. Do not make the mistake of becoming cynical and thinking that the occupational and political aspects are all that matter, and that rational arguments are merely rationalizations to defend a particular position. The arguments by which the Personnel Manager, for example, resists a diminution in the department's functions will be real ones, even though they will inevitably be suffused with occupational and political considerations.

Principle Four: Change is most likely to be acceptable and effective in those people or departments who are basically successful in their tasks but who are experiencing tension or failure in some particular part of their work. They will have the two basic ingredients of confidence in their ability and motivation to change. The next most likely to change are the successful. They will have the confidence but must be interested in developing the motivation. The least likely to understand and accept change are the unsuccessful. They will attempt to protect themselves by their rigidity.

These principles are very important in designing a change process, in deciding where to start and what methods to use.

For effective change to take place, therefore, a manager must *anticipate* the need for change so that time is available, and *manage* the process over that time so that the two relevant characteristics of the people involved (i) their confidence in their ability and (ii) their motivation to change, can be maintained and developed.

Here are six rules for managing change effectively:

Rule One: Work hard at establishing the need for change. This may seem hardly necessary to the change proposer, but what may be an obvious need to him/her may not be seen as such by the others involved. What may be seen as an obvious need for improvement in their control procedures by the accountants may be seen by the marketing staff as yet another attempt to reduce their autonomy and responsibilities.

Effective reasons for changes are those that can be accepted by many of the interest groups and people who will be involved. For example, needs which can be demonstrated to flow from changes in the firm's environment (changes in customers' behaviour, competitors' tactics, Government policies) will find greater acceptability as being relevant to all, than purely internally generated changes which are more likely to be viewed in the political system.

Rule Two: Don't only think out the change, THINK THROUGH IT. It is not enough to think out what the change will be and calculate the benefits and costs from the proposer's point of view. The others involved will almost inevitably see the benefits as less and the costs as greater. By 'thinking through' is meant the need to consider consciously and systematically what the change will mean for all the parties involved, or what they will see as their costs and benefits.

For example, consider systematically for all groups involved:

- will the change alter job content;
- will it introduce new and unknown tasks;
- will it disrupt established methods of working;
- will it rearrange group relationships;
- will it reduce autonomy or authority;
- will it be perceived to lower status;
- will it be established without full explanation and discussion?

It is in the answers to these questions, which identify the potential points of resistance to the change, that the manager can get a fuller understanding of what is involved for all. And on the other side he needs to ask what are the benefits in pay, status, job satisfaction, career prospects which are generated as well as the increase in performance.

Rule Three: Initiate change through informal discussion to get feedback and participation. No one person or group can hope to foresee correctly all the ramifications of a real change in policy, structure, procedures or products. So it is important to get discussions going to get feedback to enable the manager to evaluate the proposal fully from all points of view. He/she needs to discover whether the change is correct in principle or not, and what modifications, if any, will improve it.

In addition, in modern organizations effective change is a participative process. Early discussion allows the necessary participation of those affected to take place, since this is what generates commitment to the changes and develops the motivation to make them work. The change proposer has participated a lot if it is his/her idea, that is why he/she is committed to it. Others must have the opportunity to go through this process too.

Rule Four: Positively encourage those concerned to give their objections. This rule may be regarded as rather perverse by an enthusiastic manager who is pushing the change proposal and whose natural inclination is to ride over or belittle objections. But it is an important part of an effective change process for two reasons.

First, because people who have a change pushed on them without account being taken of their objections inevitably lose some confidence in their abilities ('If we are good, why is it that nobody listens to us?'). This leads to rigidity. Flexibility is encouraged by people seeing that they can contribute and make an impact.

Second, any current situation is the resultant of a balance of forces. If the forces pressing for change are increased, the forces resisting change do not go away even if they are not brought out into the open. It is important to ensure that the resisting forces are identified and dealt with in their own right.

For example, a change proposal may lead a departmental group to be concerned with their ability to work a new system or to doubt its appropriateness. This may be tackled as a problem in its own right by means of a trial run and a training programme. Or a proposal which leads to a reduction in autonomy on one aspect of a job may be compensated for by increased autonomy in another aspect.

Rule Five: Be prepared to change yourself. This is probably the most important rule of all. Modern managers cannot afford the luxury of believing that 'change is for other people', since a manager who proposes to initiate change joins in the process and must himself/herself be prepared to change.

There are two corollaries to this rule. *Don't fall in love with your own idea.* It may be good, but it could well be improved after the discussions and objections are taken into account. Overcommitment by the manager at too early a stage leads to rigidity again.

It is essential to split a proposal into its general and specific aspects, starting the discussion on the more general aspects of principles and approach. Do not overplan the details at this stage, leave this until the feedback has shown that the direction is accepted as appropriate. The detailed planning may then take account of the information generated by the whole process.

The second corollary is that change *may be* 'bottom up' *as well* as 'top down'. Change does not have to be initiated from above. A manager who is prepared to change may well consider ideas initiated from below. A very good way of obtaining ideas for improvement is to carry out a survey of subordinates' views. Many managers have been surprised at the quality of proposals which can be unlocked by this method.

Rule Six: Monitor the change and reinforce it. When the change has been carried through, check after a suitable time to see if it is working well and giving the benefits that were argued. If it does not, minor modifications will be in order (but beware of changing in a major way again too quickly).

If the change is working well and the benefits can be demonstrated in, for example, improved efficiency, higher turnover, more satisfaction, *tell every one that this is the case.* This is most important as it gives reinforcement to those involved (who are otherwise more likely to remember the dislocation than the benefits) and for others helps to set up an organizational climate in which change can be seen to be beneficial.

(This chapter was developed from an article which originally appeared in *Accountancy Age.*)

PART 3:

Implementing Change

PART 3:
IMPLEMENTING CHANGE

The four papers in this part of the collection together address one of the key aspects of successful change; that is, the processes of implementation when action takes over from talking and planning. Yet one shared underlying message rings through them all, namely, the importance of effective consultation and involvement as a means of generating the ownership and commitment which is a prerequisite of well-managed change.

In drawing out attention to 'process consultation', Coghlan brings out the role of consultants, whether internal or external, in change, and their prominent role in organization development (OD). The discussion in which he explores the different influences on the ideas of consultation, diagnosis and intervention further extends our picture of the post-war historical context in which so many of today's approaches to change have their roots.

In contrast to the other papers in this section, the chapter by Leonard-Barton and Kraus links change to technological innovation, and in doing so, provides a perspective on one of the most difficult features of change in contemporary life – the real and 'unknowable' complexity of technological innovation. Their own explanation of resistance addresses the issues of risk and judgement, giving us an insight into the fully justifiable reasons for resistance to change.

The article from Owen is another retained from the first edition. The presentation of strategy supports the argument for a systemic approach, such as that developed within The Open University course, and described in the paper by Mayon-White. This has three roles. The first is to rectify an omission from the first volume which contained only the barest references to the content of The Open University course. The paper contains a description of the intervention strategy which is used extensively as a framework for managing change. This has proved itself to be effective and robust in a range of change settings, and has given rise to other variants of the approach. Development work continues as new ideas and tools are developed and some of these are included in the new Open University course. The second role is that of emphasizing the importance of teamwork in change settings; the third being to set the development of the ideas embodied in the methodology in the context of systems thinking and OD, and provides a further extension to the discussion of the context in which these ideas have developed.

10

IN DEFENCE OF PROCESS CONSULTATION

David Coghlan

In his *Organizational Psychology*, Schein defines the role of the organization development (OD) consultant in terms of helping the organization improve its inherent capacity to cope by helping it diagnose itself, select its own coping responses and determine its own progress (Schein 1970). The first, *Process Consultation* was published in 1969 (Schein 1969). Its aim was to articulate a mode of organizational consultancy that paralleled the client-centred approach in counselling and contrasted with consultancy models that were centred on expertise. This little book quickly became a standard text and a classic in the field of organizational processes. The term 'process consultation' became a technical term in organization development for the concept and practice of working with groups in OD interventions. In the standard OD texts, there is a section on process consultation in the 'group intervention' section (Burke 1982, Harvey and Brown 1982, French and Bell 1984, Huse and Cummings 1985). The effect of this, to my mind, is to confine the notion of process consultation to one particular intervention process. This does not do justice to what is fundamentally a philosophy of a helping relationship. The core of the process consultation approach is not so much its applicability to group situations as its articulation of a philosophy, and its implications. This is what has been neglected in the literature; process consultation has been degenerated into a group intervention approach. This article attempts to restate some of the key principles and practices of process consultation with a view to emphasizing its role in providing a model for the helping relationship rather than a confinement to group interventions.

PROCESS CONSULTATION

Schein defines process consultation as 'a set of activities on the part of the consultant which help the client perceive, understand and act upon process events in the client's environment' (Schein 1978 p. 341). His underlying assumptions are that managers often do not know what is wrong in an organization and need a special kind of help to diagnose what their problems actually are. They often do not know what kinds of help consultants can give and so need help in knowing what kind of help to seek. They need help in being able to identify what needs improving and what does not. The consultant must work jointly with the manager so that the manager can learn to see the problem for him/herself, share in the diagnosis and be actively involved in creating a solution. On the basis of such assumptions it can be seen that the process consultation model is in direct contrast with the 'expert' models of consultation. Schein makes this comparison as he places the process consultation approach in juxtaposition with what he refers to as the 'doctor-patient' model and the 'purchase' model. The process consultant, in contrast, is an expert in building an effective helping relationship, which is contingent on working jointly with the client so that the client can solve his/her own organizational problems. The process consultant is an expert in organizational processes and can help the client develop diagnostic and intervention skills in this area.

The crucial human processes for organizational effectiveness are: communication, member roles and functions in groups, group problem solving and decision making, group norms and development, leadership and authority, intergroup co-operation and competition, intrapsychic processes, cultural rules of interaction, and initiating and managing change. Finally, the process consultant passes on his/her skills to the client so that the client becomes, in essence, a 'process consultant' in his/her own organization.

While process consultation is a skill for the consultants, it is also a key skill for managers. Managers who are judged to be effective are those who are perceived to be the kind of people who get the job done and who are able to build their human organization at the same time, so that jobs continue to get done. Effective managers behave in such a way that subordinates, peers and supervisors can get the help they need in order to get things done. A manager's role is frequently that of helping others do their jobs well. As expertise becomes more narrowly based, a subordinate can have more expertise than the boss. The boss's job is to integrate, co-ordinate and blend the expertise of others into a coherent decision. The manager becomes a facilitator of good process. The higher one climbs in an organization, the more general the role, and so the skills of helping others do their jobs well become more needed. A manager may also need to be able to be of help to his/her own boss. A good deal of a manager's interpersonal time is spent helping others. From this brief description of the process consultation approach, its theory and practice, it can be seen how there is a complementary relationship with the person-centred counselling approach. There is a fundamental complementarity regarding the nature of the person and of the helping relationship, with a definition in terms of a facilitative accompaniment, as contrasted with a more authoritative expert approach.

The conceptual origins of process consultation are described by Schein (1969). The insight of Lewin and his colleagues at the famous seminar in

Connecticut in 1946, that attention to the here-and-now process in a group is a significant way of learning, is well documented as the significant origin of organization development. Out of that insight came the laboratory method of learning as enshrined in the T-group, which, for many years, was a core OD intervention (Schein and Bennis 1965). The concepts 'diagnosis' and 'intervention' derive directly from the concept of laboratory training. Yet, there is a difference between the process consultant and the group trainer. The process consultant does not have the environmental support of a laboratory, nor the intensive involvement of a group. He/she may not have the commitment to learning of a laboratory group participant. The process consultant must built involvement and commitment as he/she works. He/she must gain acceptance for the value of looking at process.

Schein's own development is intimately tied up with his entry on to the faculty of the Sloan School of Management in the Massachusetts Institute of Technology at the personal invitation of Douglas McGregor, by whom he was deeply influenced (Sashkin 1979). *Process Consultation* (1969) originated through a remark about his work. As he tried to explain what he was doing he found his listener did not understand.

> I angrily went home and wrote down what I was doing in a ten-page paper. About a year later that paper became *Process Consultation* . . . the motivation to do it really came from being goaded on one hand by McGregor's not writing and, on the other hand, by colleagues misunderstanding what I was doing (Sashkin 1979 p. 409).

McGregor's seminal work on management and organizations is best summarised in his concepts of Theory X and Theory Y (McGregor 1960, 1967). What is of relevance in this context is Schein's lecture at the symposium held on the occasion of the 50th anniversary of the original Hawthorne studies in which he articulated his own philosophy of the person (Schein 1975). In this lecture, he corrected the often-mistaken notion that Theory X and Theory Y describe modes of behaviour. Rather, they are theories of motivation, and assumptions about human nature on which behaviour is based. Schein clearly comes down in favour of Theory Y, which affirms the person's inner self-directedness in relation to achieving goals and personal satisfaction. It is Theory Y assumptions that provide the framework by which managers can believe in groups in the first place, and learn skills in handling them. From such a base comes the process consultation approach.

In his work on careers and individual development in organizations, Schein develops the process consultation approach implicitly in his concept of the 'career anchor' (Schein 1978, 1980, 1985a, 1986). In this approach, the individual is facilitated to decide for him/herself what his/her own career anchor is, and, in that light, to review his/her career development. Individuals, in an interaction with a consultant, superior or mentor, make their own decisions based on reflection on their own actual career choices and experience. The person accompanying them in an acceptant, supportive and facilitative manner provides a mirroring function by which the individuals can review their past and their present (Schein 1985, Coghlan 1987). The process is clearly in the hands of the individuals concerned. This whole approach is seen as a key managerial skill on the individual level of organizational behaviour (Rashford and Coghlan 1987).

Schein's approach to change is firmly Lewinian (Schein 1961, 1979, 1987a). The creation of the motivation to change ('unfreezing' in Lewin's terms) arises from the experiences of disconfirmation in which the self-image interests with a situation, and an image of other people and aspects of the self-image fail to be confirmed. The reaction is a feeling of inadequacy or anxiety. With a reduction of threat and the creation of psychological safety, change can take place. The unfreezing process is a process of becoming open to certain kinds of information which are actually or potentially available. The changing process is the assimilation of this new information leading to a cognitive redefinition, new attitudes and new behaviour. This process occurs through one of two mechanisms. The information can come from multiple sources. This mechanism is primarily a scanning process (reading books, observing other people, etc). It can produce a lot of irrelevant information and is basically non-interactive. It implies attention to content, and the client may have difficulty in locating reliable and useful information.

The other mechanism of change is through a single source. This is the utilisation of an interpersonal process through a change agent – such as a consultant, therapist, counsellor or friend with whom the client identifies. In such a relationship, there are the tensions of positive and negative identification. The client should not be the captive of the change agent, dependent on his/her power for change to occur. The client learns from the freedom and support afforded in the relationship. He/she experiences autonomy and a sense of his/her own power. He/she can terminate the relationship. Learning from the change agent is what he/she assimilates from the model in the interpersonal process. Learning is not only on the cognitive level. The refreezing process is the stabilisation of change in the normative pattern of the client's life that is congruent with the self-image. Such a stabilisation is often contingent on reward from the social environment.

The single-source change agent process is fundamental to the assumptions underlying process consultation. That the consultant is in relationship with the client is a sign of some degree of unfreezing. The process consultant enters the relationship with a view to working jointly with the client so that the client can develop his/her own diagnostic and intervention skills in solving problems. The consultant may utilise a scanning approach as he/she provides the framework by which the client can select his/her own information sources which he/she then fits into his/her own situation and personality. This helps the refreezing process. Identification alone may not provide what is useful. At the same time, there are some elements of the identification process operative in the relationship between the consultant and client. For the process consultant, the identification process differs from that of a therapist primarily through the difference of agenda. Through the collaborative interaction the client is exposed to learning process consultation skills.

INTERVENTION

In process consultation the guiding principle for the consultant is the collaborative working with the client in a manner that enables the client to develop his/her own diagnosis of the situation and the skills to act on it. Argyris uses the term 'organistically oriented research' to express the collaborative contract between an interventionist and a client, as contrasted with 'mechanistically oriented research' (Argyris 1970). Schein describes the 'clinical' method of enquiry and contrasts it with ethnographic method (Schein 1987b).

The tasks of the consultant are to gather valid information, help create the conditions for the client to make free and informed choices and be internally committed to the choices he/she has made (Argyris 1970). Valid information reflects information that is useful and needed by the client. By free choice, Argyris means that the locus of decision making is in the client and that the client has options from which to choose. By internal commitment is meant that the client owns the choice he/she has made and feels responsible for implementing it. These three tasks, which Argyris calls, 'primary tasks', are the essence of the process consultation approach. They are primarily achieved through the collaborative working with the client. For Argyris this means a firm grounding in the three tasks as governing variables (Argyris and Schon 1974) and through interventions that emphasise minimal inference, minimal attribution, and the public testing of assumptions and conclusions (Argyris 1985). Through this approach, the client receives consistent feedback as to where the consultant's questions are coming from, and thereby consultant power is minimised.

Schein is more concrete on consultant intervention behaviour (Schein 1987a). He attempts a typology of interventions, distinguishing exploratory, diagnostic, action alternatives and confronting interventions. Exploratory interventions are based on active listening in which the consultant encourages the client to tell the story and tries to see the uniqueness of what the client is talking about, develops empathy and tries to understand the client's perspective. Diagnostic interventions focus on helping the client to think about what is going on through forcing historical reconstruction, concretisation, process emphasis, and, through the consultant, testing what he/she has heard and understood. Action alternative is a shift in focus to what the client might want to consider on the assumption that if the client can begin to solve his/her own problem, he/she will also have learned something about the process of how to solve problems.

Confronting interventions focus on the client's own behaviour in juxtaposition with his/her stated goals. Schein suggests that it is only after a good deal of joint enquiry has taken place that suggestions or recommendations about content or structure are appropriate. The core of the process consultation approach is grounded in a focus on intervention rather than on diagnosis. Diagnosis and intervention are simultaneous activities and are inseparable. Consultants make diagnostic interventions through asking questions which provoke the clients to form their own hypotheses as to why events have occurred and what might be done. Such an emphasis on intervention takes away the pressure from the consultant or manager of having to be the expert and provide solutions. The consultant is never just diagnosing but always intervening to some degree.

In his seminal work on organizational culture Schein applies this process to the work of uncovering organizational and group cultural assumptions (Schein 1985). The consultant acts as a mirror in helping organizational members see the assumptions under which they operate. These assumptions arise from the organization or group's history of success in dealing with problems of internal integration and external adaptation. As the assumptions are taken for granted, they are not easily available to consciousness. The process by which a group or organization comes to realise and manage its culture is fundamentally a process consultation approach (Schein 1987a).

In process consultation, there have been some controversial issues regarding practice. One such controversy has focused on the use of structured experiences as a sort of intervention. Structured experiences can be manipulative and controlling, and ultimately diminish the freedom of the client. As we have seen Schein considers the use of structured interventions as rare intervention for possible use only after considerable use of the primary facilitative intervention behaviours, and when it is clearly accepted that the consultant is managing the process and not the solution. In a recent article he expresses his alienation from a notion that defines OD in terms of the application of techniques (Schein, in press).

A second controversial issue has focused on the consultant's use of self in working with the client. The challenge came primarily from the practice of Gestalt therapy. Nevis (Nevis 1982) expressed the difference in approach in terms of 'provocative' and 'evocative' modes of influence. In another article, Nevis articulated the Gestalt approach to process consulting through the image of the TV detective, Columbo, who models a provocative mode of intervention (Nevis 1980). In process consultation the client controls the process and the consultant works out of respect for the client's own self-determination.

RESEARCH

Schein (1987b) reflects on the gap between traditional scientific knowledge of what goes on in organizations and what is known from experience in organizations. He comments on how positivist empirical experimental and survey research frequently does not fit what is experienced from consulting and fieldwork experiences. This reflection leads him to elaborate the distinction between quantitative and qualitative research further by describing the differences between different qualitative approaches. In this work he focuses on the difference between the 'clinical' approach and the ethnographic approach.

The clinical approach is defined in terms of the process consultation approach in which the researcher/consultant is invited into the system to help, and gathers data through interaction and intervention from within in terms already described. This contrasts with other forms of research in which the researcher initiates the process and is present in the system as observer or data gatherer. In the clinical approach the consultant is client and problem centred and scientific results are secondary to helping. Through this approach, in Schein's experience, the consultant is more likely to find out what 'really goes on' in an organization. Process consultation as a clinical approach to research is a form of 'action-research' and 'action-science' (Lewin 1948, Lippitt *et al.* 1958, Argyris *et al.* 1985).

CONCLUSIONS

For Schein (1987a) process consultation is a 'philosophy of how to provide help to human systems' (p. 205). It is not the only helping model, and Schein clearly advocates choice and decision as to what model is appropriate in a given situation. In process consultation skills workshops for personnel managers I have found there exists a basic block in participants to grasp the process consultation insight. In role-plays they universally get hooked into feeling they have to solve problems and prescribe magic solutions instantaneously. In these role-plays these prescriptions are typically rejected, and those playing the parts of process consultants then tend to revert to a form of intervention that can appropriately be described as reflecting the patterns of intervention of many radio and TV journalists. Such interventions emphasise the closed and manipulative question: 'Don't you think that you should have . . .?' Their effect is to close the client to the intervener and to the help he/she can provide. In the light of this experience I am more convinced of the need for exposure to, and training in, process consultation skills so as, at least, to provide managers with intervention choices (Lippitt *et al.* 1958). Process consultation as a catalytic form of intervention is the ground on which other interventions can be made.

Discussion of process consultation in organization development texts is usually confined to a section on group intervention. This limitation to a single form of organizational intervention does not do justice to the depth of the process consultation approach. Process consultation is a philosophy of helping that is accessible to those who find themselves in a helping role, whether formally or informally. It provides a structure for learning key management helping skills that are based on an attitude of collaborative problem solving. It is a consultation approach that is authentic to the original concept and spirit of organization development (Schein, in press). It is an approach to organizational research that gets inside organizational culture and opens the possibility of uncovering basic assumptions (Schein 1987b). It is a deeper, more sophisticated concept than the simple group intervention accreditation it receives, with far-reaching implications for the use of authority and expertise. For its full potential process consultation deserves a higher profile.

REFERENCES

Argyris, C. (1970) *Intervention Theory and Method*, Reading, Mass. Addison-Wesley.
Argyris, C. (1985) *Strategy, Change and Defensive Routines*, Marshfield, MA: Pitman.

Argyris, C. and Schon, D. (1974) *Theory-in-Practice: Increasing Professional Effectiveness.* San Francisco: Jossey-Bass.

Argyris, C., Putnam, R. and Smith, D. (1985) *Action Science,* San Francisco: Jossey-Bass.

Burke, W.W. (1982) *Organization Development: Principles and Practices.* Boston: Little, Brown.

Coghlan, D. (1987) Consultation on organisational levels: an intervention framework, *Leadership & Organization Development Journal,* 8 (3), 3–8.

French, W. and Bell, C. (1984) *Organization Development,* 3rd ed., Englewood Cliffs, NJ: Prentice-Hall.

Harvey, D. and Brown, D. (1982) *An Experimental Approach to Organization Development,* Englewood Cliffs, NJ: Prentice-Hall.

Huse, E. and Cummings, T. (1985) *Organization Development and Change.* St Paul: West.

Lewin, K. (1948) *Resolving Social Conflicts.* New York: Harper and Row.

Lippitt, R., Watson, J. and Westley, B. (1958) *The Dynamics of Planned Change.* New York: Harcourt, Brace and World.

McGregor, D. (1960) *The Human Side of Enterprise.* New York: McGraw-Hill.

McGregor, D. (1967) *The Professional Manager.* New York: McGraw-Hill.

Nevis, E.C. (1980) 'Gestalt awareness process in organizational assessment', *Sloan School of Management Working Paper,* 1,142–80, Massachusetts Institute of Technology.

Nevis, E.C. (1982) Evocative and provocative modes of influence in the implementation of change. *Gestalt Journal,* 6 (2), 5–12.

Rashford, N. and Coghlan, D. (1987) Enhancing human involvement in organisations – a paradigm for participation. *Leadership & Organization Development Journal,* 8 (1), 17–21.

Sashkin, M. (1979) Interview. *Group and Organization Studies,* 4 (4), 400–17.

Schein, E.H. (1961) *Coercive Persuasion.* New York: Norton.

Schein, E.H. (1969) *Process Consultation: Its Role in Organization Development,* Reading, MA: Addison-Wesley.

Schein, E.H. (1975) The Hawthorne group studies revisited: a defense of Theory Y. In: E. Cass and F. Zimmer, *Man and Work in Society.* New York: Van Nostrand Reinhold.

Schein, E.H. (1978) *Career Dynamics: Matching Individual and Organizational Needs.* Reading, MA: Addison-Wesley.

Schein, E.H. (1979) Personal change through interpersonal relationship. In: W. Bennis, J. Van Maanen, E.H. Schein and F. Steele, *Essays in Interpersonal Dynamics.* Homewood, Ill: Dorsey.

Schein, E.H. (1980) *Organizational Psychology,* 3rd edn. Englewood Cliffs, NJ: Prentice-Hall.

Schein, E.H. (1985a) *Career Anchors: Discovering your Real Values.* San Diego: University Associates.

Schein, E.H. (1985b) *Organizational Culture and Leadership.* San Francisco: Jossey-Bass.

Schein, E.H. (1986) Individuals and Careers. In J. Lorsch (ed.), *Handbook of Organizational Behavior,* Englewood Cliffs, NJ: Prentice-Hall.

Schein, E.H. (1987a) *Process Consultation, Volume II: Lessons for Managers and Consultants.* Reading, MA: Addison-Wesley.

Schein, E.H. (1987b) *The Clinical Perspective in Fieldwork,* Sage University Paper on Qualitative Research Methods Series, Vol. 5. Beverly Hills: Sage Publications.

Schein, E.H. (in press) Back to the Future: Recapturing the OD Vision. In F. Massarik (ed.), *Advances in Organization Development.*

Schein, E.H. and Bennis, W. (1965) *Personal and Organizational Change through Group Methods.* New York: Wiley.

11

IMPLEMENTING NEW TECHNOLOGY

Dorothy Leonard-Barton and William A. Kraus

(This material has been excerpted from the original.)

Introducing technological change into an organization presents a different set of challenges to management than does the work of competent project administration. Frequently, however, the managers responsible for shepherding a technical innovation into routine use are much better equipped by·education and experience to guide that innovation's development than to manage its implementation.

In the following pages, we describe some of the challenges managers must overcome if companies are to absorb new technologies efficiently. We also suggest strategies managers can use to address these difficulties. Although the examples we cite are all computer-related and come from the experience of large manufacturers, the issues raised and strategies proposed apply every bit as well to small businesses, to service operations – in fact, to any organization where technological innovation flourishes.

Our findings derive from our combined research and consulting experience with more than 20 large multinational corporations and with some 70 organizations within General Electric. Our focus is on internally developed technologies; but as vendors of advanced manufacturing equipment have found in their efforts to help implement the systems they market, new technologies, no matter what their origin, confront managers with a distinctive set of challenges.

A DUAL ROLE

Those who manage technological change must often serve as both technical developers and implementers. As a rule, one organization develops the technology and then hands it off to users, who are less technically skilled but quite knowledgeable about their own areas of application. In practice, however, the user organization is often not willing – or able – to take on responsibility for the technology at the point in its evolution at which the development group wants to hand it over. The person responsible for implementation – whether located in the developing organization, the user organization or in some intermediary position – has to design the hand-off so that it is almost invisible. That is, before the baton changes hands, the runners should have been running in parallel for a long time. The implementation manager has to integrate the perspectives and the needs of both developers and users.

Perhaps the easiest way to accomplish this task is to think of implementation as an internal marketing, not selling, job. This distinction is important because selling starts with a finished product, marketing, with research on user needs and preferences. Marketing executives worry about how to position their product in relation to all competitive products and are concerned with distribution channels and the infrastructure needed to support product use.

Adoption of a marketing perspective encourages implementation managers to seek user involvement in the: early identification and enhancement of the fit between a product and user needs; preparation of the user organization to receive the innovation; and shifting of ownership of the innovation to users. We discuss the first two of these issues in this section of the chapter, the third we cover later.

Marketing perspective

That involving users in a new technology's design phase boosts user satisfaction is quite well-known, but the proper extent, timing and type of user involvement will vary greatly from company to company. For example, software developers in an electronic office equipment company established a user design group to work with developers on a strategically important piece of applications software when the program was still in the prototype stage. Prospective users could try out the software on the same computer employed by the program's developers. The extremely tight communication loop that resulted allowed daily feedback from users to designers on their preferences and problems. This degree of immediacy may be unusual, but managers can almost always get some information from potential users that will improve product design.

A marketing perspective also helps prepare an organization to receive new technology. Many implementation efforts fail because someone underestimated the scope or importance of such preparation. Indeed, the organizational hills are full of managers who believe that an innovation's technical superiority and strategic importance will guarantee acceptance. Therefore, they pour abundant resources into the purchase or development of the technology but very little into its implementation. Experience suggests, however, that successful implementation requires not only heavy investment by developers early in the project but also a sustained level of investment in the resources of user organizations.

A very promising implementation effort in a large communications and computer company went off the rails for many months because of inadequate infrastructure in the user organization. New computerized processing control equipment was ready for shipment to prospective users enthusiastically awaiting its arrival, but a piece of linking software was not in place. Arguments erupted over who should pay for this small but critical piece of the system. Equally troubling, there were no resources for training because the developers did not see providing these resources as part of their normal responsibilities. No-one in the user organization had prepared the way for the innovation, so there was no-one to whom developers could hand it off.

Framework for information

Just as marketing managers carefully plan the research through which they will gather critical product-information, so implementation managers must develop an iterative, almost accordion-like framework to guide decisions about when and how to collect needed information from all groups affected by an innovation. We say 'accordion-like' because the process necessarily involves a search for information, a pause to digest it, and then another active period of search – cycle after cycle. What information is important – and who has it – may vary at different stages of the implementation process, but someone must coordinate the iterative work of gathering it – and that someone is the implementation manager.

MULTIPLE INTERNAL MARKETS

The higher the organizational level at which managers define a problem or a need, the greater the probability of successful implementation. At the same time, however, the closer the definition and solution of problems or needs are to end-users, the greater the probability of success. Implementation managers must draw up their internal marketing plans in light of this apparent paradox.

As these managers identify the individuals or groups whose acceptance is essential to an innovation's success, they must also determine whom to approach, when, and with which arguments. Top management and ultimate users have to buy into the innovation to make it succeed, but marketing an idea to these two groups requires very different approaches. How, then, can an implementation manager foster general acceptance of an innovation from such a range of constituencies? We believe this executive must view the new technology from the perspective of each group and plan an approach to each accordingly.

Top management, most concerned with an innovation's likely effect on the bottom line, is accustomed to receiving proposals that specify return on investment and paybacks. Many of today's computerized technologies, however, do not lend themselves to justification in traditional financial terms, yet they may be essential to a company's future. Amid growing calls for the accounting profession to provide better means to assess the value of robots, CAD and computer-integrated manufacturing, some companies are beginning to realize the limitations of traditional capital budgeting models.

Selling top management on the case for new technology – without simul-taneous involvement of user organizations in the decision-making process – is not enough. It is equally important for users of an innovation to develop 'ownership' of the technology. The meaning of this term depends largely on the scope of the project. Although it is patently impossible to involve all users in the choice and/or development of an innovation, that is no excuse not to involve their representatives.

Perhaps even more important is to plan for the transfer of knowledge from the old operation, in which people knew the materials and the product very well, to the new process, which outsiders may initially design and run. The developers of the new process (especially when it is computer software) often know their tools very well, but rarely do they understand the materials and processes to which their software is applied as well as the people on the plant floor who have been working with both for years. At the very least, managers should provide some mechanism and time for such knowledge to flow from experienced worker to developer.

RISKY SITE, SAFE INNOVATION

There are two reasons for conducting a pilot operation before introducing an innovation across the board in a large organization: first, to serve as an experi-ment and prove technical feasibility to top management and, second, to serve as a credible demonstration model for other units in the organization. These two purposes are not always compatible.

If the innovation must succeed at the pilot site in order to survive politically, the implementation manager may choose a site that poses virtually no risk but that neither offers real benefit to the organization nor establishes a model for other units. At the same time, however, if the trial is to be a credible test, it cannot take place among the most innovative people in the corporation. Suc-cess at this kind of site is vulnerable to the criticism that these users are far from typical.

Testing the new technology at the worst performing unit, even though it may be where the innovation is most needed and would show the most spectacular results, is no better a choice. If the project fizzles, the implementation manager will not know how much of the failure was caused by extraordinary problems with the site and how much by the inherent properties of the technology. If the project succeeds, critics will be quick to note that anything would have helped operations at that site.

The solution, therefore, is to be clear about the purpose of the test – experi-mental or demonstration – and then to choose the site that best matches the need. The customized end of one large computer manufacturer's business suf-fered from a problem. If customers cancelled orders, the partially built systems were either totally scrapped – that is, broken down into components and sent back to the warehouse – or matched with incoming orders to determine if the fit was close enough to warrant retrofitting. When this matching process, which had been done manually, was computerized, the first applications site was an operation with an enthusiastic champion, but it was to be phased out in a matter of months. The site was politically risk-free but not useful for a demonstration. Although the first application was successful, the operation closed down before the site could serve as a demonstration for other plants, and the implementation manager in charge of the next site had to start all over.

Obviously, it is not always possible to site new equipment for everyone's convenience. Even so, the placement of an innovation frequently determines who uses the new technology first and most. If the equipment is located farther away from older or more reluctant potential users, they have a ready excuse for avoiding it. Consequently, managers who do not consider physical layout in their implementation strategies may, by default, select as first users people with little or no influence in the organization.

As noted earlier, involving leaders in the planning process helps to smooth the path of implementation. If the first users of a new technology are credible role models (neither extraordinarily adept nor very poorly skilled), their demonstration has heightened meaning for a wide audience. Sometimes these opinion leaders strongly resist the technology, and getting even one of them to use it can create the necessary crack in the dam. Getting them to try the innovation may require nothing more elaborate than a well-paced and tactfully presented training session.

Often, however, an implementation manager has to create new role models by siting the innovation where the workers most open to change can demystify the technology for others by using it themselves. Although it is definitely a mistake to correlate resistance with age per se, it remains true that people with a long-term investment in certain routines and skills often hesitate to give up the security of those habits. Again, it is best to avoid extremes and to site new technology near workers who are fairly open to change but not so different from those whose resistance makes them poor models.

When a large warehouse installed a materials-handling system, it relied on its so-called 'hippy' crane operators instead of workers on the loading platform. Once the crane operators had worked out the wrinkles, management could progressively install the system throughout the plant. The crane operators were not opinion leaders at first because of their relative youth and different backgrounds, but they were both receptive to innovation and not so very different as to be unacceptable role models.

THE MANY AND THE ONE

If an innovation is to succeed, the implementation team must include: a sponsor, usually a fairly high-level person who makes sure that the project receives financial and manpower resources and who is wise about the politics of the organizations; a champion who is salesperson, diplomat, and problem solver for the innovation; a project manager, who oversees administrative details; and an integrator, who manages conflicting priorities and moulds the group through communication skills. Since these are roles, not people, more than one person can fulfil a given function, and one individual can take on more than a single role.

Even if all these roles are filled, however, the project can still stall if the organization does not vest sufficient authority in one person to make things happen. One of these individuals – usually the sponsor or the champion – must have enough organizational power to mobilize the necessary resources, and that power base must encompass both technology developers and users.

There are, of course, many ways to mobilize supplies and people. By encouraging ownership of an innovation in a user organization, for example, skilful advocates can create a power base to pull (rather than push) the innovation along. But enthusiasm for a new technology is not enough. New technology usually requires a supportive infrastructure and the allocation of scarce resources for preparing the implementation site. A champion based in the development group with no authority among the receivers must rely on time-consuming individual persuasion to garner the necessary resources. Further, even if prospective users believe in an innovation's worth, they may have to convince their superiors to free up those resources.

A short case will illustrate the point. A manufacturer of engineering test-equipment was in trouble because many orders for its customized products reached the plant floor missing vital components. Technical experts were able to catch omissions and incorrect selection of parts before the orders went into production, but the mechanics of checking orders and cycling them back through the purchase-order process cost enormous amounts of time, money and customer good will. Customers were angry at the delay of orders for weeks when manufacturing bounced them back to the initial salespeople and were even more dismayed when price quotations had to be revised upward because of a part forgotten in the first go-round.

An internally developed technology offered a partial solution: a computer program could automatically check the orders before salespeople issued quotations. Although the people who placed the orders were enthusiastic about the concept, the work of implementing the system was fraught with problems. No sales manager was willing to function as either sponsor or champion for the innovation. Although a user group funded its development, the appointed champion in that organization was too low in the hierarchy to control the resources necessary to install the system. Moreover, he lacked a clear endorsement for the project from his superiors and had mixed feelings toward the innovation. He believed in its purpose but was not certain it was being developed correctly and was afraid to stand behind it wholeheartedly lest it fail in the field. He was, therefore, slow to seek the resources and upper management support that would have moved the project forward quickly. Ultimately, an innovation has to be one person's responsibility.

A WORD ABOUT HEDGERS

Besides the champions and assassins in an organization, there will always be some 'hedgers', individuals who refuse to take a stand against an innovation so that others can address their objections but who also refuse to support the new technology. They straddle the fence, ready to leap down on either side to declare that they had foreseen the value of the innovation all along or that they had known it would fail from the start. These risk-averse managers can affect the future of a new technology when they are a key link in the implementation plan. Because these hedgers are usually waiting for signals to tell them which way to leap, astute implementation managers will see to it that they receive the appropriate signals from those higher up in the organization.

Like product assassins, hedgers can be found at any level in an organization and dealing with them effectively requires a sequence of actions. The first, and the easiest, is to persuade top management to take some kind of quick symbolic action in support of the innovation. Whether the action takes the form of a memo, a speech or a minor policy change, it must send a signal that top management will stand behind this technology even in a budget crisis.

The second step, which is harder, is to help managers at all levels send out the right signals. If, for instance, the first step was an announcement of a new drive for quality, the second should be to increase the emphasis on quality throughout the company. If workers hear an announcement about a new quality program but continue with impunity to ship products that they know are inferior, the initial symbolic gesture loses potency. Worse, all future gestures lose credibility too.

The third step is the hardest – and the most necessary. Managers must bring the criteria used to judge the performance of innovation users into conformance with the demands of the new technology. New technologies often require new measures. If, for example, a new, structured software·technique requires more time than did the old, managers must evaluate programmer-analysts less on the basis of the quantity of output than on the basis of its quality.

Further, because productivity commonly declines whenever a new technology is introduced, more accurate measurements of productivity in the old sense may lead supervisors to fear that their performance will look worse – not least because, with a fully automated system, direct labour drops but indirect labour grows.

Other adjustments might include a phase-in period for the new technology during which the usual output measurements do not apply. It might also make sense to reward people for preventing rather than just solving problems and for developing work behaviour identified with the new technology. Although operators do not respond well when they view technological systems as controlling their behaviour, they respond quite well when a system gives them feedback on their performance and the performance of their machines. Information increases the amount of control people have over their environment.

Converting hedgers into believers is not a simple task, but it is one more of the inescapable challenges managers face as they try to implement new technology. Indeed, as the competitive environment changes and as the systematic effects of new technologies become even more pronounced, the work of implementing those technologies will increasingly pose for managers a distinctive set of challenges – not least, the task of creating organizations flexible enough to adjust, adapt and learn continuously.

12

PROBLEM-SOLVING IN SMALL GROUPS:
Team Members as Agents of Change

Bill Mayon-White

Drawing upon experience in the use of an intervention method developed by Mayon-White (1986) this chapter discusses the role of a facilitator in a task force or study group engaged in group problem-solving. The facilitator is seen in relation to the client in the framework of transactional analysis. In addition the development of several approaches to problem-solving is discussed. Many of these methods attempt to blend the hard disciplines of systems engineering and operational research with soft approaches.

One such transferable framework is the systems intervention strategy (SIS). This is taught over a six-month (50-hour) part-time Open University management course in the UK and is designed to overcome the limitations of traditional approaches to problem-solving and change management. From the client's point of view, the attraction of this framework derives from its role as a common language and way of working for resolving problems which can be put into place across a whole organization.

It has proved extremely difficult to extract a clear description of the processes which take place inside any group engaged in change management. All the dynamics that one would predict from an understanding of the theories of group behaviour are present, but it is more difficult to pinpoint the ways in which a team uses particular techniques within the methodology. Figure 1 shows some of the processes used, and in practice they seem to be easy for change management teams to learn and to use.

THE FACILITATOR'S ROLE

One way of attempting to model the role of the facilitator as he/she works alongside a team of managers is to call on transactional analysis (Berne, 1964). The ideal form of communication between team and facilitator is 'adult–

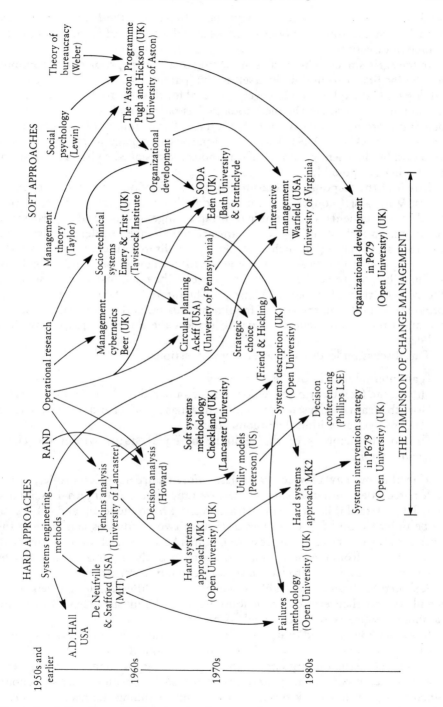

Figure 1 A 'family tree' of hard and soft approaches

adult', in which any advice is sought, not offered and the facilitator increasingly becomes a 'sounding board' for ideas and a source of clarification, not a source of directives.

In the early stages of analyzing the setting of a change problem it is common for the facilitator to find him/herself in the 'parent' role of tutor as the methodology is first explained. However it is usual for this role to disappear once an initial iteration through the methodology has been completed. Some methods demand more initial explanation than others. For example soft systems methodology (Checkland, 1981) uses special-purpose language which must be understood by the client group. Other methods are designed to be as transparent to the client as possible.

Much of the response is determined by the behaviour of the team of managers. With a self-confident team of middle-level managers (that is, section heads or equivalent) who are able to bring a range of skills and experience to the common task of solving an organizational change problem progress can be rapid and exciting. In such a setting, the facilitator quickly settles into the role of adviser and acts as a 'sounding board' for new ideas. In addition he or she may be able to contribute as a member of the team instead of restricting the role to that of impartial chair and facilitator. When members of the organization take on the role of facilitator, this transition is usually immediate and other team members seem to respect the dual role played by their colleague.

This discussion leads us to several new questions:

Is an internal facilitator to be preferred?
Should the facilitator be of senior status compared to the team members?
Does the team need a senior executive to act as a patron and to give the team some protection within the organization?
Should all members of the team be of equal status within the client organization?

The facilitator may play several roles: tutor, chairperson, controller, counsellor, recorder, initiator, summarizer, or rapporteur. An internal facilitator may be preferred if he or she (a) attracts respect from the team, and (b) is seen to be unbiased and fair to all views. If these two conditions can be met, the questions raised above can be resolved. Status becomes irrelevant for the facilitator, though from the viewpoint of other parts of the organization, it may be advantageous to be seen to have a senior person in control.

A skilled facilitator is also able to manage status differentials between group members and elicit effective contributions from the most reticent, while containing the more extroverted members of the team.

It is sometimes argued (but usually by consultants!) that an external facilitator brings an objective view to the organization and that he or she can avoid becoming enmeshed in arguments about content by focusing on process. It is also fairly common for organizations to use such consultants as scapegoats when things do not work out as planned, thus avoiding the need to allocate blame internally!

Against this must be set the knowledge of a firm and its workings which a good internal consultant has in addition to a knowledge of the personalities of the team members and of other personnel in the organization. It is this knowledge which must always give the good internal facilitator an edge over an outsider, providing that the skills needed can be made transferable.

A stronger argument in favour of the external consultant is that the demands of the 'process' of running a group or team are so high that it requires a long apprenticeship to understand and cope with the pressures that this generates. Running a meeting then demands the full attention of the facilitator or process consultant during a session, leaving little time for other forms of intervention or contribution to the debate. Some methods, notably decision conferencing (Phillips, 1989) and SODA (Eden, 1989), use more than one facilitator in order to counter this problem. In these methods one facilitator concentrates on managing process and one on managing content analysis.

Despite the increasing tendency for organizations to use some kind of computer support for planning, simpler methods are sometimes the best way of helping an organization to plan and make decisions. Those methods which rely heavily on computer support have been defined by Huber (1984) as group decision support systems (GDSS). At the present time some facilitators argue that there are advantages in the client organization having a robust process that is known and understood by internal staff and is not clouded by the 'magic' of computer support, whereas other authors argue that computers can help a group manage more complexity without recourse to 'backroom' work.

Encouraging experiments

From the preceding discussion it is clear that a facilitator needs a formidable set of skills. She or he needs to understand and operate a methodology and also will need to be able to deal with new questions of procedure intuitively. For example:

When to use particular techniques from within the methodology.
When to abandon the framework and ad lib.
When to use well known in-house methods which are familiar to team members.
When to suppress discussion and move the debate in a new direction.
When to break off the discussion and call for a pause and refreshments.

The courage to experiment with group processes is derived from self-confidence and experience rarely seen in the leaders of the 'occasional' task forces and committees which spring up in organizations in times of crisis and change. All too often, such work groups follow a sterile process of debate loosely based on the conventional committee protocol. Creativity is stifled and contributions are frequently assessed by the status or rank of the individual from whom they derive, and are not studied for their value to the organization and its problems. A simple framework which is easily learned could transform such groups and make them much more effective.

Table 1　The key features and methods of the change management strategy

The three phases of the strategy	The steps of the strategy	What kinds of actions are appropriate to each step?	What tools and techniques are available to help?
Remember that iteration is helpful when using this strategy			
Diagnosis	0 Entry	Start by recognizing that change is a complex process.	Make use of the concepts of 'mess' and 'difficulty'.
	1 Description	Structure and understand the change in systems terms.	Use diagrams.
		Get other points of view on the change problem or opportunity.	Set up special meetings (NGT, DELPHI, etc.) Create a model of things as they are.
		Set up some objectives for the systems you are examining.	Set up an 'objective tree'.
	2 Identify objectives and constraints	Think of the objectives of the change itself.	Prioritize your objectives for change.
	3 Formulate measures for your objectives	Decide on ways of measuring if an objective is achieved.	Use '£s' or quantities where possible. Scaling or ranking methods elsewhere.
Design	4 Generate a range of options	Develop any ideas for change as full options. Look at a wide range of possibilities. Your objectives may suggest new options.	Brainstorming. Idea writing. Interviews and surveys. Comparisons with best practice in other organizations.
	5 Model options selectivity	Describe the most promising options in some detail. Ask of each option: What is involved? Who is involved? How will it work?	Diagrams are simple models. Cost-benefit analysis. Cash flow models. Computer simulations.
Implementation	6 Evaluate options against measures	Test the performance of your options against an agreed set of criteria.	Set up a simple matrix to compare the performance of your options. Score each option against the measures.
	7 Design implementation strategies	Select your preferred options and plan a way of putting the changes into place.	Look for reliable options. Check back to the 'problem owners'. Plan time and allocate tasks.
	8 Carry through the planned changes	Bring together people and resources. Manage the process. Monitor progress.	Sort out who is involved. Allocate responsibility. Review and modify plans if necessary. (Critical Path Analysis etc.)

Table 1 is one guide which has been used to help the facilitator choose a technique for a given stage in the analysis. Its limitation is that it can become restrictive if it is simply used as an algorithm and not as a means of generating learning and understanding about a set of changes for an organization. The good process consultant will take cues for moving to another stage in the analysis from the group and not from a table of instructions.

The consultant as trainer and 'parent' to the group

An added dimension to the business of being a facilitator is the change of role demanded by the process of analysis. At an early stage in the diagnosis, a more directive instructional role (in transactional analysis the 'parent' role) may be permissible (Harris, 1973). Later in the design phase a more 'laid back' approach is needed to encourage creative thought. Finally, in the implementation phase, a new sense of leadership is needed as the project moves ahead with a programme of changes being put into place. For the facilitator this third phase of implementation may take place some time after the two previous activities. If an external consultant is being used, he or she may become detached from the project at this stage as the organization takes over and begins to drive the change forward. It is also fairly common for a project leader to emerge from amongst the group members as the earlier phases of analysis and planning proceed. The processes help to build commitment to the theme of a change and for some individuals this may lead to a decision to commit their careers to the management of a particular set of changes. Clearly the consultant has a crucial role in helping such individuals with these choices, and in training them in the methodology.

This may, in effect, amount to a change in facilitator and brings with it two new ideas. Those of the 'leaderless', but autonomous, group and the notion of rotating leadership as the initiative and responsibility for process is handed from one group member to another.

In all groups or teams all these things happen to some degree; the concern of those involved in designing methodologies should be to recognize this and to help teams to use it to the best advantage. Each member of a group brings a set of skills to the activity. Part of the facilitator's role is to recognize these skills and bring them to bear on the problems being reviewed.

Facilitating and managing the client

Throughout this discussion is the implicit assumption that there is a benefit for the project team to think of the parent organization as its client. Thus the team is in effect an internal group of advisers and problem-solvers, drawn from across the organization and not from a single specialist department. This has implications for the choice of project team, the choice of venue for the working sessions, and the frequency of meetings.

Members of a project team or task force are expected to be prepared to forgo their departmental loyalties in favour of a commitment to the 'best interests' of the organization. This is rarely easy to achieve since the role of task force members will be seen as a temporary one and the gains and losses of any change to a 'parent' department are readily assessed. Thus all too frequently the wrong individuals are put forward as task force members. Instead of putting forward individuals who are imaginative and open in their attitudes, individuals who can be trusted to defend a department's interests at all costs are offered instead. A good facilitator will use the patron inside the client organization to prevent this from happening.

The choice of venue and frequency of meetings will be affected by the urgency and importance of the task in hand. Ideally an off-site venue should be used to ensure that the group is free from distractions. It also helps to create a sense of identity amongst the members of a group. Comfortable surroundings, good lighting and ventilation, and ample wall space for charts and displays are essential. Most company boardrooms tend to fall short on all of these requirements. Special environments for decision support work are now being created and even the simplest of these increases the effectiveness of group interaction.

Finding enough time for group work is difficult. Ideally two to five days are needed to work through complex problems effectively. These sessions may need to be repeated at fortnightly or monthly intervals over a period of up to six months. Persuading busy executives to keep their diaries clear is difficult. When the initial meetings are being set up, some direction from senior staff in the company may be needed. For example, the initial approach to individuals could be made by the patron, but after that the commitment and intrinsic challenge of the problems should be sufficient to maintain momentum. In many circumstances the group is self-selecting as individuals will already have an interest in the issues being considered; in such circumstances the more usual task is that of identifying any other interested parties which should be represented in the work group.

Letting go

The external consultant faces one unique problem, that of letting go and accepting that the later stages of the project can be managed with a diminished or zero contribution from the facilitator. Indeed one criterion of success may be the ability of the organization to do without external help in the final stages of the implementation of changes. If this happens, the ideas of change and methodology have indeed been transferred. One of the earliest signs of this occurs when a task group reconvenes and the facilitator discovers that the debates have been progressed by informal meetings and discussions. This can be disconcerting to the consultant but shows that a commitment to the work has been achieved.

A MODEL OF CHANGE METHODS

In the course of developing these ideas it has become clear that some kind of framework which encompassed several methods would help in understanding the relationship between the work of different practitioners and the context in which some of the well known so-called 'rational' approaches to managing change have developed.

One way is to look at the origins of methodologies and at the predecessors to the present generation of methods. A 'family tree' which attempts to do just this is offered in Figure 1. It shows how parallel developments appear to have taken place more or less simultaneously on both sides of the Atlantic and within different academic fields. There seems to be convergence between various systems engineering methods as they have progressively been 'softened' by practitioners who appear to have been working independently of one another.

The two poles of 'hard' and 'soft' approaches in Figure 1 are a scale in which the figure is set. The figure must be interpreted with some care. The links mean 'influenced the development of', which in some cases means: 'as a result of difficulties with "x", we came up with "y" as a more promising way of dealing with certain kinds of issue'.

But in most instances the reasoning is simple. Thus, for example Warfield originally worked as a systems engineer at the University of Virginia and developed his approach as a means of dealing with the complex management issues which frequently emerged from the technical projects with which he was concerned.

In a similar manner Checkland (1981), Eden et al. (1983) and Ackoff (1974) appear to have developed their respective approaches as a reaction to the shortcomings of systems engineering and OR methods. In the work of Ackoff it would seem that it was the limitations of operations research and statistics that spurred the development of his ideas, which now have wide application to the areas of corporate planning and management.

The right-hand side of the figure is deceptively simple, for in reality there are a very large number of practitioners of organizational development (OD) each following the tenets of slightly different schools of thought. For the purposes of illustration only those which relate directly to the ideas presented in the Open University course, 'Planning and Managing Change' (Open University, 1986), are shown. This course teaches both OD and systems methods to its management students.

The scale on the left-hand margin is approximate, but serves to illustrate the manner in which consultants, managers, and the academic community have been able to respond to the practical problems of managing change as they are presented in industry, in corporations, and in public sector bodies. Over this same time scale, we can also argue that social norms have changed, along with the nature of the technology employed by organizations in every aspect of their work. Both of these trends are generating new kinds of problem for the manager.

Organizational Development is shown in the figure, and increasingly OD seems to be dependent on the formation of teams within the workplace for the successful conduct of particular stages in the change process. This emphasis on participation is also present in SIS, and prompts the question: 'why so?'

The most appealing reply would be that it reveals some important theory about organizations. In fact the probable answer is less sanguine. It seems more likely that a change in social behaviour has changed the nature of the control process inside organizations and groups. Rigid organizational hierarchies are now less common, higher levels of education prevail, and in some cultures the traditions of trade unionism have led to management styles which employ negotiation and consensus, and avoid management by dictat. Together these ideas may add up to an important statement about communication and control in the 'evolution of the organization'.

Success in managing change is not achieved by chance, and a positive proactive approach is clearly important. Often this can be achieved by relying entirely on resources within a company or organization but sometimes outside help is needed. All the approaches in Figure 1 attempt to help those who use them to control their own destiny, and to know the boundary of the areas over which they do have control. With these approaches there seems to be a tendency to use consultants near either pole, whilst towards the centre some 'self-operating' or 'consultant-free' methods may be emerging.

Again this could merely reflect social and cultural norms. The 1960s and 1970s may have been a time in which organizations willingly followed the advice of 'experts'. The 1980s and 1990s may be the time of the internal change agent and of the 'do-it-yourself' OD practitioner. (Pritchard 1984 Rickards 1986). These tend to suggest that many organizations do have considerable skills available to them; the facilitator merely helps the organization to make good use of its human resource.

Hard versus soft

The main argument behind many methods (including the systems intervention strategy method) is that both 'hard' and 'soft' methods have weaknesses which can be overcome by using methods that draw from both. For example, the basic structure of SIS reflects its origins in systems engineering. The delineation of three distinctive phases of work and the use of iteration to refine and test the output of each stage set it apart from the traditional formal methods for systems analysis. Superficially the early stages of description appear to match Checkland's rich picture construction. Both build models of the situation as perceived by the task force. However SIS makes explicit use of systems concepts in this stage whereas the rich picture explicitly avoids using the concept of system. This is an important distinction. Checkland claims that his soft approach avoids the assumption that systems exist 'out there' and await discovery by not using the terminology of 'system'. SIS uses the concept of system to impose a shared structure on the problem setting and so makes the initial analysis possible. Once the debate is under way this representation may be modified or discarded but remains as a common reference point. In SIS the use of diagramming enables the participants to build an agreed, shared model of problems, thus immediately creating a sense of shared ownership.

In its later stages SIS can make direct use of several well-known techniques such as brainstorming and objective setting. However, these techniques are used precisely because they are familiar and can thus be adopted and used efficiently by any task force.

Qualitative methods

The importance of process cannot be overestimated. The idea of a change methodology as a learning system is captured by Churchman's concept (1971) of an 'inquiring system'. As the company evolves, organizational learning is taking place. Any team attempting to manage change will itself be learning about the organization, its environment and about the skills possessed by the team itself. Thus a team acquires confidence in its ideas and proposals, rather than verifiable proofs which state that their preferred course of action is the best.

For example, the SIS process makes extensive use of qualitative techniques to test agreement and to search for common ground. Nominal group technique (Delbecq et al., 1975) and its variants is always used together with a variety of voting procedures.

Wrap-round: phenomenology and positivism in the world of engineering and the social sciences

Another interpretation of Figure 1 is that the two extremes reflect a reductionist view of the world, with positivism and a mechanistic world view emerging in the 'hard' paradigm, and the social sciences attempting to use the methods of the natural sciences to explain their objects of study. If this deterministic world view is associated with the earlier methods shown at the poles, then those methods shown in the centre of the figure reflect the outlook of phenomenology, even though most of the practitioners would admit to being reconstructed positivists. The two ends of the continuum thus reflect the same outlook and the central area represents a contrasting paradigm. It may be helpful to think of the figure as representing the surface of a cylinder in an 'evolutionary space' in which ideas and paradigms spiral through time.

If we pursue this idea further it becomes clear that if we choose other slices through this space some of these will intersect the cylinder, others will touch, and other slices will not have any contact with the surface described. We can then imagine that those intersecting surfaces include artificial intelligence, expert systems, and other emerging fields such as software engineering.

CONCLUSIONS: WHERE NEXT?

Possible future developments of most methodologies in the 'soft *and* hard' categories may be (a) in the direction of computer-aided decision support; and (b) some simplification of the methodology so that it can be used by an individual manager to help with problem structuring in the course of day-to-day work.

The skills of the consultant are vital and more work is needed to understand how the processes of decision are helped by the facilitator. Some internal consultants are very successful, others fail when using well established frameworks and more investigations are needed to understand the mix of craft skills which are needed to ensure success for most work groups (Cropper, 1984).

The team members themselves are the main source of ideas in any change exercise. It is perhaps appropriate that the balance of thinking shifts from focusing on the consultant as the change agent to give the team members greater recognition for their role in the process of managing change.

REFERENCES

Ackoff, R.L. (1974) *Redesigning the Future.* New York: Wiley.

Berne, E. (1964) *Games People Play.* New York: Grove Press.

Checkland, P.B. (1981) Towards a systems-based methodology for real world problem solving. In: Open Systems Groups (eds) *Systems Behaviour.* London: Harper & Row.

Churchman, C.W. (1971) *The Design of Inquiring Systems.* New York: Basic Books.

Cropper, S.A. (1984) *Ways of Working.* Brighton: OR Group, University of Sussex.

Delbecq, A.L., Van de Ven, A.H. and Gustafson, D.H. (1975) *Group Techniques for Program Planning.* Glenview, Illinois: Scott Foresman.

Eden, C. (1989) Strategic options development and analysis – SODA. In: J. Rosenhead (ed) *Rational Analysis for a Problematic World.* London: Wiley.

Eden, C., Jones, S. and Sims, D. (1983) *Messing about in Problems.* Oxford: Pergamon.

Harris, T.A. (1973) *I'm OK, You're OK.* London: Pan Books.

Huber, G.P. (1984) Issues in the design of group decision support systems. *MIS Quarterly,* 8(3), 195–204.

Mayon-White, W.M. (ed.) (1986) *Planning and Managing Change.* London: Paul Chapman.

Open University (1986) *Planning and Managing Change.* Milton Keynes: Open University Press.

Phillips, L.D. (1989) People-centred group decision support. In: G.I. Doukidis, F. Land and G. Miller (eds) *Knowledge-based Management Systems.* Chichester: Ellis Horwood.

Pritchard, W. (1984) What's new in organizational development. *Personnel Management,* July, 30–33.

Rickards, T. (1986) Making new things happen. *Technovation,* 3, 119–131.

Warfield, J.N. (1974) *Societal Systems Planning, Policy and Complexity.* New York: Wiley.

13

HOW TO IMPLEMENT STRATEGY

Arthur A. Owen

Senior managers today are mostly familiar with the jargon of strategic planning, and systematic approaches to the planning of business strategies are now being used by many professionally managed corporations. Terms such as 'business unit', 'competitive position', 'industry maturity' and 'experience curve', all of which evolved during the 1970s, are an accepted part of management language, and the techniques of planning have been sufficiently well-developed, in one form or another, to produce strategies for most corporations. But even top-class strategies are worth nothing if they cannot be implemented – and in the 1980s more and more attention is being given to ways of improving the rate of success in implementation: better a first-class implementation procedure for a second-class strategy than *vice versa*.

In real life, all too many strategic plans have ended up as mere documents on the chief executive's shelf, while the corporation plods on in its old familiar ways. The value of strategic planning, and the positions of those who use it, will be called into grave question unless more effective approaches are developed to ensure the success of strategies. These can be defined as the key intentions of top management, towards which corporate resources must be directed so as to achieve specific objectives relevant to the competitive environment; such as broadening the product line, moving into embryonic technologies or increasing manufacturing efficiency.

'Intentions' do not exist as strategies unless the management has thought through what needs to be done, by when and by whom, using which resources, to achieve what objectives. Strategies are specified in relation to the market place or in relation to internal organization and efficiency. The strategic plan involves specifying the implications of strategies: and, to be meaningful, strategies must be communicated to, agreed to and supported by management.

Problems of successful implementation centre on how well or badly the existing organization responds and how adequate or otherwise its reporting proves to be. In practice, the problems fall into four main categories. The first difficulty is that, although strategies need to be developed around the 'business units' of the corporation, these units often (alas) do not correspond to parts of the organization structure. Business units have an external market place for goods and services, and their managements can plan and execute strategies independent of other pieces of the company. On the other hand, the organization structure – and how that functions – derives from its history of takeovers, tax considerations, shareholder considerations, economies of scale, personnel strengths and weaknesses, personal relationships, ambitions, national legal requirements and so on. Strategic planners must attempt to cut through this 'culture' and to plan in relation to the various competitive environments by identifying the strategic business units (SBUs) and developing strategies for them. The catch is that the strategies still have to be implemented by the organization as a whole.

As an example of the mismatch between business units and organization, one highly diversified corporation in Europe consisted of about 140 operating companies. We identified within the corporation about 85 SBUs. But only 30 of these consisted of complete operating companies. The remaining 55 all contained bits of the latter. While half the operating companies fell clearly into SBUs, the other 70 or so had their activities split across units.

In addition, the corporation had grouped its companies into four divisions by broad category of activity, while SBUs often incorporated companies from more than one division. Naturally, top management is not keen to reorganize the whole corporation drastically in order to implement strategies – thus, unless responsibility for strategies is clearly defined, nothing will happen. In the above case, getting business-unit strategies implemented through the divisions and operating companies demanded the development of new techniques to improve strategy control and communication.

A second problem area is that traditional management reports are not sensitive enough to monitor the implementation of strategies. Such reports are designed to help manage operations, working through the organization structure represented by 'profit centres', 'cost centres' or other forms of responsibility or reporting centre. These reports should reflect the detail of all planning (but often do not); and therefore cannot be used to monitor individual strategies. Even if performance turned out as planned, it would not be clear which strategies had worked out as intended; a better than expected performance of strategy A could have compensated for underperformance of strategy B. For example, did the stock reductions take place because of the new material-requirements-planning system, or as a result of the product rationalization programme?

Since responsibility centres frequently do not coincide with SBUs, the effects of strategies can only be noted, if at all, by looking at several of the traditional reports. As the latter are required for regular periodic control, they are 'calendar-driven' and cover a different time-frame from strategy implementation controls, which are 'event-driven'. Often, implementation will cover several cycles of traditional reporting, whose mechanisms, anyway, contain far too much detail and swamp the key measures required to monitor particular strategies. There are many examples of reporting systems which are inappropriate for this purpose; indeed, very few serve it well.

WHY STRATEGIES DON'T MATERIALIZE

Companies face many problems in introducing change. They find that:

1. Implementation of their chosen strategies cuts across traditional organization units;
2. Information available for monitoring implementation is not adequate;
3. The organization resists change;
4. Payment systems are geared to past achievements, rather than future goals.

STRATEGIES MUST BE MONITORED

Once again, top management, naturally enough, will not want to make drastic changes to the traditional reporting systems just to control strategies over a specific time-period of a year or two or three. But unless strategies can be monitored, the success of the strategic plan cannot be evaluated – and the planning process is further diminished if lessons cannot be learned for future planning.

Implementing strategies involves change, and change involves uncertainty and risk. Managers will happily agree to change in the cosy confines of the planning meeting; but when the crunch comes, there are always excuses, relating to the pressures of day-to-day operations, that justify putting off the process. Unless the corporation ensures that management is committed at the most senior levels, change will not take place. Any system for implementing strategy must maintain the motivation that is often generated during the planning process itself.

Finally, management systems are seldom adapted to ensure the success of strategies. Management systems involve review and reward processes, communication channels, management and personnel development and so on. These systems are often in place as a result of past strategies; they are rarely tuned or revised to meet the needs of new ones.

So how can successful implementation of strategies be ensured? How can management be sure that the assumptions underlying its strategy remain valid, that planned progress is maintained, that specific intermediate goals are being met, that variances from plan are dealt with effectively? The implementation process, as used by Arthur D. Little, recognizes that strategies are similar in nature to projects, that is, an objective has to be realized, with a given set of resources, within a given time-scale. The techniques of project management can therefore be applied to assist the successful implementation of strategies by focusing management's attention on achieving strategic objectives. Project-management techniques do not mean complex computer-based critical path analyses (although these have their place in helping to implement extremely complex strategies); but they do include five basic principles:

1. Allocation of clear responsibility and accountability for the successful outcome of the overall strategy project;
2. Limiting the number of strategies pursued at any one time;
3. Identifying actions to be taken to achieve the strategic objective, allocating and getting agreement to the detailed responsibilities for the actions;
4. Identifying a list of 'milestones' or major intermediate progress points;
5. Identifying key performance measures to be monitored throughout the life of the strategy project, and creating an information system to record progress.

Since the organization cannot be changed significantly in the short term, and many of its aspects and its reporting system need to be retained, these five basic principles should be superimposed on the existing organization. The techniques of project management can then be tailored to suit the strategy being implemented. A material-requirements-planning system to reduce manufacturing costs and inventory will need different management from a strategy to diversify into related, but different industries; the management and controls for implementing various strategies can then come and go with the strategies themselves. However, our experience has shown that several general organization and control steps, derived from project-management techniques, can be systematically followed to promote successful implementation.

First, what are the implications of the strategies for the existing responsibility centres in the traditional budgets – what is the impact on revenue, costs, capital, personnel and so on? These basic mechanisms for controlling the organization must take into account what resources are required to implement each responsibility centre's contribution to strategies. Planners and management accountants must look for a fit between what the strategic plan requires and what revenue and resource assumptions are contained in the traditional budgets. Minor changes or 'revectoring' of one or the other may well be required to pull them into line. A manager is then given responsibility for the success of the strategy.

As mentioned, implementing strategy cuts across organizational boundaries. Thus, one client who was following a rationalization strategy found, while attempting to prune a major product line, that the strategy had implications for its marketing division, manufacturing side and the central raw materials purchasing department. Another client, a Dutch construction group, has domestic divisions for civil engineering, road-building, pipe-laying and housebuilding; while pursuing a strategy of overseas penetration, it has had difficulty in developing foreign markets as a full-time contractor and in promoting its activities as a homogeneous group – all because of the divisionalized profit centres in its national market.

The chief executive or the corporate management team must make one manager responsible for the successful outcome of the strategy. The 'strategy manager' takes on this responsibility in addition to his/her normal executive role. He/she will be the person most concerned with the successful outcome of the strategy, even though some of the resources to implement it may lie outside his/her organizational jurisdiction. As an added incentive, it may be necessary to provide new financial rewards for the management and other staff closely associated with a strategy's success.

The strategy manager draws on the help of the corporate planners, management accountants and other managers of responsibility centres associated with the plan. He/she starts with the agreed strategic objectives, resources and financial implications agreed upon and prepares a detailed implementation plan. It will include:

1. Specific activities and actions to be performed, allocation of responsibility for achieving these actions and time-scales within which they must be achieved;
2. Physical resources to be consumed or made available;
3. Manpower level requirements, manpower development programmes and compensation systems and incentives appropriate to achieve success;
4. Levels of investment required to implement the strategy;
5. Revised effects on responsibility centre budgets;
6. Performance factors to be monitored continuously to ensure successful implementation of the strategy, including assumptions made about aspects of the external environment that can affect the outcome of the strategy – national economic considerations, responses of the competition, external raw material costs and so on;
7. Milestones to be recognized as progress points or checkpoints to ensure that the strategy proceeds within the planned time-scale, and that the effects on the business can be measured.

These benchmarks also provide opportunities to reassess the plan and make any adjustments as a result of variances.

HOW TO MAKE STRATEGIES WORK

Project-management techniques can be used which involve:

1. Allocating clear responsibility and accountability for the success of the overall strategy project;
2. Limiting the number of strategies pursued at any one time;
3. Identifying actions to be taken to achieve the strategic objective, allocating detailed responsibilities for the actions – and getting agreement to them;
4. Identifying a list of 'milestones', or major intermediate progress points;
5. Identifying key performance measures to be monitored throughout the life of the strategy project, and creating an information system to record progress.

FINAL TOP APPROVAL AND GO-AHEAD

The plan is submitted for final approval and go-ahead to the top management, which will already have made the initial broad decisions to allocate resources, and will be kept informed throughout the development of the plan – so there should be no major surprises. Nevertheless, detailed planning of strategic projects may have implications for other projects, and corporate management may require some final changes – for example, if less money is available for investment than was expected.

The successful implementation of the approval project is then monitored – as the overall strategy manager watches the performance factors and reports on milestone achievement to top corporate management. He/she may need to set up a temporary information system, and the data-processing department may be able to help by abstracting results from the traditional operating reports. Data-processing departments which have successfully promoted database techniques will be better able to respond quickly to short-term needs than others. (A 'data base' is a file or collection of files designed for sharing several users.) Indeed, one US client was advised to structure its data base around the 'planning model' at SBUs as the 'fundamental building blocks' of the corporation. Reports by responsibility centres and by planning units can then be produced from the same statistical base.

There is no general rule about which measures of performance should be used to monitor success – they depend on the strategy. However, the choice of the appropriate measures should be carefully considered by the strategy manager, planners and management accountants. Often, the best approach is to monitor physical measures separately from external factors such as inflation, energy costs and financing. The latter are subject to different influences and fall less easily within the corporation's control. By separation, the true causes of variance from plan can be measured and acted on. Progress reviews at milestone points may lead to a review of initial assumptions and of changes in the environment, and thus to some replanning.

Communications may well have to be improved to ensure the success of the strategy – especially if the strategy manager depends on other managers outside his/her control. All corporations have their means of communication, both formal and informal, but these may not suit the specific purposes of the strategy which is being implemented. It may be necessary to set up a project committee (initiated by the strategy manager) to coordinate activities during strategy implementation or key phases of it. Any conflicts that arise between a manager's implementing responsibility and his/her other priorities should normally be resolved by the strategy manager and department head concerned. Higher management should be called in to arbitrate if they fail.

THE CHIEF EXECUTIVE AS LYNCHPIN

The chief executive remains the lynchpin of both strategic planning and strategy implementation. His/her role is to ensure that the corporation will be servicing market needs in three, five or 10 years time – or whatever time-scale is appropriate to the industry. Without his/her full commitment to the strategic development of the corporation, the planning and implementation processes will not work: he/she and corporate management must ensure that managers are brought out of their day-to-day tasks to take part in developing the business unit plans. Obviously, the chief executive and corporate management are deeply involved in the development of the corporate plans. The chief executive appoints the strategy project managers and reviews and authorizes the project plans, and then reviews strategic progress at milestones and coordinates reactions to variances.

The planner administers the planning process and acts as an 'information broker', passing information between managers and the chief executive and *vice versa*, acting as an adviser to both and as a strategy evaluator looking for realism, consistency and desirability from the corporate point of view. He/she also assists strategy managers to prepare their plans, identifies performance measures and advises on an appropriate project information system. During strategy implementation, the planners act as the eyes and ears of the chief executive.

HOW TO IMPLEMENT STRATEGY

Management accountants must be prepared to adopt a flexible approach to providing information for planning meetings and subsequently in assisting strategy managers to track the key factors for controlling implementation. In this, management accountants are likely to work very closely with the data-processing department. The planning process revolves round the profit centre managers; they contribute their market knowledge, ideas and experience. They then take on the strategic development role as discussed and agreed at the planning meetings.

How does the complete process work in practice? One European client recognized that a major profit-improvement strategy – indeed, one that was crucial for survival – was to improve manufacturing efficiency by reducing stocks and costs. The method was to introduce an integrated materials requirements planning and production control system. The chief executive realized that implementing the strategy would cut across several divisions and change established work practices. He made the manufacturing manager responsible for its successful outcome. A detailed plan along the lines outlined above was prepared as a basis for implementation. The activities of marketing, sales forecasting, data-processing, manufacturing, accounts and purchasing departments were clearly specified and agreed.

The amounts of capital to be invested in computers, shop-floor recording service, stores recording and the like were quantified, agreed to by top management and carried through into departmental budgets. Performance factors such as levels of project expenditure, raw material purchases and stock and shop-floor turnaround were chosen to monitor the success of the strategy and several milestones were agreed for monitoring implementation – availability of key computer program, completion of training schedules, achieving an agreed level of stock improvement. This approach paid off, and the strategy has worked. Many companies would have taken the easy way out and left it to the data-processing department: but other clients which did indeed adopt the latter approach paid for it by spending considerable sums without achieving their objective.

Adopting a systematic project management approach to strategy implementation has a number of significant advantages:

1. It allocates clear responsibility for the strategy. Someone has responsibility to cut across the organization boundaries, pull the pieces together and make sure it happens.
2. A more formal and impersonal reporting procedure tracks progress both for the benefit of the strategy manager and, more important, for the chief executive. Without such a procedure, management is dependent on informal comment, which is often inaccurate reflecting the reluctance of managers to identify problems early because this may be seen as reflecting on their personal abilities.
3. The system redresses the organization's desire to keep going in the same direction and to resist change. It overcomes the need to make dramatic changes in organization, traditional reporting or managerial behaviour, all of which take time and money. The process is added to the normal behaviour pattern and provides a timely control mechanism. As implementation proceeds, more fundamental changes to the organization and management processes can be made in the confidence that the strategy is on course and that the risks associated with change are minimized.
4. Manpower development and compensation can be planned to achieve strategic goals.

All of these benefits lead to greater confidence by the chief executive in his/her ability to control and monitor the implementation of strategy. This in turn will make possible the most aggressive initiatives which the current times surely demand.

PART 4:

Examples of Change

PART 4:
EXAMPLES OF CHANGE

Any reader on the management of change would be incomplete without reference to contemporary examples of organizations where new or revised ways of operating have been attempted. Elaborate models, frameworks and change techniques are fine, but the practitioner wants to know what works in practice and why. Conferences, journals and books abound with stories of successful organizational change, and any such choice for a volume like this is bound to be selective and somewhat arbitrary. However, we have chosen for this section descriptions that meet three broad criteria: practicality, realism and variety. Each of the accounts specifies in some detail the change principles employed as well as the practical steps taken to design and implement a recent change effort. As with much of the change management literature, the authors rely on anecdotal and unsystematic evidence, but they are not entirely celebratory: they are realistic enough to readily admit faults and weaknesses in the methods and mechanisms adopted as well as some of the painful lessons attending the overall change process.

Finally, the five case studies deliberately represent a wide range of sectors and organizations. While the challenge to work more effectively and make better use of resources is common to each scenario, the context and scope varies enormously – from a company-wide organisation development programme at British Airways with a workforce of 37,000 to the building of a small interagency drug team in East Dorset. It is hoped that most readers will be able to identify with at least one of the organisations described.

Colin Price and Eammon Murphy were both – at the time of the changes they report – internal agents of change in the Western London District of British Telecommunications plc. Here the stimulus for improving their quality of service was both overwhelming and complex. Emerging from the relative comfort of protected monopoly, not only did BT need to radically overhaul its operational systems and structures, but traditional staff attitudes and organizational culture also needed to adapt rapidly to the new competitive environment. The authors describe how Richard Beckhard's classic OD framework was utilized to guide the change programme, noting a range of transitional activities that were set in motion to move the District to where it needed to be. Of necessity, the account is brief and perhaps deceptively simple, but it does much to demystify the practice of OD. The British Airways case also concerns a recently privatized service industry, and here the scope of the proposed changes are – if anything – even more ambitious. This time, the authors call upon another tried and tested model to describe the BA change effort: Lewin's stages of unfreezing, movement and refreezing. It is not clear whether this methodology was used to guide those managing the change at the time, or was utilized subsequently as an analytical device for organizing the article. Either way, it provides a valuable insight into multi-faceted change across all levels of all organisations. Noteworthy is the apparently precipitative role of training at each stage of the OD process.

The article by Paul Iles and Rhandir Auluck introduces a dramatically different context and focus. Their concern is the effectiveness of working teams in social work practice in the UK. They usefully summarize a number of team-building techniques, particularly as they relate to multi-disciplinary and inter-agency teams. Finally, they go on to apply some of these change processes to one particular Community Drug Team, made up of five professional groups drawn from three different employing agencies. Although typically located under the OD banner, such team-building techniques have currency in virtually any change effort; neither is their utility restricted to public sector environments.

The central office of Billiton International Metals situated in The Hague, Holland, is the case example explored by Graham Benjamin and Christopher Mabey. Again, it draws upon Beckhard and is an illustration of OD in practice, spelling out some of the steps taken by the 250 staff to restructure their organization, renegotiate their roles with the rest of the business and bring their own attitudes into line accordingly. The authors emphasize the pivotal position of change managers and the need for them to be open to behavioural and attitudinal change themselves as they attempt to lead employees into new ways of thinking and doing things. Successful change is as much about harnessing the creativity and energy of the workforce as it is about devising enlightened business plans.

In the last article of this section, Walsham describes an all too common change scenario at an anonymous processing company: the introduction of a new information system (material requirements planning) which, after 18 months of chaos, finally fails. Citing the work of Peter Checkland on soft-systems and Andrew Pettigrew on the need for a contextualist approach, the author argues that this abortive outcome was all but inevitable because a number of important change principles were neglected. Indeed, this post mortem serves as a useful summary for Part 4 as a whole. For example, it emphasizes the need to consider the historical and cultural context before embarking on change; the need to build informal networks, procedures and lines of communication to facilitate change; the need to cater for differing stakeholder perspectives on the requirement for and outcomes of change; and the need to devote as much energy to the process – as to the content – of proposed changes. Despite the contrasting nature of the organizations selected it is perhaps reassuring that several such critical success factors run consistently through each account, regardless of sector, size or scope of proposed change.

14

ORGANIZATION DEVELOPMENT IN BRITISH TELECOM

Colin Price and Eamonn Murphy

A good deal of attention has focused, in recent years, on 'excellence' as a desirable goal for organizational zeal (and indeed passion!) and on the Japanese and American companies who have 'shown the way' by sustaining very high standards over many years. Inevitably the implication of much of the research has been – despite the carefully expressed caveats of the various authors – that one can achieve similar successes by imitating the most attractive characteristics of these top companies. The plain fact is that success is only likely to result if the desired future state of the organisation is visualised with sufficient clarity and the hard work of getting closer to it is done each working day by the managers and staff who are committed to a shared vision of the future. This article describes the methodology, results and lessons learned from the management of an organizational change programme which has concentrated on this less glamorous and more painstaking approach.

THE ORGANIZATION

British Telecom Western London District (BTWLD) is a major operating unit of British Telecom employing over 6,000 staff and having a turnover of several million. BTWLD provides telecommunications services to both residential and business users over approximately one fifth of the area of Greater London. The District is structured in a relatively traditional way, having a District Board and Divisions within the District for Business Systems, Consumer Products, Network Business, Marketing, Finance and Personnel/Support Services.

THE NEED FOR CHANGE

BT has been subject to radical change over the last few years. Those changes include: privatisation, liberalisation and deregulation; increasing competition and significant technological advances. In response to these changes in the external environment BT has realized the need, and grasped the opportunity, to change its own internal environment. Change programmes have been initiated company-wide to improve: quality of service; customer response time; ease of customer contact; management control of cost; etc, etc. These programmes have focused primarily on the systems of management and have produced some quite outstanding results. However, the attitudes, perceptions, skills and core behaviour of staff are subjects which the centre of BT have left largely as the province of local management. In order to get to grips with these fundamental characteristics of the organization, BTLWD has initiated an Organization Development Strategy.

MAKING THE CONNECTION

The first steps in the OD strategy were taken by the Board of the District (then called an Area) calling in consultants from the BT Management College to help them 'get a feel for where we should be headed.' This request for help resulted in a series of two and three-day residential workshops for the Board, where they asked themselves the question shown in Figure 1.

The 'where are we now?' question was answered by the Board analysing, in some depth, data gathered by the consultants through extensive individual interviews, group interviews and questionnaire application. The data was collected from all levels of management, together with representative samples of employees. The results were certainly interesting and produced quite a stimulus for change. The dimensions of organization culture that gave greatest cause for concern were:

- A public service orientation rather than a business orientation towards the customer with insufficient distinction made between sectors of the market.

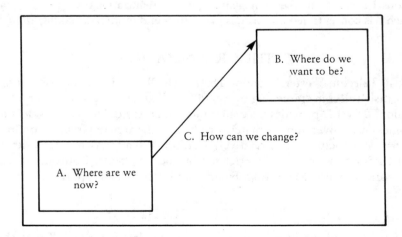

Figure 1   Questions the members of the Board asked themselves

- Little or no identification with Business aims as newly expressed, among staff generally.
- A punitive management style encouraging subordinates to 'keep the lid on the dustbin.'
- Extensive indulgence in blame laying – it was always 'the other Division's fault.'
- Alienation of junior management – 'we are just the meat in the sandwich.'

However, not all was gloom and doom. Willingness to change was evident and loyalty to the organization was high. Dedication to customer service was widespread.

The 'where do we want to be?' question took some time to answer it. It may seem that the obvious answer is to change those aspects of our present situation which cause concern – ie take more effort to involve Junior Managers etc – and to retain the advantageous aspects. This is not the case. There is no guarantee that our present situation will contain within it all the elements which will determine future success. The appropriateness of the culture can only be determined by the environment the organization is operating in – what was 'good' in the past may not be 'good' now or in the future – for example, the concept of public service for its own sake is deeply embedded in the thinking of many employees and, whilst it manifests itself in dedication to customer service now it is likely to cause more and more problems when the quite different demands of customer satisfaction within the context of a private company arise.

One aspect of the desired future state is that all customers should be able to feel that they have been treated well and that this should be compatible with an approach which recognises the differences in needs between large, medium and small users. In the transition phase staff may feel that residential customers are no longer of importance and that their new environment is simply 'unfair' and unacceptable.

Hence the Board, with the help of the Senior Managers and the consultants, designed their ideal future climate, including within it their ideas on the dimensions of the culture which needed to be modified and developed if the organization was to fulfil its potential.

THE 'TRICKY' BIT

So, we knew where we were and where we wanted to be. The 'tricky' bit is actually moving from A to B. The consultants agreed on three criteria for a series of actions necessary to produce the desired change:

1. Change from the top.
   The commitment of senior management, particularly the 'top person' – in this case the District General Manager – is an essential pre-requisite for the change initiative. As the change programme develops, this commitment needs to be mirrored in the behaviour of Board members and their senior managers. The characteristics must be evident in:

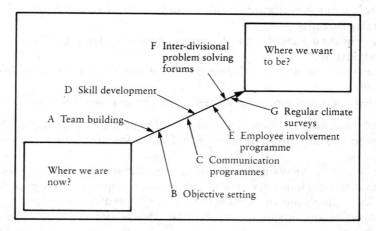

Figure 2   The 'fishbone', showing strategy

  a. deeds and not just words – this means the use of personal time in being
     seen to participate actively.
  b. willingness to take the initiative in developing the programme rather
     than waiting for cues from consultants – the ownership of activities
     must lie with management if lasting change is to take place.
2. Real not feel.
     In change programmes that are concerned primarily with 'perceptions',
     'attitudes' and 'emotions' there is a great temptation to measure suc-
     cess by 'counting smiles on faces.' Smiles are all very well but they are
     only of value to the organization if they are turned into more output,
     better customer service or decreased cost.
3. Don't tinker.
     In a large organization the strength and reinforcement capabilities of cul-
     ture can be extremely powerful. Tinkering around at the edges, changing
     the odd policy here or improving relationships there, is unlikely to work.
     The force of change has to be pretty substantial to break the mould.

With these criteria in mind the Organization Development Strategy was designed. The main activity areas within the strategy cannot be described fully
here but are summarised in Figure 2.

  A. Team Building has generally followed the action research model – data
     collection on an inter- and intra-group basis, feedback to whole teams
     and actions arising out of the energy created as a result of feedback. The
     Finance division, for example, were able to take a long hard look at how
     they were meeting the needs of the business and local managers and
     established a sufficiently clear focus to provide a more customer orien-
     tated service in a short space of time at a point where it was particularly
     valuable for them to be able to do this (devolved budgets, increased local
     autonomy etc.).

B. Objective-setting programmes have proved difficult to evolve in practice. The clarity provided by the McKinsey's 7-S model was useful in the initial stages to demonstrate how difficult it was to achieve common understanding from District General Manager down to first line managers about the goals of the organization. Eliciting meaningful detail from the existing 'Business Plan' – such as it was – and cascading this down to managers was a near impossible task. It was all too evident that the Business was only just *beginning* to think in terms of real goals. The level of detail was woefully inadequate. We found it useful to start a simultaneous *upward* movement in the goal setting programme, looking closely at the actual day-to-day priorities of first line managers and using the insights gained to change, reshape and redefine agreed goals. In addition we are now concentrating on specific managers' situations, seeking to perfect the feedback mechanisms which are, or should be, in operation to help them get results. The success gained from these studies can then be duplicated for the benefit of managers in equivalent situations across the District.

C. Communication programmes have included team briefing on a monthly basis, an audit of the other communications systems (internal post, electronic mail etc) and the development of a quarterly video magazine which has sought to keep off staff informed of major developments whilst retaining a lighter element (competitions on improvement suggestions etc).

D. Skill development has concentrated on the training of first line managers in the technique of resource management, enabling them to prove to themselves that significant monetary savings can be achieved in a relatively short period – typically 3 months or so. In addition to the skills of these managers in handling their interpersonal interactions, those of their staff in customer situations are also being developed. Higher level managers have been trained to carry out a support and reinforcing role in order to progress these projects and ensure that training needs are identified and addressed.

The last three items of our 'fishbone' on Involvement, Inter-Divisional Forums and Climate Surveys take us to our current 'present state.' Our strategy is to provide more opportunity for front line staff to become actively involved in the change processes. A particular problem area is the way in which the boundaries between different divisions or departments can become significant barriers to organizational effectiveness. A causal factor for many of these problems may well lie in the cultural legacy from the past – overbureaucratic division of work processes, clear divides between work hierarchies etc – but little genuine progress can be made until large numbers of staff become committed to the changes. So far only small numbers have been involved in workshop events and climate surveys. These surveys suggest that much more work needs to be done to make the necessity for change more evident and the opportunity of involvement more real. The next planned step is to hold a series of interactive seminars with the District General Manager during which the current business realities will be discussed and staff will have the opportunity to explore the implications for them and their work.

SO IS IT WORKING?

The OD programme *does* seem to have been significant help so far. Evaluation results from each activity show extremely positive results, subjective evaluation from senior managers is overwhelmingly positive, and commercial performance is well up (coincidence or causal?).

But the real test of success is being capable of responding to continual change in the environment. We are not at that stage yet. We *are* getting there. One thing is sure though – that the organization and the consultants have learned many lessons from the strategy. Here are just a few:

- Think big – it is difficult but necessary to visualise a quantum leap. In BTLWD we need to change, in a short period, the culture which has developed over decades. It *is* possible to sustain enthusiasm for long-term change provided that the milestones are visible.
- Simplify and publicise – make sure everyone knows what's going on; if the ground rules are changing then let people know why, but do not crush them under the weight of the full details of a large-scale change strategy. Strike the balance between information which generates commitment and information which generates a headache!
- Do not 'mystify' change – do not let OD be something people do late at night in hotels. Get it into the workplace, publish notes of meetings, talk about it in a matter-of-fact way.
- Don't rely on 'top down' cascades – they can end up as a trickle! Starting change at the top is crucial but the downward momentum can only be sustained if you check progress, regularly rethink your strategy and introduce new initiatives when they are needed.
- Don't over-rely on consultants – they can be useful catalysts but can all too readily become 'the person driving the change initiatives.' When this happens all lasting benefits may be lost. Make sure that it is the senior manager who announces all the major change activities, who opens workshops, bangs heads or taps shoulders when needed, rewards effort etc. In the early stages many senior managers will want to be non-committal: 'let's try it and see.' This is fine to start with. Stop and rethink if it goes on.
- Do not rely on groups – a group never changed anything. Participative decision making – yes. Group problem solving – yes. Group responsibility for action – no. Make sure that every action in a change programme is tied down to one individual. Change requires the single-mindedness of an individual to drive action through.
- Do not forget to refreeze – the emphasis in much OD work is on unfreezing the system. This is fine but make sure that, once the system is liquid and change has happened, you refreeze. Establish processes and systems

that 'institutionalise' new ways of doing things – the consultants will not always be around to keep an eye on things.

- The installation of a steering group who can grasp the right moment when refreezing can happen – when enthusiasm is still high and workable strategies have been established to take the next few practical steps – is one way of refreezing. In our case this group consists of several line managers who are located in key operational situations in each Division across the District.
- Time and energy – do not underestimate the amount of time required to produce change or the amount of energy needed to shift a little closer to the ideal. Watch for the signs of 'reversion to type' among managers – disproportionate lengths of time spent on the budget, in-trays etc, rather than on spending time with staff solving real problems.

NEXT STEPS?

The next few steps will be to instil the active pursuit of organization development as just another part of the strategic processes of BTLWD. Towards the end of 1987 the District will make less use of external consultant resources and concentrate on the development of the steering group members as change consultants – co-running workshop events etc. As line managers in their own right they are well placed to provide effective role models for the management of change as an integral component of their leadership styles.

It will not be easy for managers throughout the District to sustain the momentum gained, nor will it be easy for them to lead their staff into a new and quite stressful environment in such a way that the opportunities and threats which will inevitably arise can be handled with energy, enthusiasm and creativity. Essentially this is a leadership issue and, on the basis of our experiences so far, the combination of a clear end vision and sustained hard work on the journey towards it seems to be helping managers resolve it with satisfying success.

15

CREATING SUCCESSFUL ORGANIZATION CHANGE

Leonard D. Goodstein and W. Warner Burke

In 1982 Margaret Thatcher's government in Great Britain decided to convert British Airways (BA) from government ownership to private ownership. BA had regularly required large subsidies from the government (almost $900 million in 1982), subsidies that the government felt it could not provide. Even more important, the Conservative government was ideologically opposed to the government's ownership of business – a matter they regarded as the appropriate province of private enterprise.

The growing deregulation of international air traffic was another important environmental change. Air fares were no longer fixed, and the resulting price wars placed BA at even greater risk of financial losses.

In order to be able to 'privatize' – that is, sell BA shares on the London and New York Stock Exchanges – it was necessary to make BA profitable. The pressures to change thus exerted on BA by the external environment were broad and intense. And the internal organizational changes, driven by these external pressures, have been massive and widespread. They have transformed the BA culture from what BA managers described as 'bureaucratic and militaristic' to one that is now described as 'service-oriented and market-driven.' The success of these efforts over a five-year-period (1982–1987) is clearly depicted in the data presented in Table 1.

This table reflects BA's new mission in its new advertising slogan – 'The World's Favorite Airline.' Five years after the change effort began, BA had successfully moved from government ownership to private ownership, and both passenger and cargo revenues had dramatically increased, leading to a substantial increase in share price over the offering price, despite the market crash of October 1987. Indeed, in late 1987 BA acquired British Caledonian Airways, its chief domestic competitor. The steps through which this transformation was accomplished clearly fit Lewin's model of the change process.

Table 1 The British Airways success story: creating the 'world's favorite airline'

	1982	1987
Ownership	Government	Private
Profit/(loss)	($900 million)	$435 million
Culture	Bureaucratic and militaristic	Service-oriented and market-driven
Passenger load factor	Decreasing	Increasing – up 16% in 1st quarter 1988
Cargo load	Stable	Increasing – up 41% in 1st quarter 1988
Share price	N/A	Increased 67% (2/11/87–8/11/87)
Acquisitions	N/A	British Caledonian

LEWIN'S CHANGE MODEL

According to the open-systems view, organizations – like living creatures – tend to be homeostatic, or continuously working to maintain a steady state. This helps us understand why organizations require external impetus to initiate change and, indeed, why that change will be resisted even when it is necessary.

Organizational change can occur at three levels – and, since the patterns of resistance to change are different for each, the patterns in each level require different change strategies and techniques. These levels involve:

1. Changing the *individuals* who work in the organization – that is, their skills, values, attitudes, and eventually behavior – but making sure that such individual behavioral change is always regarded as instrumental to organizational change.
2. Changing various organizational *structures and systems* – reward systems, reporting relationships, work design, and so on.
3. Directly changing the organizational *climate or interpersonal style* – how open people are with each other, how conflict is managed, how decisions are made, and so on.

According to Lewin, a pioneer in the field of social psychology of organizations, the first step of any change process is *to unfreeze* the present pattern of behavior as a way of managing resistance to change. Depending on the organizational level of change intended, such unfreezing might involve, on the individual level, selectivity promoting or terminating employees; on the structural level, developing highly experiential training programs in such new organization designs as matrix management; or, on the climate level, providing data-based feedback on how employees feel about certain management practices. Whatever the level involved, each of these interventions is intended to make organizational members address that level's need for change, heighten their awareness of their own behavioral patterns, and make them more open to the change process.

Table 2   Applying Lewin's model to the British Airways (BA) change effort

Levels	Unfreezing	Movement	Refreezing
Individual	Downsizing of workforce (59,000 to 37,000); middle management especially hard-hit. New top management team. 'Putting People First.'	Acceptance of concept of 'emotional labor'. Personnel staff as internal consultants. 'Managing People First.' Peer support groups.	Continued commitment of top management. Promotion of staff with new BA values. 'Top Flight Academies.' 'Open Learning' programs.
Structures and systems	Use of diagonal task forces to plan change. Reduction in levels of hierarchy. Modification of budgeting process.	Profit sharing (3 weeks' pay in 1987). Opening of Terminal 4. Purchase of Chartridge as training center. New, 'user friendly' MIS.	New performance appraisal system based on both behavior and performance. Performance-based compensation system. Continued use of task forces.
Climate/ impersonal style	Redefinition of the business: *service*, not *transportation*. Top management commitment and involvement.	Greater emphasis on open communications. Data feedback on work-unit climate. Off-site, team-building meetings.	New uniforms. New coat of arms. Development and use of cabin-crew teams. Continued use of data-based feedback on climate and management practices.

The second step, *movement*, involves making the actual changes that will move the organization to another level of response. On the individual level we would expect to see people behaving differently, perhaps demonstrating new skills or new supervisory practices. On the structural level, we would expect to see changes in actual organizational structures, reporting relationships, and reward systems that affect the way people do their work. Finally, on the climate or interpersonal-style level, we would expect to see behavior patterns that indicate greater interpersonal trust and openness and fewer dysfunctional interactions.

The final stage of the change process, *refreezing*, involves stabilizing or institutionalizing these changes by establishing systems that make these behavioral patterns 'relatively secure against change,' as Lewin put it. The refreezing stage may involve, for example, redesigning the organization's recruitment process to increase the likelihood of hiring applicants who share the organization's new management style and value system. During the refreezing stage, the organization may also ensure that the new behaviors have become the operating norms at work, that the reward system actually reinforces those behaviors, or that a new, more participative management style predominates.

According to Lewin, the first step to achieving lasting organizational change is to deal with resistance to change by unblocking the present system. This unblocking usually requires some kind of confrontation and a retaining process based on planned behavioral changes in the desired direction. Finally, deliberate steps need to be taken to cement these changes in place – this 'institutionalization of change' is designed to make the changes semi-permanent until the next cycle of change occurs.

Table 2 presents an analysis of the BA change effort in terms of Lewin's model. The many and diverse steps involved in the effort are categorized both by stages (unfreezing, movement, and refreezing) and by level (individual, structures and system, and climate/interpersonal style).

Unfreezing

In BA's change effort, the first step in unfreezing involved a massive reduction in the worldwide BA workforce (from 59,000 to 37,000). It is interesting to note that within a year after this staff reduction, virtually all BA performance indices had improved – more on-time departures and arrivals, fewer out-of-service aircraft, less time 'on hold' for telephone reservations, fewer lost bags, and so on. The consensus view at all levels within BA was that the downsizing had reduced hierarchical levels, thus giving more autonomy to operating people and allowing work to get done more easily.

The downsizing was accomplished with compassion; no one was actually laid off. Early retirement, with substantial financial settlements, was the preferred solution throughout the system. Although there is no question that the process was painful, considerable attention was paid to minimizing the pain in every possible way.

A second major change occurred in BA's top management. In 1981, Lord John King of Wartinbee, a senior British industrialist, was appointed chairman of the board, and Colin Marshall, now Sir Colin, was appointed CEO. The appointment of Marshall represented a significant departure from BA culture. An outsider to BA, Marshall had a marketing background that was quite different from that of his predecessors, many of whom were retired senior Royal Air Force officers. It was Marshall who decided, shortly after his arrival, that BA's strategy should be to become 'the World's Favorite Airline.' Without question, critical ingredients in the success of the overall change effort were Marshall's vision, the clarity of his understanding that BA's culture needed to be changed in order to carry out the vision, and his strong leadership of that change effort.

To support the unfreezing process, the first of many training programs was introduced. 'Putting People First' – the program in which all BA personnel with direct customer contact participated – was another important part of the unfreezing process. Aimed at helping the line workers and managers understand the service nature of the airline industry, it was intended to challenge the prevailing wisdom about how things were to be done at BA.

Movement

Early on, Marshall hired Nicholas Georgiades, a psychologist and former professor and consultant, as director (vice-president) of human resources. It was Georgiades who developed the specific tactics and programs required to bring Marshall's vision into reality. Thus Georgiades, along with Marshall, must be regarded as a leader of BA's successful change effort. One of the interventions that Georgiades initiated – a significant activity during the movement phase – was to establish training programs for senior and middle managers. Among these were 'Managing People First' and 'Leading the Service Business' – experiential programs that involved heavy doses of individual feedback to each participant about his or her behavior regarding management practices on the job.

These training programs all had more or less the same general purpose: to identify the organization's dysfunctional management style and begin the process of developing a new management style that would fit BA's new, competitive environment. If the organization was to be market-driven, service-based, and profit-making, it would require an open, participative management style – one that would produce employee commitment.

On the structures and systems level during the unfreezing stage, extensive use was made of diagonal task forces composed of individuals from different functions and at different levels of responsibility to deal with various aspects of the change process – the need for MIS (management information systems) support, new staffing patterns, new uniforms, and so on. A bottom-up, less centralized budgeting process – one sharply different from its predecessor – was introduced.

Redefining BA's business as service rather than transportation represented a critical shift on the level of climate/interpersonal style. A service business needs an open climate and good interpersonal skills, coupled with outstanding teamwork. Off-site, team-building meetings – the process chosen to deal with these issues during the movement stage – have now been institutionalized.

None of these changes would have occurred without the commitment and involvement of top management. Marshall himself played a central role in both initiating and supporting the change process, even when problems arose. As one index of this commitment, Marshall shared information at question-and-answer sessions at most of the training programs – both 'to show the flag' and to provide his own unique perspective on what needed to be done.

An important element of the movement phase was acceptance of the concepts of 'emotional labor' that Georgiades championed – that is, the high energy levels required to provide the quality of service needed in a somewhat uncertain environment, such as the airline business. Recognition that such service is emotionally draining and often can lead to burnout and permanent psychological damage is critical to developing systems of emotional support for the service workers involved.

Another important support mechanism was the retraining of traditional personnel staff to become internal change agents charged with helping and supporting line and staff managers. So too was the development of peer support groups for managers completing the 'Managing People First' training program.

To support this movement, a number of internal BA structures and systems were changed. By introducing a new bonus system, for example, Georgiades demonstrated management's commitment to sharing the financial gains of BA's success. The opening of Terminal 4 at Heathrow Airport provided a more functional work environment for staff. The purchase of Chartridge House as a permanent BA training center permitted an increase in and integration of staff training, and the new, 'user friendly' MIS enabled managers to get the information they needed to do their jobs in a timely fashion.

Refreezing

During the refreezing phase, the continued involvement and commitment of BA's top management ensured that the changes became 'fixed' in the system. People who clearly exemplified the new BA values were much more likely to be promoted, especially at higher management levels. Georgiades introduced additional programs for educating the workforce, especially managers. 'Open Learning' programs, including orientation programs for new staff, supervisory training for new supervisors, and so on, were augmented by 'Top Flight Academies' that included training at the executive, senior management, and management levels. One of the Academies now leads to an M.B.A. degree.

A new performance appraisal system, based on both behavior and results, was created to emphasize customer service and subordinate development. A performance-based compensation system is being installed, and task forces continue to be used to solve emerging problems, such as those resulting from the acquisition of British Caledonian Airlines.

Attention was paid to BA's symbols as well – new, upscale uniforms; refurbished aircraft; and a new corporate coat of arms with the motto 'We fly to serve.' A unique development has been the creation of teams for consistent cabin-crew staffing, rather than the ad hoc process typically used. Finally, there is continued use of data feedback on management practices throughout the system.

Managing change

Unfortunately, the change process is not smooth even if one is attentive to Lewin's model of change. Changing behavior at both individual and organizational levels means inhibiting habitual responses and producing new responses that feel awkward and unfamiliar to those involved. It is all too easy to slip back to the familiar and comfortable.

For example, an organization may intend to manage more participatively. But when a difficult decision arises, it may not be possible to get a consensus decision – not at first, at least. Frustration to 'get on with' a decision can lead to the organization's early abandonment of the new management style.

In moving from a known present state to a desired future state, organizations must recognize that (as noted earlier) the intervening *transition* state requires careful management, especially when the planned organizational change is large and complex. An important part of this change management lies in recognizing and accepting the disorganization and temporarily lowered effectiveness that characterize the transition state.

In BA's change effort, the chaos and anger that arose during the transitional phase have abated, and clear signs of success have now emerged. But many times the outcome was not all clear, and serious questions were raised about the wisdom of the process both inside and outside BA. At such times the commitment and courage of top management are essential.

To heighten involvement, managing such organizational changes may often require using a transition management team composed of a broad cross-section of members of the organization. Other techniques include using multiple interventions rather than just one – for example, keeping the system open to feedback about the change process and using symbols and rituals to mark significant achievements. The BA program used all of these techniques.

Process consultation

In addition to the various change strategies discussed above, considerable use was made of all the usual organizational development (OD) technologies. Structural changes, role clarification and negotiations, team building, and process consultation were all used at British Airways to facilitate change.

In process consultation – the unique OD intervention – the consultant examines the pattern of a work unit's communications. This is done most often through direct observation of staff meetings and, at opportune times, through raising questions or making observations about what has been happening. The role of the process consultant is to be counternormative – that is, to ask why others never seem to respond to Ruth's questions or why no one ever challenges Fred's remarks when he is clearly off target. Generally speaking, process consultation points out the true quality of the emperor's new clothes even when everyone is pretending that they are quite elegant. By changing the closed communication style of the work teams at British Airways to a more open, candid one, process consultation played an important role in the change process.

IMPLICATIONS AND CONCLUDING REMARKS

We very much believe that an understanding of the social psychology of the change process gives all of us – managers, rank-and-file employees, and consultants – an important and different perspective for coping with an increasingly competitive environment. Our purpose in writing this article was to share some of this perspective – from an admittedly biased point of view.

The change effort at BA provides a recent example of how this perspective and this understanding have been applied. What should be apparent from this abbreviated overview of a massive project is that the change process at BA was based on open-systems thinking, a phased model of managing change, and multiple levels for implementing the change. Thus both the design and the implementation of this change effort relied heavily on this kind of understanding about the nature of organizations and changing them.

The change involved a multifaceted effort that used many leverage points to initiate and support the changes. The change process, which used transition teams with openness to feedback, was intentionally managed with strong support from top management. Resistance to change was actively managed by using unfreezing strategies at all three levels – individual, structural and systems, and interpersonal. Virtually all of the organizational change issues discussed in this article emerged in some measure during the course of the project.

It is quite reassuring to begin to find empirical support for these efforts in field studies and case reports of change efforts. Moreover, the recent meta-analyses of much of this work are quite supportive of what we have learned from experience. We need to use such reports to help more managers understand the worth of applying the open-systems model to their change efforts. But we also need to remember that only when proof of the intervention strategy's usefulness shows up on the firm's 'bottom line' will most line managers be persuaded that open-systems thinking is not necessarily incompatible with the real world. The BA success story is a very useful one for beginning such a dialog.

As we go to press, it seems clear that many of the changes at British Airways have stabilized the company. Perhaps the most important one is that the company's culture today can be described as having a strong customer-service focus – a focus that was decidedly lacking in 1982. The belief that marketing and service with the customer in mind will have significant payoff for the company is now endemic to the corporate culture. Another belief now fundamental to BA's culture is that the way one manages people – especially those, like ticket agents and cabin crews, with direct customer contact – directly impacts the way customers will feel about BA. For example, during 1990, Tony Clarry, then head of worldwide customer service for BA, launched a leadership program for all of his management around the globe to continue to reinforce this belief.

Yet all is not bliss at British Airways, which has its problems. Some examples:

- American Airlines is encroaching upon BA's European territory.
- The high level of customer service slips from time to time.
- Those who can afford to ride on the Concorde represent a tiny market, so it is tough to maintain a consistently strong customer base.
- Now that BA has developed a cadre of experienced managers in a successful company, these managers are being enticed by search firms to join other companies that often pay more money.

Other problems, too, affect BA's bottom line – the cost of fuel, effectively managing internal costs, and the reactions of the financiers in London and on Wall Street, to name a few. It should be noted that since 1987 and until recently, BA's financials have remained positive with revenues and profits continuing to increase. During 1990 this bright picture began to fade, however. The combination of the continuing rise in fuel costs, the recession, and the war in the Persian Gulf have taken their toll. Constant vigilance is therefore imperative for continued success.

It may be that BA's biggest problem now is not so much to manage further change as it is to manage the change that has already occurred. In other words, the people of BA have achieved significant change and success; now they must maintain what has been achieved while concentrating on continuing to be adaptable to changes in their external environment – the further deregulation of Europe, for example. Managing momentum may be more difficult than managing change.

16

TEAM BUILDING, INTER-AGENCY TEAM DEVELOPMENT AND SOCIAL WORK PRACTICE

Paul Iles and Randhir Auluck

Good teamwork is an essential component of effective social work delivery, and an integral ingredient of many aspects of social work practice. It is also a necessary constituent of effective allocation meetings. Many social workers appreciate fellow team members as a valuable source of support. Increasingly, social workers may work in a variety of multi-agency and multi-disciplinary teams with health, education, housing and other professionals. However, many social workers recognize that their team work may not be as effective as it should or could be. A variety of team building techniques exist, and there is considerable evidence of their effectiveness in improving team members' skills and team and organizational effectiveness. Such techniques, however, may not be totally transferable to multi-disciplinary and inter-agency teamwork, as these situations present new problems of co-ordination, communication and collaboration.

TEAM BUILDING TECHNIQUES

A variety of team building techniques have been devised, in addition to standard techniques such as brainstorming and force field analysis. In most such interventions, the classic action research model of problem identification, data gathering, data feedback, diagnosis, action planning, action taking, and evaluation is followed. Actions taken might focus on goal-setting, mission identification, or prioritizing. Other actions might focus on role analysis and role clarification, in order to resolve issues of role conflict or role ambiguity. One such technique, the role analysis technique of Dayal and Thomas (1968), seeks to define and clarify role requirements. An individual occupying a 'focal' role initiates an analysis of that role and its rationale and duties. Behaviours are added or subtracted until the role incumbent and the group are satisfied with the role description. A role profile is then constructed, and other roles are then analysed and clarified in turn. A further technique developed by Harrison (1972) called 'role negotiation' arranges for each party to change some of their work behaviours in return for changes in the other's behaviour, in terms of behaviour they would like the other to keep doing, stop doing, or start doing. These behaviour changes are written down and agreed in the form of a written contract, with a follow-up meeting to determine whether contracts have been honoured and to evaluate their effectiveness.

Other techniques focus on improving relationships *between* groups rather than within groups, especially in terms of reducing intergroup conflict. One technique, the 'organizational mirror' involves a host group receiving feedback from representatives of several other organizational groups about how it is perceived. Another, known as the 3D image exchange, involves two separate groups building and sharing two lists, one concerning perceptions of the other group and one predicting what the other group will be saying in its list. After meeting separately to discuss what has been learned, each group then makes a list of priority issues to be resolved, shares these lists, and constructs a new list prioritizing issues. Together the groups then devise action plans (Blake *et al.*, 1965). An alternative used by Fordyce and Weil (1971) is to get each group to build three lists, a 'positive feedback' list containing things the group likes and values about the other group and wishes it to keep doing, a 'bug' list containing things the group dislikes about the other group and wishes it to stop doing, and an 'empathy' list containing a prediction of what the other group is saying in its list. The two groups then share their lists, and the total group then builds a key list of unresolved issues and priorities. Subgroups are formed to work on each item and to report back to the whole group for action planning and action evaluation.

It is possible to use this technique to address equal opportunity issues, such as facilitating successful joint work by male and female or black and white co-workers. Such a use has been described in relation to gender by Donleavy (1985) in Ireland and Glucklich (1985) with the British Civil Service, and by Patten and Dorey (1972) in relation to race relations in the US Army. We have presented elsewhere a comprehensive review of such interventions in the equal opportunity field (Iles and Auluck, 1988).

TEAM BUILDING APPROACHES AND SOCIAL WORK PRACTICE

Team building interventions are rarely employed in isolation from other OD techniques. For example, Hall (1985) reports a study which used survey feedback to diagnose problems of trust and morale in a Texas mental health/mental retardation centre, and used team building to address such problems. Alongside survey feedback and other interventions, Boss and McConkie (1981) describes an intergroup team building design which attempted to resolve problems between the associate director of a US social service agency and his nine first line supervisors. Each party exchanged images of themselves and the other party, as well as predictions of their image in the other's eyes, and attempted to plan various actions that would reduce director-supervisor conflicts. Though positive improvements in organizational climate and group functioning were detected, the supervisor group apparently became so cohesive and developed such a strong sense of identity that it neglected wider organizational concerns and priorities. This illustrates the need for careful initial diagnosis and appropriate follow up, and the danger of prescribing team building indiscriminately as a remedy for all organizational ills.

Team building approaches might also be employed alongside mission definition and strategy implementation approaches. An attempt may be made to identify the core mission of the organization, formulate strategic objectives, and assess environmental threats and opportunities to accomplishing the mission successfully. An assessment of organizational strengths and weaknesses in meeting environmental demands may also be conducted, perhaps with the help of 'open systems planning' techniques. For example, Smith and Theaker (1987) report an intervention with Waltham Forest Social Services Department. Workshops with senior management personnel focused on perceptions of the current state of the organization, its culture, strengths and weaknesses. The desired future state of the organization was also identified in response to current and future environmental trends and pressures. This raised such issues as community care, a change in political control, devolution, links with ethnic minority communities, and ethnic minority needs. The kinds of organizational objectives, systems, policies, procedures and relationships needed to achieve this desired future state were also identified. Other workshops with senior management personnel focused on welding them into a cohesive team with a corporate sense of identity, with role analysis and role negotiation techniques being used to enable senior managers to clarify what they needed from each other and compare this to self-perceptions. Mutual contracting and the identification of needs for support, advice, information and co-operation followed. Further workshops with middle managers focused on role and teamwork issues, with particular attention on the behaviours team members felt others should start doing, stop doing, and keep doing.

That OD techniques such as team building can work well in a 'radical' local authority like Sheffield is shown by projects with the direct works department (Kilcourse, 1985) and the library services (Blanksby, 1987). Many of the themes and issues identified, such as the need for cultural change, decentralization, a client-centred approach promoting wider access to services, and greater employee and community participation, seem also very relevant to social work practice. The techniques used, such as mission definition, team building, and climate reviews, also seem highly appropriate.

INTER-AGENCY TEAM DEVELOPMENT

Most team building interventions have been conducted in single organizations, whether with intact work teams or with new teams such as units, new departments, or project teams. Often, however, organizations, especially in the public sector, seek to achieve co-ordination and co-operation by setting up small joint committees, teams, or planning groups, with members drawn from each of the co-operating organizations. These teams, such as National Health Service health care planning teams drawn from their social services, health authorities and housing departments, may often result in greater conflict and frustration rather than co-operation (Sims, 1986a).

Often, team members appear to perceive, and wish to have accepted, differing issues, and appear unsure of which issues should be discussed. The *multiple disciplines* of team members, with their different interests, priorities, perspectives and even languages, such as 'client' vs. 'patient' vs. 'resident', and the *multiple structures* members are drawn from, make co-operation problematic. Negative views may be held by many professionals, due to their socialization and training, of the value of other professionals' contributions (Fried and Leatt, 1986). There may be a lack of respect for other disciplines and different rules about what counts as valid information. Sheppard (1986) reports that, though primary health care workers such as GPs, health visitors, and district nurses in general accepted the legitimacy of the social work role, they were in many cases unaware of the range of tasks social workers could perform. In addition, a significant minority saw some tasks, especially those closest to their own domain, as performed incompetently. This suggests not only a lack of knowledge but negative stereotyping based on a desire to protect professional domains. Auluck (1986) shows how some maternity unit nurses held negative images of social work staff and their competence, and were unaware of the range of services social workers could offer maternity unit users. Those expressing such views seemed less likely to make referrals to the hospital social work department.

The *multiple employers* of members, such as different health authorities and social services departments, may contribute to a lack of commitment, as ultimately careers, reference groups, and rewards are elsewhere, with inter-organizational team activity often counting as 'semi-legitimate'. The *multiple interests* of members, such as different perspectives on appropriate care for the elderly, may engender difficulties, as might the *multiple constituencies* of members, with other members only having a cursory knowledge of these constituencies and pressures. The *multiple power levels* present in an inter-organizational team and the differing extent to which members could commit resources and take binding decisions might also affect team effectiveness. Some participants may have to take issues back continually for departmental approval. More 'senior' members may query the value of their participation, given the 'junior' level of other members. Sims (1986b) discusses such issues arising with a Certificate in Social Service Joint Management Committee, where social service department representatives expressed concern about the limited extent to which college representatives could commit their colleges to specific courses of action. One issue emerging was whether it was better to have members actually involved in course teaching but junior, or members with greater responsibility but less direct involvement. Diagramming the meeting and mapping the relationship of various contributions to the agenda enabled the meeting to make progress.

Sims (1986a) also identifies the issue of *multiple rules for procedure* as a problem, with members used to different ways of conducting meetings, allowing discussion, and taking minutes. He comments on the issue of *multiple expectations of the chairperson* as an additional complicating factor, with much dissatisfaction and scapegoating likely when progress is slow.

Sims (1986a) does acknowledge, however, that many participants consider such teams useful as a way of drawing the attention of other professionals to issues they feel important, and as a way of collecting pressure group support. Social workers may, for example, find them a useful forum in which to demonstrate their distinctive contribution.

INTER-AGENCY TEAM DEVELOPMENT IN A COMMUNITY DRUG TEAM

An intervention designed to promote more effective teamwork has been undertaken in an East Dorset Community Drug Team (Bennett, 1988b). This team consisted of members of five professions: a clinical psychologist, a community psychiatric nurse, a probation officer, a social worker, and an occupational therapist, drawn from three different agencies, health, social services and probation. The intervention used a particular approach, 'task oriented team development', devised initially by Rubin *et al.* (1978) from their work in US community health care settings. This approach asserts that teams need to resolve certain issues before others. These are, in order of priority: issues of goals, roles, procedures and interpersonal relationships. Many team building approaches, such as those based on sensitivity training, often target relationships or procedures, whereas goal or role conflicts may be more fundamental. Particular attention needs to be given to goal and priority issues, such as the degree to which such community teams should be concentrating on direct services to clients, on providing support, advice, training and consultancy services to primary workers, on service development, on service co-ordination, or on liaison and research, monitoring and evaluation of service provision. External pressures from line managers, other professionals and clients, as well as internal interests, experience and career goals may push team members to engage in more direct work with clients. This may be necessary to establish credibility with other workers, but may cause wider goals to be neglected.

The East Dorset Community Drug Team faced not only such standard issues as how to develop effective teamwork and how to maintain it through changing circumstances such as changes of personnel, but how to do this in the context of a team composed of members of five professional groups drawn from three different employing agencies. The Community Drug Team, operating as the most recent component in a network of services which included the Drug Advisory Service, a residential rehabilitation centre for women drug users, a branch of Narcotics Anonymous and an outpatient prescribing clinic, aimed to provide a specialist non-medical treatment and rehabilitation service. It aimed to do this within this network of established services and in co-ordination with other agencies. A Drug Interest Group has enabled drug workers to meet at regular lunchtime meetings. The team, aiming to ensure that drug users receive the specific help they require, decided to operate an open referral system but to advertise only to professionals. It shares a large office and has offices in which to see clients on health service and social services department premises. Operating on a key worker basis, any team member is able to make initial assessments, and the cases are discussed at weekly clinical meetings. As well as work with individuals, it runs some opiate user groups and training courses for generic workers, as well as carrying out several research projects.

In order to work as an effective team (in one instance members of one agency wanted the team to mail details of training courses to them separately, as they did not trust 'colleagues' to pass the information on!) several team building interventions have been undertaken. In order to clarify *goals and missions*, the team, set up with initially ill-defined goals, attempted to set specific objectives (such as setting up specific user groups and setting up a family support service) and to get these endorsed by a meeting of managers. In order to clarify *roles*, the team attempted to define profession-specific and generic skills and get agreement about who does what based on individuals in post. Recurring problems included the specific demands placed on some team members, such as the requirement of the probation officer to find acceptable placements, and appear before the courts at short notice. Other members seemed more able to develop more long-term therapeutic commitments. Given that team members are also members of other teams, some degree of role conflict is also inevitable, and this required negotiation and agreement with the respective managers so that team activities were seen to contribute to professional responsibilities rather than to act in competition with them. The team chose to adopt a 'co-ordinated team' arrangement (Ovretveit, 1986) where the team leader, the clinical psychologist, obtained agreed authority and accountability over allocation of priorities, monitoring, external liaison, induction and training.

In order to clarify *procedures* the team agreed to record new referrals, arising through different routes, in a common referral book, and to allocate cases by agreement according to workload and case characteristics. A key worker system was agreed, by which all members carried out initial assessments and brought these to weekly meetings, which decided who should take on the case as key worker. Though in practice most members were competent to take on most cases, only the health service workers could take on certain clients. All cases were reviewed at clinical meetings, which also took decisions about case closures. It was also agreed to have minuted weekly meetings, to address all relevant incoming correspondence to all team members, and to have one set of notes accessible to all.

In order to improve *relationships* between team members, the team attempted to recruit and select committed staff, to meet frequently, to share projects, to include everyone at monthly lunches, to train together by having monthly training days, and to identify joint training needs. Training included outside facilitators and workshops on groupwork and specific drug problems.

A particularly helpful event was spending the first week together as a full team at a Drug School in Scotland, which generated a common knowledge base, a wider perspective and a corporate identity. This corporate identity has continued to be developed through corporate public relations work and through articles in relevant professional journals. Given new developments such as the initiation of a women's group and changes in staffing, the team has felt the need for periodic team maintenance work.

Further details of the team and the team building interventions can be found in Bennett (1988a). Further details of community drug teams and community alcohol teams can be found in Clement (1988) and Schneider *et al.* (1988), whilst Bennett (1988b) gives further details of the East Dorset Community Drug Team.

DISCUSSION

Team building techniques can be very useful in enabling teams to diagnose blocks to team effectiveness and to take action to remove those blocks. Particularly useful are strategies aimed at ensuring that the team reaches consensus on its core mission and its priorities, and achieves commitment to its objectives. Such commitment and clarity are only fully achievable through the participation of all team members in setting goals and objectives. Strategies aimed at clarifying and agreeing team roles, such as role clarification and role negotiation techniques, are also useful. Teams should regard team building not as a one-off developmental event, but as something that involves periodic review, re-evaluation and maintenance. It is important continually to assess and revise the ways teams make decisions, solve problems, exercise leadership, and relate to other teams and groups both in the organization and externally. Attention also needs to be given to the ways team members communicate with each other, and to relationships between subgroups within working teams, whether based on task or identity. Particularly important here are power/status differences and their influence on team effectiveness. Such differences may be based on task, hierarchical position, function or role differences, or on differences based on divisions salient in the wider society as well as in the team itself, such as those based on race, ethnicity, gender or disability.

Such considerations apply also to working in multi-disciplinary or multi-agency teams. Working in these teams introduces additional complications, related to differences in professional perspectives, interests, knowledge, skills, perceptions, and external demands. Social workers may be particularly well placed to actively promote inter-agency relationships, given their possibly greater experience and training in ensuring effective liaison between organizations, in outplacement work with other agencies, and in operating a 'key worker' system. Effective inter-agency teamwork requires considerable organizational support from managers and professional superiors, however, and demands attention be given in particular to issues of team organization, workload management and case co-ordination.

REFERENCES

Auluck, R. (1986) The referral process: a study of the working relations the antenatal clinic nursing staff and hospital social workers. Unpul dissertation, University of York.

Bennett, G.A. (1988a) Multidisciplinary teamwork issues in community drug teams. Paper presented to conference on community drug teams: clinical and organizational issues, University of London, 17 March 1988.

Bennett, G.A. (ed.) (1988b) *The Treatment of Drug Abuse: Recent Developments*. London: Stoughton.

Blake, R.R., Shepherd, H.A. and Mouton, J.S. (1965) *Managing Intergroup Conflict in Industry*. Ann Arbor, Michigan: Foundation for Research on Human Behavior.

Blanksby, M. (1987) Changing a bureaucracy into an open organization. *Journal of European Industrial Training*, 11, 21–27.

Boss, W.R. and McConkie, M. (1981) The destructive impact of a positive team-building intervention. *Group and Organization Studies*, 6, 45–56.

Clement, S. (1988) The community team: lessons from alcohol and handicap services. In: G.A. Bennett (ed.) *The Treatment of Drug Abuse: Recent Developments*. London: Stoughton.

Dayal, I. and Thomas, J.M. (1986) Operation KPE: Developing a new organization. *Journal of Applied Behavioral Science*, 4, 473–506.

Donleavy, R. (1985) Antidote to Babel: organizational and personal renewal through women and men working together. *Management Education and Development*, 16, 230–237.

Fordyce, J.K. and Weil, R. (1971) *Managing with People: A Manager's Handbook of Organization Development Methods*, Reading, Mass: Addison-Wesley.

Fried, R.J. and Leatt, P. (1986) Role perceptions amongst occupational groups in an ambulatory care setting. *Human Relations*, 39, 1155–1174.

Glucklich, P. (1985) Women's management training in a ghetto? *Personnel Management*, September 39–43.

Hall, J. (1985) Productivity improvement through teambuilding and organizational redevelopment: evaluating the experiences of a human services agency at the county level. *Public Personnel Management*, 144, 409–416.

Harrison, R.C. (1972) When power conflicts trigger team spirit. *European Business*, Spring, 27–65.

Iles, P.A. and Auluck, R. (1988) Managing Equal Opportunity through strategic organization development. *Leadership and Organization Development Journal*, 4.3, 3–10.

Kilcourse, T. (1985) How culture can be the key to management development. *Personnel Management*, December 33–35.

Ovretveit, J. (1986) Organization of multidisciplinary community teams. *BIOSS*, Brunel University.

Patten, T.H. and Dorey, L.E. (1972) An equal employment opportunity sensitivity workshop. *Training and Development Journal*, 26, 42–53.

Porras, J.I. and Berg, P.O. (1978) Impact of Organization Development. *Academy of Management Review*, 3, 349–366.

Rubin, I.M., Plovnick, M.S. and Fry, R.F. (1978) *Task Oriented Team Development*. New York, McGraw Hill.

Schneider, J., Nuzum, W. and Bennett, G.A. (1988) The community drug team: current practice. In: G.A. Bennett (ed.) *The Treatment of Drug Abuse: Recent Developments*, London: Stoughton.

Sheppard, M. (1986) Primary health care workers' views about social work, *British Journal of Social Work*, 16, 459–468.

Sims, D. (1986a) Interorganization: some problems of multiorganizational teams. *Personnel Review*, 15, 27–31.

Sims, D. (1986b) An interorganizational intervention. *Leadership and Organization Development Journal*, 7, i–iii.

Smith, B. and Theaker, W. (1987) Building teams and managing change in a local government authority. *Industrial and Commercial Training*, 19, 14–21.

17

FACILITATING RADICAL CHANGE:
A Case of Organization Transformation

Graham Benjamin and Christopher Mabey

INTRODUCTION

While the primary stimulus for change in organizations remains those forces in the external environment, the primary motivator for *how* change is accomplished resides with the people in the organization. As the pressing need to remain profitable, the introduction of new systems and technologies, and demographic trends combine to insist upon fewer and more skilled employees, so the flexibility and adaptability of the workforce becomes more important. One of the effects of this is to encourage employees to question the ethos and strategic direction of their organization more readily. In view of their increasing value as staff, whether it be in project management skills, software knowledge or some other form of indispensable competence, those proposing and managing change in organizations (especially radical change) need to be able to give satisfactory answers.

The basis upon which an organization acts, adapts and implements changes is coming to interact more and more closely with personal values. As all employees play a more vital part in the organization's life so their learning – conscious and unconscious, explicit and implicit – becomes of greater consequence; and as learning in itself becomes more valued in organizations, and therefore more visible as an activity, questions about organizational purpose become more urgent and necessary to address. This, again, has implications for the leadership of organizations. People need to believe firmly in their leaders if they are to agree to planned radical change, and if their involvement and participation in change processes is to become active and earnest. As much attention needs to be given to the political dimension as it does to the technical and financial dimensions, because change invariably involves a redistribution of power in the organization.

Radical change invariably touches on the core purpose of the organization: it causes people to ask, 'What are we in business for and how do we want to behave to achieve our business objectives?' The need to address change at this fundamental level is becoming all the more insistent as employees increase their flexibility and become more discerning about where they choose to use their indispensable skills. For them it is not just 'What for, but also who for?' Employees can perhaps see the rational justification for change, but do they care enough about those proposing the change and sufficiently value the promised benefits to invest their time and energy in attaining them? Having raised the issues we now put forward some ways in which real – rather than cosmetic – change can be facilitated.

FACILITATING CHANGE

A key prerequisite seems to be the preparedness of those involved in organizational change to accept the possibility that they themselves will need to revise their attitudes and behaviours (and perhaps even their values) if the process is to be successful. This is particularly true of those leading and/or managing the change.

In recent years a fashion has developed for leadership training to include outdoor, group activity, known in the UK as 'outward bound'. This experience can be insightful, beneficial and effective. When it comes to leading change at an organizational level, it seems to us that at least the key figure or figures need, as part of their preparation, to go through a counterpart exercise which we could call 'inward bound'.

This would involve the management team in two parallel processes. First, they need to envisage the future, arriving at a vision statement for the organization that defines how they will stay ahead of, or respond to, forces and circumstances in the competitive environment. Second, they need to describe in detail the present state of the organization: this, in effect, is a diagnosis of strengths and weaknesses, current driving and restraining forces and an estimate of the organization's capacity for change. The next and vital step is to plot the gap between these present and desired 'states'. This might involve data-gathering by surveys, establishing some strategic milestones and setting up change management activities for co-ordinating the transition (Beckhard and Harris, 1987; Beckhard, 1989).

The parallel process involves defining the internal situation and some articulation of the culture and core values required by the enterprise. Then, some understanding and clarifying of what the organization currently stands for and how the beliefs, attitudes, and behaviours of its people relate to, demonstrate and reinforce the desired future values. Then, as before, the gap between present and desired states can be plotted, identifying activities that will help to reorientate attitudes and values in the appropriate direction. This may well comprise a range of behavioural, structural and cultural strategies for change.

Radical change processes are, by definition, so far-reaching for organizations and for individuals, that this kind of joint attention to both aspects is essential: the core purpose as related to the environment and the core values as related internally to the ethos of the organization. It is the task of the individual as leader or change-agent to not only demonstrate the impelling logic of the proposed changes but also to appeal to the values of those involved. In this way it is more likely that emotional commitment will be won, and the latent creative energies of the workforce will be harnessed. This calls for consistent and clear communication of the alignment between personal and organizational values throughout the transition period. During this time, the self-esteem of participants will be buffeted and it is helpful to anticipate the sequence of reactions typical of disruptive transition (Adams *et al*, 1976).

It may be that external consultants could help the change-agents in this task. For a management team, process facilitation may be called for to optimise planning meetings, and ensure that the performance of the task is appropriately matched by attention to how the group is developing the task in relation to underlying assumptions, beliefs and values. At the organization level, provision has to be made for individuals in work groups, old or new, to come to terms with the nature of the change and its impact upon them and their lives.

These, then, are some of the issues and principles of bringing about change – but how do they work in practice?

A CASE EXAMPLE

The first author was recently involved, as a consultant, in a successful example of radical change which occurred in the central office of Billiton International Metals in The Hague. Billiton is the metals industry division of the Royal Dutch Shell Group. After seven years of fundamental over-supply in the metals market the company, with a turnover at that time of around $1.5bn, had accumulated losses of $750m. The parent company was considering disposal as an option when a new President was appointed in 1986. He advised that the business had to be put in better shape, even to sell it. Every operation in Billiton, world-wide, was reviewed 'to determine what businesses we were in and why we were in them'. A survival plan resulted, whereby product-oriented divisions were to be scrapped in favour of four core business segments. The management organization needed to be changed from a typical metals industry structure, heavily centralized to permit significant authority and responsibility to be transferred into the operating companies. Consequently, the role of central office had to change from command and control to a dual role which was very different, being more subtle and complex. The roles embraced first monitoring and auditing on behalf of the shareholder (Shell) and second provision of advice to operating companies on request, and at market competitive rates. The radical change in attitude required could be described as being from 'we're in charge' to 'no one owes us a living'. The change in role also required a reduction by half of staff numbers in central office, with some transferring to the operating companies and some taking redundancy, mainly on a voluntary basis.

The clear view of where the future of the business lay and the role of central office had been reached by the directors after some six months of review and planning, involving senior central office and operating company management with some consultancy support. The directors acknowledged that they had been profoundly challenged by the review, professionally and personally, and recognized that the results could well have a similar impact for staff in the office. The President became convinced that structural reorganization alone was not enough, and a new approach to work was required.

> As the roles of the people in the organization were changing we decided we had to change behaviour and attitudes as well. [From the top down] we would like to trust each other. We wanted individuals to tell their bosses what the problems really were, not what they thought their bosses wanted to hear.

In order to effect change, to accomplish the dual role successfully, the smaller number of people would have to work across organizational boundaries in a quite new way for Billiton, multi-disciplinary and integrative in form and therefore attitudinally different.

The key features of the transformation were:

- the directors in consultation with key stakeholders had reviewed and redefined the business, its purpose and future and the necessary distribution of role and responsibility to achieve that;
- the directors took care to learn from their own experience the implications for change for staff in central office and what was needed to help them accomplish it;
- the President led from the front;
- a programme was designed which, firstly, gave information on plans and reasons; secondly, space was created for feelings and attitudes to be expressed and be given consideration; and thirdly, the task of implementing structural reorganization was begun.

The initial programme was designed by the directors with advice from internal specialists from Shell. It involved every member of staff within work groups, across organizational boundaries. The programme:

- gave information about the review and planning process, the need for change and the plan for the future;
- encouraged expression of current feelings and perceptions;
- defined the issues to be addressed at local, inter-departmental and whole organization or board level;
- focused colleagues, management and consultant attention on the resolution of issues;
- gave responsibility for detailed design and implementation to those closest to the work;
- offered outplacement counselling and support to those leaving;
- ensured continuous feedback to management and directors so that leadership could be given through the change process and resources made available based on accurate data.

The programme process was accomplished by several means used in combination:

- an attitude survey of the whole office (250 staff) was commissioned to provide:
    full expression to current feelings, attitudes and perceptions, at a tense and stressful time;
    valid information with which to begin the change process in human terms;
    a baseline from which to measure or assess progress;
- commitment to further surveys, initially at a six-monthly interval and thereafter annually, to monitor progress, providing data for all;
- work groups, formed in each department to receive first survey output, to validate it and to define the issues to be worked upon (these may have been attitudinal, structural or skills related) – the issues were then allocated by the working group to themselves, to management or to the board, as appropriate, and by agreement;
- an inter-departmental, multi-disciplinary follow-up team, formed to monitor the work groups' progress, give support to the groups and to line management and to ensure that issues which crossed organizational boundaries were properly addressed;
- specific consultancy skills, deployed to support the directors, management groups, the follow-up team and, in some instances, work or departmental groups and individuals identified as encountering particular difficulty or distress.

This intensive period of work enabled underlying attitudes and perceptions to be brought to the surface and faced; it lasted for about three months and took up to 30% of staff time. It was iterative in nature as persons and groups learned how to tackle the raw expression of issues that precedes change. It was also recursive in its simultaneous involvement of staff throughout the organization on key issues, as in the later part of 1987, and through 1988, when the detail of structural and attitudinal change was systematically addressed.

The first survey assessed the present state and uncovered powerful and difficult feelings of distress, and also anxiety for the future, which were worked through. The second survey gave key data on progress, which was made available for all staff, and subsequent work in all departments was aimed at bridging the gap between present and future states. This included the planning and provision of training and meeting other resourcing needs.

The third survey, like the second, produced predominantly positive data on progress and gave impetus to renewed effort, which helped to move people beyond the shock of restructuring and reorganization. This transition process was helped by training in teamworking and new behavioural and technical skills together with further overt discussion in divisions and departments concerning the values and modes of working which were becoming necessary.

This brief description summarises some of the key change events in the central office transformation. Since then, development work has continued in departments and ABC (Attitude, Behaviour, Communication) as the initiative was known, has become a byword in the organization. Business planning is now customarily accompanied by the question, what does this mean for ABC? Furthermore, values are now explicit and well understood, leading to ever increasing consistency between what we are here to do and how we need and wish to do it.

For the international business as a whole, return on capital rose from 2% in 1987 to 13% in 1988 and 16% in 1989, with a capital employed of $1.7bn and a profit after tax of $262m. Although record metal prices account for much of this, as the market changes again in 1990 the flexibility of the new organization and its people is proving its worth.

In review, the management team, which has retained the same personnel throughout the period, have by their own open admission significantly changed the way they individually and collectively behave in business over this period of time. Every member of the central office has attested to a significant rethinking of who they are, where they are leading people, and how this related with the business. Most say that the process of radical change, and the ultimate survival of the business, was significantly affected by the close attention to vision, direction and strategy, alongside the implications for the values, expectations and assumptions of each person involved.

CONCLUSION

Transformation of business objectives and work practices implies significant, even profound change. A major alteration in strategic direction inevitably implies a reassessment of an organization's core purpose, which in turn prompts individuals to question their own work values, and the extent to which they are aligned with those of their employer. Effective and radical change is best facilitated by planned processes which first of all acknowledge and make explicit these views of corporate and individual vision and, second, provide time and resource for people's values, attitudes, beliefs and behaviours to be worked upon participatively, alongside the business and organizational imperatives. Finally, and crucially, leaders of change need to be open to personal change in such a way that they themselves are models of the newly espoused behaviours and values.

REFERENCES

Adams, J., Hayes, J. and Hopkins, B. (1976) *Transition: Understanding and Managing Personal Change.* London: Martin Robertson.

Beckhard, R., and Harris, R.T. (1987) *Organisational Transition: Managing Complex Change.* London: Addison-Wesley.

Beckhard, R. (1989) A model for the executive/management of transformational change. *The 1989 Annual: Developing Human Resources,* University Associates.

18

MANAGEMENT SCIENCE AND ORGANIZATIONAL CHANGE:
A Framework for Analysis

G. Walsham

1. INTRODUCTION

The practice of management science normally involves recommending changes to existing organizational practices and procedures and it is well known that, in some cases, such changes are not successfully accomplished. The description of applied work in the literature is often silent on whether proposed changes actually took place. Some authors do reflect on the difficulties of achieving change but admissions of implementation failure are rarely published. The discussions and explanations concerning change, where they are present in the management science literature, are often inadequate and, in particular, suggest a limited conceptual understanding of organizations and of the processes of organizational change. However, there is a rich literature on organizations, and it will be argued in this paper that management science research and practice would benefit from a more formal analysis of organizational change using ideas and approaches drawn from organization theory.

This paper is concerned with the management of the process of organizational change and its dynamic linkages with context. A specific framework for the analysis of organizational change is outlined in the next section of the paper and the relevance of the framework for management science is discussed. Some detailed conceptual elements are introduced, linked to the analytical framework, and designed to provide specific guidelines for research and practice. A particular case study of the introduction of a material requirements planning system into a manufacturing company is then described, and the case study is used to illustrate the value of the analytical framework and the associated conceptual elements.

2. A FRAMEWORK FOR ORGANIZATIONAL CHANGE

Outline framework

The basic theoretical framework referred to above is drawn from research on organizational change carried out by Pettigrew and others at the University of Warwick in the UK (Pettigrew 1985, 1989). The work has involved the development of theory, a large programme of field work in both the public and private sectors taking the form of longitudinal case studies, and the generation of consequent prescriptions for the management of organizational change. It is not possible here to give a full description of the 'contextualist' work carried out at Warwick, but some key theoretical ideas of relevance to management science are now outlined.

The main thrust of the work is that theoretically sound and practically useful research on organizational change should involve the continuous interplay between ideas about the *context* of change, the *process* of change and the *content* of change. Organizational change should be seen as linked to both intra-organizational and broader contexts, and one should not try to understand projects as episodes divorced from the historical, organizational or economic circumstances from which they emerge. The management of organizational change is not seen as a straightforward, rational process but as a jointly analytical, educational and political process. Power, chance and opportunism are·as influential in shaping outcomes as are design, negotiated agreements and master-plans. It is also noted that implementation cannot be separated from policy formulation and that these processes should not be viewed as discrete or chronological but as interactive and muddled. In short, organizational change and its implementation is viewed as a complex, messy process inseparable from its intra-organizational and broader contexts.

Contextualism and management science

Management science is concerned with intervention to bring about beneficial organizational change. However, with reference to the above contextualist framework, management scientists can be seen to have concentrated largely on the content of change and to have placed much less emphasis on the context and process of change, despite the existence of a significant body of work two decades ago (e.g. Radnor *et al.* 1970) suggesting the need for management scientists to pay more attention to analyses of the environment and process of projects.

Although much traditional management science remains acontextual, ahistorical and aprocessual, there has been some movement over the last decade towards a consideration of the context and process of change in the work of the 'soft systems' school, and notably that of Checkland (1981). It is interesting to observe some parallels between Checkland's work and Pettigrew's contextualism where Checkland emphasizes that the initial analysis of the situation, or his 'rich picture' phase, should be done by recording elements of slow-to-change structure and continuously changing process and how structure and process relate to one another. It is beyond the scope of this paper to attempt a full analysis of the links between the two bodies of work above, but similar conclusions are reached in both cases in terms of the need to see 'problems' in their broader situational context and to try to understand the subtle links between process and context or structure. Checkland (1981) notes that (p. 166):

> The relationship between structure and process, the 'climate' of the situation, has frequently been found to be a core characteristic of situations in which problems are perceived.

The argument to date is that context and process and their interaction are important in understanding organizational change, but management science researchers and practitioners will want to know how to operationalize these concepts in a way which can be drawn on in descriptions and prescriptions for particular projects. There is no unique way of doing this and, in this paper, the 'recipe' approach to analysis, which looks for a list of necessary and sufficient ingredients, is avoided. Such an approach will fail since real situations exhibit infinite variety and require attention to their special features. Nevertheless, certain elements of context, process and their interaction can be identified as valuable guidelines for analysis and, in the remainder of this section, these elements are discussed in detail.

Elements of context

The concepts in this sub-section are partly drawn from the work of Kling (1987) in the area of computer-based information systems. Kling's 'web-models' draw broader boundaries around the focal computer system and examine how their use depends upon a social context of complex social actions. The models emphasize the history of commitments made in the course of computing developments and the infrastructure that supports the deployment of computer-based technologies. As with both contextualism and soft systems, web models see the need to locate the focal project within a much broader context.

Specific concepts which can be identified for the analysis of the contexts of management science projects include different *stakeholder perspectives* and the social relations between participants and others affected by a project. Secondly, it is essential to gain a rich understanding of the *history* of existing procedures and systems. Thirdly, the importance of *informal networks and procedures* is often a significant contextual element in addition to, and sometimes in conflict with, formal organizational hierarchies and systems. Finally, *infrastructure needs* should be analysed; these include not only physical aspects, such as appropriate computing resources for example, but also experience and skills and the management authority needed to produce resources as and when required.

Elements of process

At the level of process, the concern is with the dynamics of interaction between the participants in a project and others who are affected by it or can affect it. According to contextualist theory, it is necessary to have a model or set of perspectives on human behaviour in order to operationalise an analysis at this level. In this article, two main perspectives on human behaviour are considered. The first is a *power/politics perspective* (e.g. Keen 1981, Kling 1987) which views organizational change as a product of a legitimation process shaped by the interests and commitments of individuals and groups, although these interests are often expressed in rational/analytical terms.

A complementary, although interlinked model of human behaviour is a *cultural perspective* (e.g. Peters and Waterman 1982, Smircich 1983) which focuses on shared meanings and norms of behaviour. The different sub-cultures within an organization can have radically different core assumptions about the nature of the organization, its goals and their role within it. For example, one would typically expect a certain homogeneity of view within a group of computer specialists in contrast to a group of marketing people. In trying to bring about organizational change, management scientists are agents of cultural change and transformation, even if they do not always see themselves explicitly in this light.

Interactions between context and process

Some elements of both context and process have been described, which provide guidelines for analysis of a particular project. However, both contextualism and soft systems emphasise the importance of the linkage between these two levels of analysis. A sophisticated theoretical treatment of the linkage between the level of action/process and the level of context/structure is given in structuration theory (Giddens 1984). Space restriction permits only a very brief outline of this theory here. A fuller description of the application of the theory to the specific domain of information systems if given by Walshman (1991).

According to structuration theory, action at the level of process is viewed as producing or reproducing context or structure, and context is viewed as conditioning action. Thus process and context are inextricably interlinked and should be viewed together as different aspects of the same reality. Linkage between the two levels, in structuration theory, is provided by three dimensions which can be loosely described as meaning, power and morality. Actors draw on schemes of meaning, sources of power and standards of morality or norms in order to get others to carry out actions. In so doing, they produce new structures or reproduce old structures of signification, domination and legitimation.

The relevance of the above theory to this paper is to note that the process perspectives of power/politics and culture described earlier are an amalgam of the three dimensions of structuration theory. As outlined above, they provide a means of linking process with structure since they may be viewed as elements of either level. In other words, political and cultural structures can be seen as elements of context and, at the level of process, actors can either reinforce these structures or produce new structures of power and meaning. One insight from this abstract theory of immediate practical relevance is to see context as produced by human action. Thus, for example, when we intervene as management scientists and attempt to introduce change in products or systems, we may well not change political alliances or cultural attitudes which will leave fundamental social structure unchanged. This can have negative consequences in terms of achieving effective organizational change associated with the proposed technological changes.

3. CASE STUDY OF THE INTRODUCTION OF AN MRP SYSTEM

The framework for organizational change and associated conceptual elements are summarised in Table 1, and will now be illustrated using a specific case study. A brief description of the case history is outlined below and the case material is then used to illustrate and enlarge on the theoretical and methodological ideas presented in the previous section.

Outline case history

The *Processing Company* was a wholly-owned subsidiary of a large international manufacturing organization; in the early 1980s it had about 450 employees and a turnover of £25 million. Its original area of business was the manufacture of a product for which the market had gradually shrunk since the 1970s with the entry of newer, technically superior products manufactured by multinational firms. Increasing competition therefore forced the Processing Company to switch from making to buying in base material, and to diversify into the expanding market for converted products which, by 1986, accounted for about half of total sales. Traditionally the Processing Company had had a small range of products with few customers and a limited number of large orders. Lead times were long and no stocks were held without an order. By the

Table 1 Analytical framework and associated conceptual elements

Key components of change framework	Associated conceptual elements
Content	Technology/products/systems.
Context	History of existing systems. Stakeholder perspectives. Informal networks. Infrastructure needs.
Process	Power/politics perspective. Cultural perspective.
Context/process interaction	Action draws on structures of power and meaning and thereby produces or reproduces social structure.

early 1980s, the situation was radically different; there were about 2000 converted products of which approximately half were manufactured for stock and half to customer order. The number of customers had increased dramatically and orders had become smaller and more numerous, with shorter lead times.

In the 1970s, information systems for business control included manual card systems, software for stocks of manufactured base material running on a Data General minicomputer, and an accounts and statistics package run on an IBM mainframe at Divisional Headquarters located over 50 miles away. By the early 1980s, it had become clear that the existing information systems for converted products were inadequate. Unacceptably large differences between book and physical stock showed that the business was not in effective control of finished product stocks and work-in-progress; the same applied to stocks of packaging materials, and there was no effective system of work measurement. Customer service was slipping and delivery dates were not being met on the majority of orders. Management determined that improved computer-based information systems were needed to increase their control over the business and, in particular, started the process of looking for a material requirements planning (MRP) system suited to their needs.

The evaluation and choice of suitable software and hardware was a complex process which has been described previously (Symons and Walsham 1989, Symons 1990). The main choice in the end was between a proposal from *Systems House* for *ProSys* software running on Data General equipment and a package requiring significant bespoke development running on IBM hardware. The former was chosen although not without significant resistance from the holding company who pressed the case for IBM equipment since IBM were one of their two preferred suppliers. Finally, in August 1985, it was reluctantly agreed by the holding company to award the contract to Systems House.

The contract was signed in September 1985, and installation of the Data General hardware and transfer of existing systems was completed two months later. Work had already started on drawing up specification documents for modifications to the standard ProSys modules. The departments involved were identified and a 'key user' was appointed in each to represent the users in discussions on modifications, training and implementation. The sales order processing module was to be implemented first, followed by purchasing and manufacturing, with the aim of completing the project by the end of 1986. The specification work for sales order processing and purchasing continued over several months as many more modifications were required than had originally been envisaged. Software began to come in from Systems House in May 1986, and over the summer the internal Project Team were extremely pressured in trying to simultaneously test software, set up the database and revise procedures. One major change involved the replacement of the old 4-digit part numbering system with a precise 13-digit one; attempts to persuade users of the importance of this met with considerable resistance.

Pressure from management to implement the system was building up, and in October 1986 the sales order processing department started dual running. This proved extremely difficult: the workload involved in using old and new procedures in parallel was excessive, and sales clerks made many errors due to their lack of understanding of how to use the new part number codes. In addition, the Project Team had not finished testing the software and they were not satisfied that the system was robust enough. Management decided, however, that switch over could not be delayed any longer and the switch was made to the new system, in December 1986 for home orders and January 1987 for exports. The following period saw 'total chaos' in order processing and despatch; hundreds of orders were late and a lot of business and several customers were lost.

Repetitive training in the importance of the systems and continual stock takes to improve the accuracy of records gradually increased staff familiarity and confidence, until by April 1987 error rates and delivery times were considerably improved. At this stage, work was resumed on specification for the manufacturing modules and the Project Team and senior management attended a three-day MRP workshop run by Systems House personnel. It was then that they began to understand the systems as not simply hardware and software but 'a whole new philosophy of working'.

Management was now concerned that the company did not have the experience, skills and resources required to undertake system implementation even within a new extended timescale. Consultants were brought in and produced reports on a revised organizational structure, an implementation plan, and an education and training programme. Soon after this, the Processing Company was merged with another subsidiary, its board members were replaced, and a new strengthened senior management structure was imposed. A re-evaluation was started on the information systems for both finance and manufacturing.

Contextual analysis

The implementation of the MRP system in the Processing Company was largely unsuccessful and the argument in this paper is that a formal consideration of the context and process of organizational change and the links between them is valuable in helping to understand some of the problems which occurred. A number of analytical elements of context were identified earlier and these concepts are now illustrated using the case material.

With respect to *history*, it is of key importance to see the Processing Company in its broader context. The business had suffered from underinvestment and a rapidly changing market. The holding company had not given it any significant attention and local senior management were largely demotivated. Morale among the workforce was generally low and they lacked confidence in the abilities and vision of their senior management. According to one of the new management team of the late 1980s, the 'business had been pushed into a dusty corner and largely ignored'. The company was undermanaged at the senior level and this contributed significantly to other negative aspects of context.

Essential *infrastructure* for an information system project includes experienced and skilled staff and the management authority to produce physical and human resources when required. There were deficiencies in all these areas in the case study. The internal Project Leader had significant experience of computers and information systems but his team did not. Senior management were keen to have the system up and running but were not themselves knowledgeable about computer systems and, crucially, did not appreciate the extent of organizational change involved. They did not provide adequate support and authority for the Project Leader, either in terms of resources for the Project Team or in encouraging and motivating users to be actively involved in the specification and implementation of the new systems.

The case study can also be used to illustrate the importance of *informal networks and procedures*. They were an integral part of the old systems in the company and, although it was expected that the new systems would minimise the use of informal approaches, the increased regulation was not successful. For example, while senior management viewed the new system as a tool by which to increase their overall control of the business, to the warehousemen it appeared as an institution which removed much of their discretion over their work. They no longer had responsibility for transport arrangements and for making the best use of scarce warehousing space, but because they could see where improvements in these areas would save money for the company, they found ways of working round the new systems. The need for analysis of the informal elements of current working practices and the impossibility and, indeed, undesirability of trying to eliminate the informal was recognised by the new management team of the late 1980s.

An example of the value of an analysis of *stakeholder perspectives* concerns the area of user training. The perspective of the system developers was markedly different from that of the users. The Project Team regarded the users as having no experience of computers, being rather apprehensive about them, and not being prepared to invest the time and effort in learning how to use the new systems until they were forced to do so. From the users' perspective, on the other hand, consultation and communication about the project were virtually nonexistent. There was no attempt made to improve basic discipline and procedures before implementation. The users' perception of their need for careful training and good procedures, a view which could have been picked up at an early stage of the project, was not taken into account and was a major contributor to the disastrous switch to the new system. The Project Team were aware of the need for better user involvement but, with inadequate resourcing and senior management pressure to meet deadlines arising from the contextual elements discussed above, users were largely neglected. A further contributory factor to poor communication between system developers and users, related again to senior management neglect and lack of understanding of infrastructure needs, was that the 'key user' in the sales order processing department was new to the job, was not well-equipped for it and was not computer literate.

Processual analysis

A full processual analysis of the project cannot be attempted here, but an illustration is now given of the two models of human behaviour described earlier. The first model is a *power/politics perspective* and it has already been seen how the contextual conditions of history and different stakeholder perspectives created the conditions for conflict at the level of process. The project was characterised throughout by overt or covert conflict between such groups as the system developers and the users and the warehousemen and senior management. An example of the dysfunctional aspects of these conflicts arose during system testing before switch over when orders were raised by the Customer Services Department but were not picked up in the warehouse, so the system was never fully tested. The Project Leader pointed out to senior management that the users were not relying on the system but nothing was done about it. At switch over, it was immediately discovered that the lot-number control of the system was incompatible with the method of product storage; one lot of material was split between several pallets. A major software modification was needed taking several months of programming effort. The critical point is not that conflict occurred, which is always latent in any human organization, but that no one was managing the politics of the process in a hands-on and well-informed way; neither the system developers nor the senior management of the company.

The second model of human behaviour discussed earlier was a *cultural perspective*. Fully functional MRP systems do not automate existing work in an enterprise, but involve all the workers in the company from senior management downwards in a cultural change reflected in changed ways of working and different approaches and attitudes. Strong sub-cultures in the case study included the system developers who largely saw themselves as automating procedures, the warehousemen who were loyal to the organization but sceptical of management's ability to drive effective change, and the users in sales order processing who saw the computer project as 'an enforced change for no particularly clear reason from a system they were reasonably happy with'. The critical point again is not that the process of cultural change is easy to achieve, which it is not, but that in the case study the process of cultural change was not managed. Even worse, it was not realised that management of this change was necessary, by either system developers or senior management, until after the first disastrous attempt at implementation.

4. RELATIONSHIP BETWEEN CONTEXT AND PROCESS

Intervention in organizations, as with the introduction of new information systems in the Processing Company, can create new contexts or structures. These can be changed cultural structures involving ways of working and attitudes to work, or changed political structures with different power balances and allegiances. However, in order to achieve desired structural changes, the process of change must be sympathetically managed and those doing the management must have a rich understanding of current context, a broad vision of desired changed structures, together with the behavioural skills and authority to communicate this vision and to manage the inevitable conflicts and disagreements which arise during the process. In the case study, neither the system developers nor senior management had a good appreciation of the current context, an understanding of the complex process of organizational change necessitated by the introduction of an MRP system, nor a realization of the need to manage the process of change in order to create new structures or contexts.

This case study has concerned an information systems project but the lessons from the case are of relevance to management science in general. Management scientists, in common with information systems professionals, tend not to be trained to think in the broader analytical terms that have been described here. However, all such groups are deeply involved in the process of organizational transformation, and the case study has aimed to provide an illustration of the downside risk of a lack of adequate conceptualization of the complex problems involved in the management of organizational change.

ACKNOWLEDGEMENTS

The author would like to acknowledge the contribution of Veronica Symons to the research described in this paper, particularly with respect to the field work and analysis of the case study.

REFERENCES

Checkland, P. (1981) *Systems Thinking, Systems Practice*. Chichester: Wiley.

Giddens, A. (1984) *The Constitution of Society*. Cambridge: Polity Press.

Ginzberg, M.J. and Schultz, R.L. (1987) The practical side of implementation research. *Interfaces,* 17, 1–5.

Keen, P.G.W. (1981) Information systems and organizational change. *Commun. ACM,* 24, 24–32.

Kling, P. (1987) Defining the boundaries of computing across complex organizations. In: R. Boland and R. Hirschheim (eds) *Critical Issues in Information Systems Research*, pp. 307–362. Wiley, New York.

Markus, M.L. and Pfeffer, J. (1983) Power and the design and implementation of accounting and control systems. *Acctng Organiz. Soc.* 8, 205–218.

Peters, T.J. and Waterman, R.H. (1982) *In Search of Excellence.* New York: Harper & Row.

Pettigrew, A.M. (1985) *The Awakening Giant: Continuity and Change in ICI*. Oxford: Basil Blackwell.

Pettigrew, A.M. (1987) Context and action in the transformation of the firm. *J. Mgmt Stud.* 24, 649–670.

Pettigrew, A.M. (1989) Longitudinal methods to study change: Theory and practice. In: R. Mansfield (ed.) *Frontiers of Management*, pp. 21–49. London: Routledge.

Radnor, M., Rubenstein, A.H. and Tansik, D.A. (1970) Implementation in operations research and R&D in government and business organization. *Opns Res.* 18, 967-991.

Smircich, L. (1983) Concepts of culture and organizational analysis. *Admin. Sci. Q.,* 28, 339–358.

Srinivasan, A. and Davis, J.G. (1987) A reassessment of implementation process models. *Interfaces,* 17, 64–71.

Symons, V. (1990) Evaluation of information systems: IS development in the Processing Company. *J. Infor. Tech.* 5, 194–204.

Symons, V. and Walsham, G. (1989) Evaluation of information systems: a case study of a manufacturing organization. In *Operational Research and the Social Sciences* (Edited by Jackson, M.C., Keys, P. and Cropper, S.A.), pp. 421–426. New York: Plenum Press.

Walsham, G. (1991) Stucturation theory and information systems research. *J. Appl. Sys. Anal.* Forthcoming.

PART 5:

Perspectives on Change

PART 5:
PERSPECTIVES ON CHANGE

In this final section of the book we have deliberately chosen to broaden the terms of reference, to deviate from the more predictable menu to more unusual offerings – which, if not as palatable as what has gone before, will undoubtedly provoke. Frustratingly, space only allows us to glimpse a few differing perspectives rather than explore a wider range and in fuller depth. However, if these extracts (and in all cases, they are very much selected portions) whet the appetite to investigate further, then our purpose has been served.

Jeffrey Pfeffer has been writing on the subject of power in organizations for some time, and in this extract he outlines a number of steps for implementing change drawing explicitly upon a power and influence perspective. While he stays firmly with Morgan's pluralist conception of organization, and advocates expediency for would-be managers of change, Pfeffer nevertheless offers many insights on how to get things done, especially in organizations where hierarchical power has long since evaporated and where the charismatic nurturing of a common vision is problematic. He may walk a fine line between advocating management and manipulation, but we are certain Pfeffer's realism will ring true for many readers.

Interestingly, Nigel Nicholson's essay on organization culture examines a theme which has been implicit through many of the earlier chapters in this book, as well as developing another of Morgan's metaphors: that of organizations as socially constructed realities containing a potent mix of rituals, values, norms and shared beliefs. Again, the extract provides a useful pair of spectacles through which to view attempts to mobilise and sustain change in organizations. Too often this culture dimension is attended by twin perils. On the one hand there are those who attempt to push through apparently rational changes (perhaps in the arena of technology or new operating practices) totally overlooking the 'iceberg' of cultural or subcultural resistance. On the other hand, there are those who view culture as an important variable but one which can be simplistically shaped in order to reinforce or precipitate proposed changes.

In his book, *Images of Organization*, Gareth Morgan conjures up eight different ways of construing organizations using metaphors like organisms, machines, brains, psychic prisons, instruments of domination and the like. How an organization is perceived will naturally influence the assumptions, methodologies and strategies when change is contemplated: in the minds of both change-makers and change participants. It is from his chapter on seeing organizations as political systems that we select the piece on managing pluralist organizations. This perspective proposes that interest-based activity, conflict and the role and use of power are central to understanding organizations; and since the planning and managing of change implies the re-ordering of goals, the redesigning of jobs and the re-distribution of status and rewards, the political metaphor is especially meaningful. Managing change cannot be divorced from ideology. However, Morgan does warn against overemphasizing the manipulative stance which elevates a selfish, ruthless and get-ahead-at-all-costs mentality in the so called 'corporate jungle'.

We started out in this book with a consideration of various pressures and forces for change which relentlessly bear down upon the modern manager. It is therefore fitting that in our final article we return to the individual and how he or she copes with the stresses of disruption in the workplace. Bereavement is perhaps a surprising notion to ponder in this regard, but a central thesis of Peter Marris' extract is that situations of change – even when they are desired – actually constitute loss for the participants concerned. It is in recognizing the anxieties of loss, or bereavement, that the tenacity of conservatism and the ambivalence of transitions becomes clear. We close, then, with yet another perspective on the managing of change – one that is fundamentally personal, subjective and recognizably real; it is also one which planners and would-be change agents would do well to heed.

19

UNDERSTANDING POWER IN ORGANIZATIONS

Jeffrey Pfeffer

(This material has been excerpted from the original.)

WAYS OF GETTING THINGS DONE

Why is implementation difficult in so many organizations, and why does it appear that the ability to get decisions implemented is becoming increasingly rare? One way of thinking about this issue, and of examining the role of power and influence in the implementation process, is to consider some possible ways of getting things done.

One way of getting things to happen is through hierarchical authority. Many people think power is merely the exercise of formal authority, but it is considerably more than that, as we will see. Everyone who works in an organization has seen the exercise of hierarchical authority. Those at higher levels have the power to hire and fire, to measure and reward behavior, and to provide direction to those who are under their aegis. Hierarchical direction is usually seen as legitimate, because the variation in formal authority comes to be taken for granted as a part of organizational life. Thus the phrase, 'the boss wants . . .' or 'the president wants . . .' is seldom questioned or challenged. Who can forget Marine Lieutenant Colonel Oliver North testifying, during the Iran-Contra hearings, about his willingness to stand on his head in a corner if that was what his commander-in-chief wanted, or maintaining that he never once disobeyed the orders of his superiors?

There are three problems with hierarchy as a way of getting things done. First, and perhaps not so important, is that it is badly out of fashion. In an era of rising education and the democratization of all decision processes, in an era in which participative management is advocated in numerous places (Bradford and Cohen 1984; Pasmore 1988), and particularly in a country in which incidents such as the Vietnam War and Watergate have led many people to mistrust the institutions of authority, implementation by order or command is problematic. Readers who are parents need only reflect on the difference in parental authority between the current period and 1950s to see what I mean. How many times have you been able to get your children to do something simply on the basis of your authority as a parent?

A second, more serious problem with authority derives from the fact that virtually all of us work in positions in which, in order to accomplish our job and objectives, we need the cooperation of others who do not fall within our direct chain of command. We depend, in other words, on people outside our purview of authority, whom we could not command, reward, or even punish even if we wanted to. Perhaps, as a line manager in a product division, we need the cooperation of people in human resources for hiring, people in finance for evaluating new product opportunities, people in distribution and sales for getting the product sold and delivered, and people in market research for determining product features and marketing and pricing strategy. Even the authority of a chief executive is not absolute, since there are groups outside the focal organization that control the ability to get things done. To sell overseas airline routes to other domestic airlines requires the cooperation of the Transportation and Justice Departments, as well as the acquiescence of foreign governments. To market a drug or medical device requires the approval of the Food and Drug Administration; to export products overseas, one may need both financing and export licenses. The hierarchical authority of all executives and administrators is limited, and for most of us, it is quite limited compared to the scope of what we need in order to do our jobs effectively.

There is a third problem with implementation accomplished solely or primarily through hierarchical authority: what happens if the person at the apex of the pyramid, the one whose orders are being followed, is incorrect? When authority is vested in a single individual, the organization can face grave difficulties if that person's insight or leadership begins to fail.

Another way of getting things done is by developing a strongly shared vision or organizational culture. If people share a common set of goals, a common perspective on what to do and how to accomplish it, and a common vocabulary that allows them to coordinate their behavior, then command and hierarchical authority are of much less importance. People will be able to work cooperative without waiting for orders from the upper levels of the company. Managing through a shared vision and with a strong organizational culture has been a very popular prescription for organizations (Deal and Kennedy, 1982, Peters and Waterman 1982, Davis 1984). A number of articles and books tell how to build commitment and shared vision and how to socialize individuals, particularly at the time of entry, so that they share a language, values, and premises about what needs to be done and how to do it (Pascale 1985, O'Reilly 1989).

Without denying the efficacy and importance of vision and culture, it is important to recognize that implementation accomplished through them can have problems. First, building a shared conception of the world takes time and effort. There are instances when the organization is in crisis or confronts situations in which there is simply not sufficient time to develop shared premises about how to respond. For this very reason, the military services rely not only on techniques that build loyalty and esprit de corps (Dornbusch 1955), but also on a hierarchical chain of command and a tradition of obeying orders.

Second, there is the problem of how, in a strong culture, new ideas that are inconsistent with that culture can penetrate. A strong culture really constitutes an organizational paradigm, which prescribes how to look at things, what are appropriate methods and techniques for solving problems, and what are the important issues and problems (Brown 1978). In fields of science, a well-developed paradigm provides guidance as to what needs to be taught and in what order, how to do research, what are appropriate methodologies, what are the most pressing research questions, and how to train new students (Lodahl and Gordon 1972). A well-developed paradigm, or a strong culture, is overturned only with great difficulty, even if it fails to account for data or to lead to new discoveries (Kuhn 1970). In a similar fashion, an organizational paradigm provides a way of thinking about and investigating the world, which reduces uncertainty and provides for effective collective action, but which also overlooks or ignores some lines of inquiry. It is easy for a strong culture to produce groupthink, a pressure to conform to the dominant view (Janis 1972). A vision focuses attention, but in that focus, things are often left out.

An organization that had difficulties, as well as great success, because of its strong, almost evangelical culture is Apple Computer.

Apple III had an operating system known as SOS in Sophisticated Operating System, which was actually quite similar to the system Microsoft had developed for IBM's personal computer – MS DOS (Microsoft Disk Operating System), except it was even better in some respects. Yet Apple was too wary of operating systems to try to make its system *the* standard, or even *a* standard, in personal computing. As a result the company lost out on a number of important commercial opportunities. The very zeal and fervor that made working for Apple like a religious crusade and produced extraordinary levels of commitment from the work force made it difficult for the company to be either cognizant of or responsive to shifts in the marketplace for personal computers.

THE MANAGEMENT PROCESS: A POWER PERSPECTIVE

From the perspective of power and influence, the process of implementation involves a set of steps, which are outlined below.

- Decide what your goals are, what you are trying to accomplish.
- Diagnose patterns of dependence and interdependence; what individuals are influential and important in your achieving your goal?
- What are their points of view likely to be? How will they feel about what you are trying to do?
- What are their power bases? Which of them is more influential in the decision?
- What are your bases of power and influence? What bases of influence can you develop, to gain more control over the situation?

- Which of the various strategies and tactics for exercising power seem most appropriate and are likely to be effective, given the situation you confront?
- Based on the above, choose a course of action to get something done.

The first step is to decide on your goals. It is, for instance, easier to drive from Albany, New York, to Austin, Texas, if you know your destination than if you just get in your car in Albany and drive randomly. Although this point is apparently obvious, it is something that is often overlooked in a business context. How many times have you attended meetings or conferences or talked to someone on the telephone without a clear idea of what you were trying to accomplish? Our calendars are filled with appointments, and other interactions occur unexpectedly in the course of our day. If we don't have some clear goals, and if we don't know what our primary objectives are, it is not very likely that we are going to achieve them. One of the themes Tom Peters developed early in his writing was the importance of consistency in purpose. Having the calendars, knowing the language, what gets measured, and what gets talked about – all focus on what the organization is trying to achieve (Peters 1978). It is the same with individuals; to the extent that each interaction, in each meeting, in each conference, is oriented toward the same objective, the achievement of that objective is more likely.

Once you have a goal in mind, it is necessary to diagnose who is important in getting your goal accomplished. You must determine the patterns of dependence and interdependence among these people and find out how they are likely to feel about what you are trying to do. As part of this diagnosis, you also need to know how events are likely to unfold, and to estimate the role of power and influence in the process. In getting things accomplished, it is critical to have a sense of the game being played, the players, and what their positions are. One can get badly injured playing football in a basket-ball uniform, or not knowing the offense from the defense. I have seen, all too often, otherwise intelligent and successful managers have problems because they did not recognize the political nature of the situation, or because they were blindsided by someone whose position and strength they had not anticipated.

Once you have a clear vision of the game, it is important to ascertain the power bases of the other players, as well as your own potential and actual sources of power. In this way you can determine your relative strength, along with the strength of other players. Understanding the sources of power is critical in diagnosing what is going to happen in an organization, as well as in preparing yourself to take action.

Finally, you will want to consider carefully the various strategies, or, to use a less grand term, the tactics that are available to you, as well as those that may be used by others involved in the process. These tactics help in using power and influence effectively, and can also help in countering the use of power by others.

Power is defined here as the potential ability to influence behavior, to change the course of events, to overcome resistance, and to get people to do things that they would not otherwise do (Emerson 1962, Kanter 1979, Pfeffer, 1981). Politics and influence are the processes, the actions, the behaviors through which this potential power is utilized and realized.

WHAT DOES IT MEAN, TO MANAGE WITH POWER?

First, it means recognizing that in almost every organization, there are varying interests. This suggests that one of the first things we need to do is to diagnose the political landscape and figure out what the relevant interests are, and what important political subdivisions characterize the organization. It is essential that we do not assume that everyone necessarily is going to be our friend, or agree with us, or even that preferences are uniformly distributed. There are clusters of interests within organizations, and we need to understand where these are and to whom they belong.

Next, it means figuring out what point of view these various individuals and subunits have on issues of concern to us. It also means understanding why they have the perspective that they do. It is all too easy to assume that those with a different perspective are somehow not as smart as we are, not as informed, not as perceptive. If that is our belief, we are likely to do several things, each of which is disastrous. First, we may act contemptuously toward those who disagree with us – after all, if they aren't as competent or as insightful as we are, why should we take them seriously? It is rarely difficult to get along with those who resemble us in character and opinions. The real secret of success in organizations is the ability to get those who differ from us, and whom we don't necessarily like, to do what needs to be done. Second, if we think people are misinformed, we are likely to try to 'inform' them, or to try to convince them with facts and analysis. Sometimes this will work, but often it will not, for their disagreement may not be based on a lack of information; it may, instead, arise from a different perspective on what our information means. Diagnosing the point of view of interest groups as well as the basis for their positions will assist us in negotiating with them in predicting their response to various initiatives.

Third, managing with power means understanding that to get things done, you need power – more power than those whose opposition you must overcome – and thus it is imperative to understand where power comes from and how these sources of power can be developed. We are sometimes reluctant to think very purposefully or strategically about acquiring and using power. We are prone to believe that if we do our best, work hard, be nice, and so forth, things will work out for the best. I don't mean to imply that one should not, in general, work hard, try to make good decisions, and be nice, but that these and similar platitudes are often not very useful in helping us get things accomplished in our organizations. We need to understand power and try to get it. We must be willing to do things to build our sources of power, or else we will be less effective than we might wish to be.

Fourth, managing with power means understanding the strategies and tactics through which power is developed and used in organizations, including the importance of timing, the use of structure, the social psychology of commitment and other forms of interpersonal influence. If nothing else, such an understanding will help us become astute observers of the behavior of others. The more we understand power and its manifestations, the better will be our clinical skills. More fundamentally, we need to understand strategies and tactics of using power so that we can consider the range of approaches available to us, and use what is likely to be effective. Again, as in the case of building sources of power, we often try not to think about these things, and we avoid being strategic or purposeful about employing our power. This is a mistake. Although we may have various qualms, there will be others who do not. Knowledge without power is of remarkably little use. And power without the skill to employ it effectively is likely to be wasted.

REFERENCES

Bradford, D.L. and Cohen, A.R. (1984) *Managing for Excellence.* New York: John Wiley.

Brown, R.H. (1978) Bureaucracy as praxis: toward a political phenomenology of formal organizations. *Administrative Science Quarterly*, 23, 365–382.

Davis, S. (1984) *Managing Corporate Culture.* Cambridge, MA: Ballinger.

Deal, T. and Kennedy, A.A. (1982) *Corporate Cultures.* Reading, MA: Addison-Wesley.

Dornbusch, S.M. (1955) The military academy as an assimilating institution. *Social Forces*, 33, 316–321.

Emerson, R.M. (1962) Power-dependence relations. *American Sociological Review*, 27, 31–41.

Janis, I.L. (1972) *Victims of Groupthink.* Boston: Houghton Mifflin.

Kanter, R.M. (1979) Power failure in management circuits. *Harvard Business Review*, 57, (July/August), 65.

Kuhn, T.S. (1970) *The Structure of Scientific Revolutions.* (2nd Edn). Chicago: University of Chicago Press.

Lodahl, J. and Gordon, G. (1972) The structure of scientific fields and the functioning of university graduate departments. *American Sociological Review*, 37, 57–72.

Pascale, R.T. (1985) The paradox of 'corporate culture': reconciling ourselves to socialization. *California Management Review*, 26, 26–41.

Pasmore, W.A. (1988) *Designing Effective Organizations: The Sociological Systems Perspective.* New York: John Wiley.

Peters, T.J. (1978) Symbols, patterns, and settings: an optimistic case for getting things done. *Organizational Dynamics*, 7, 3–23.

Peters, T.J. and Waterman, R.H. Jr (1982) *In Search of Excellence.* New York: Harper and Row.

Pfeffer, J. (1981) *Power in Organizations.* Marshfield, MA: Pitman Publishing.

O'Reilly, C. (1989) Corporations, culture, and commitment: motivation and social control in organizations. *California Management Review*, 31, 9–25.

20

ORGANIZATIONAL CHANGE

Nigel Nicholson

THE PARADOX OF CHANGE

Organizations are systems of action for managing our environment and fulfilling our needs. They structure effort and allocate functions, to create order out of uncertainty and stability out of turbulence. At the same time, from their internal and external environments, organizations are confronted with pressures to change, which, if ignored, may lead to their downfall. Change is therefore a foremost concern of organizations, and is always problematic.

ENVIRONMENTAL PRESSURES FOR CHANGE

Internal pressures for change stem from organizational members' motives. These may be positive, as in attempts to innovate, or negative, as in the expression of focussed discontents. Either can be in response to such factors as task demands, interpersonal relations, organizational arrangements, work conditions, management behaviours, and resource scarcities.

External pressure for change comes from whichever aspects of an organization's environment are critical. Environmental forces, systems and resources are critical to the degree that an organization depends on them, and the degree to which they are ambiguous, changeable or threatening (Pfeffer and Salancik, 1978). It can be seen that critical environmental influences form a unique array, according to an organization's goals and position in society. So, organizations are differentially attuned to such factors as: the state of the biosphere (climate, ecology, and natural resources), human demography (labour and consumer markets), economic forces (trade, taxation, financial and product markets), cultural values (legal, educational, and political developments), scientific and technological innovations, and finally, constellations of other organizations to which an organization may be bound by ties of ownership, supply, consumption or competition.

Within the literature on organizations, contingency theory has been widely adopted to explain organizational performance as a function of the fit between an organization's internal arrangements and environmental characteristics (Lawrence and Lorsch, 1967). Volatile and uncertain environments require 'organic' management systems, threatening environments require centralized control, diverse environments require decentralized organizational forms, and stable, predictable contexts make bureaucratic forms effective. However, knowledge of these contingency relations does not mean organizations can readily adapt their design characteristics to meet the demands of changing environmental conditions (Mintzberg, 1979).

There may be internal barriers to change, such as insufficient resources, expertise, time and knowledge, and in the change-resisting values, beliefs and motives of organizational members. If the principal stakeholders in the status quo are also powerful, the uncertainties of change may not be readily embraced.

HOW ORGANIZATIONS GENERATE CHANGE

So far we have talked as if forces and responses can be objectively characterized, but in reality these are not of determinate character. They are socially constructed by what organizations pay attention to and interact with. Weick has called this relationship one of 'enactment' (1979), meaning that organizations select and operationalize their environment in particular ways. So it makes a great deal of difference whether a company sees itself as, for example, an oil company or in the energy business, or whether a union sees itself as defending against threatening powers or promoting services to members. Not only is the environment socially constructed, but so too is the organization itself. Responses to the environment are not systematically determined patterns of growth or adaptation, but are acts of implicit or explicit choice. Modes of decision-making and implementation spring from the images, values, orientations, and capabilities of human agents.

Together, these observations focus our attention on psychological factors as the critical filters between environmental forces and organizational response, and, thereby, as essential components in any modeling of change. The concept of strategy summarizes the coherence and direction of choice processes in organizations, and research has identified qualitative differences between the forms this may take, and their consequences (Miles and Snow, 1978). It enables us to see how some organizations embrace change as inherent in the world that challenges them, and others as committed to the maintenance of stable operations and structures (Kanter, 1983).

The effectiveness of a strategy depends upon two principles: contingency and consistency (Child, 1984). Contingency, as described above, represents the degree to which strategic orientation matches environmental demands. Note that crises in organizations often arise because their enactment processes crucially misconstrue the real environmental pressures they face, e.g. when companies fail to realise how their markets have changed. Consistency represents the degree to which organizational sub-systems are integrated and collectively fit organizational goals.

CHANGE CONTINGENCIES

It follows from the preceding discussion that how an organization scans its environment is of major importance. Similarly the goals and interests of key agents are implicated. These can be related to a variety of factors much discussed in the organizational literature: leadership (e.g. participative vs autocratic), communications (open vs closed), decision-making style (rationalistic vs impressionistic), reward and control systems (inhibiting vs stimulating innovation), job and organizational design (high vs low discretion). How organizations differ in these characteristics can often be traced back to their historical origins; the 'mission' of their founders, the state of the environment at the time of the organization's origin, and the successes and crises it has experienced in its lifetime. The concept of organizational culture embraces these variables, by denoting how shared meanings and behaviour patterns come into being, are sustained, and evolve (Allaire & Firsirotu, 1984). The contents of culture encompass a wide range of phenomena: 'surface' features, such as values, rituals, customs, and forms of expression; 'preconscious' factors such as symbols, ideology, and norms; and 'deep' structures such as basic assumptions, world views, and cognitive/logical systems (Pettigrew, 1979; Frost *et al.*, 1985). Cultural forms evolve and are transmitted across generations of organizational membership as adaptive ways of making sense of shared existence. Cultures change in two ways: by importing new elements from the surrounding culture (Beyer, 1981) and by internal innovations to meet new circumstances. They also reproduce themselves by two means: selection and socialization. Selection (and self-selection) operates to enrol members with congruent characteristics and orientations. Socialization is the inculcation of shared meanings by formal means, such as training, induction and supervision, and by informal means, via interpersonal and intragroup influence processes (Van Maanen and Schein, 1979).

This does not mean cultural uniformity is inevitable, for these processes can also bring about diversity and conflict, through the creation of sub-cultures and counter-cultures. This raises the question of whether cultural process can be directed and controlled. The evolutionary forces we have described are too diffuse and widespread to be completely determined by organizational agents, even in the most totalitarian institutions, but at the same time it is clear that many important cultural processes are directed by those who hold power. Cultural forms are encouraged which justify and sustain the existing social order, or which legitimize and reinforce the positions of leaders.

Most writers on the subject are now agreed that cultural change is a necessary element in bringing about significant organizational change, such as radical alterations to structure or strategy. Leadership, which has been defined as the management of culture, has a crucial role to play in assisting this learning process (Schein, 1985). However, as writers have pointed out, cultures are reinforced by past success, and it takes shared trauma or the experience of crisis to unlearn deeply ingrained and historically reinforced patterns (Hedberg, 1981). By that time it may be too late. Organizations often need to undergo adaptive change well before crises hit them. This is especially difficult, since it implies that a culture that does not currently contain forces for change has to generate them. For this reason external change agents have an important role to play.

CHANGE INTERVENTION AND IMPLEMENTATION

Kurt Lewin's classic model of change intervention remains one of the simplest and most useful. First, old patterns must be unfrozen. This means creating awareness of the need for change, and, by implication dissatisfaction with the status quo. The Organization Development (OD) literature (Beckhard, 1969) is replete with examples of techniques for this purpose, such as survey feedback, training methods, and communication strategies. Second, programmatic changes must be implemented. This involves such methods as team building, retraining, participative decision making, or structural alteration to job and organizational design. Third, there must be refreezing to embed and reinforce the new patterns. This means monitoring and providing feedback on new arrangements, fine-tuning them, and often it also means implementing new systems of control, evaluation and reward.

The complexities and difficulties of such attempts at programmatic change are enormous, not least because of the 'dynamic conservatism' of most organizations: their ability to absorb and neutralize innovation; their skill in resisting change whilst appearing to embrace it; and the tendency for organizational agents to espouse theories about their own actions that conceal their real 'theories in use' (Argyris and Schon, 1978). The change agent is therefore confronted with the difficult and dangerous task of challenging fundamental assumptions, and inducing people to abandon methods, goals and frames of reference that have sustained them in the past and which justify their current existence. For this reason, top-down, rather than bottom-up, approaches to intervention are necessary to implement radical change. This makes the role of the change agent highly 'political' (Mangham, 1979). It entails awareness of the levers of power, willingness to lay hands on them, and securing the committed support of leaders in the organization.

REFERENCES

Allaire, Y. and Firsirotu, M.E. (1984) Theories of organizational culture. *Organization Studies*, 5, 193–226.

Argyris, C. and Schon, D.A. (1978) *Organizational Learning: A Theory of Action Perspective*. Reading, MA: Addison-Wesley.

Beckhard, R. (1969) *Organization Development: Strategies and Models*. Reading, MA: Addison-Wesley.

Beyer, J. (1981) Ideologies, values and decision-making in organizations. In: P.C. Nystrom and W.H. Starbuck (eds.) *Handbook of Organizational Design* (Vol. 2). Oxford: Oxford University Press.

Child, J. (1984) *Organization: A Guide to Problems and Practice*. (2nd ed). London: Paul Chapman.

Frost, P.J., Moore, L.F., Louis, M.R., Lundberg, C.C. and Martin, J. (eds.) (1985) *Organizational Culture*. Beverly Hills, CA: Sage.

Hedberg, B. (1981) How organizations lean and unlearn. In: P.C. Nystrom and W.H. Starbuck (eds.) *Handbook of Organizational Design* (Vol. 1), Oxford: Oxford University Press.

Kanter, R.M. (1984) *The Change Masters*. London: Unwin.

Lawrence, P.R. and Lorsch, J.W. (1967) *Organization and Environment*. Cambridge, MA: Harvard University Press.

Mangham, I. (1979) *The Politics of Organisational Change*. London: Associated Business Press.

Miles, R.E. and Snow, C.C. (1978) *Organizational Strategy, Structure and Process*. New York: McGraw-Hill.

Mintzberg, H. (1979) *The Structuring of Organizations*. Englewood-Cliffs, NJ: Prentice-Hall.

Pettigrew, A.M. (1979) On studying organizational cultures. *Administrative Science Quarterly*, 24, 570–581.

Pfeffer, J. and Salancik, G.R. (1978) *The External Control of Organizations: A Resource Dependence Perspective*. New York: Harper & Row.

Van Maanen, J. and Schein, E.H. (1979) Toward a theory of organizational socialization. In: B.M. Staw and L.L. Cummings (eds.) *Research in Organizational Behavior* (Vol. 1), Greenwich, CT: JAI Press.

Schein, E.H. (1985) *Organizational Culture and Leadership*. San Francisco: Jossey-Bass.

Weick, K. (1979) *The Social Psychology of Organizing*. Reading, MA: Addison-Wesley.

21

ORGANIZATIONS AS POLITICAL SYSTEMS

Gareth Morgan

MANAGING PLURALIST ORGANIZATIONS

The political image of organizations emphasizes the plural nature of the interest, conflicts, and sources of power that shape organizational life. The term
'pluralism' is used in political science to characterize idealized kinds of liberal
democracies where potentially authoritarian tendencies are held in check by
the free interplay of interest groups that have a stake in government. The
pluralist vision is of a society where different groups bargain and compete for a
share in the balance of power and use their influence to realize Aristotle's ideal
of politics: a negotiated order that creates unity out of diversity.

This pluralist philosophy stands in contrast with an older organic or 'unitary' frame of reference. The unitary view pictures society as an integrated
whole where the interests of individual and society are synonymous. This
unitary view emphasizes the sovereignty of the state and the importance of
individuals subordinating themselves in the service of society as a means of
realizing and satisfying their true interests and the common good. It is an
ideology that has grown in importance along with the development of the
nation-state and the idea that individuals should place the interests of the state
above all else.

The pluralist view also contrasts with the so-called 'radical' frame of reference, which views society as comprising antagonistic class interests, characterized by deep-rooted social and political cleavages, and held together as
much by coercion as by consent. This radical view, influenced by a Marxist
perspective, suggests that the interests of disadvantaged groups can be fur-
thered in a substantial way only through radical changes in the structure of
society that will displace those currently in power.

These three frames of reference (Table 1) have considerable relevance for
understanding organizations and the ideologies that shape management

Table 1 Unitary, pluralist and radical frames of reference. Organizations can be understood as mini-states where the relationship between individual and society is paralleled by the relationship between individual and organization. The unitary, pluralist, and radical views of organization can be characterized in the following terms

	Unitary	Pluralist	Radical
Interests	Places emphasis on the achievement of common objectives. The organization is viewed as being united under the umbrella of common goals and striving towards their achievement in the manner of a well-integrated team.	Places emphasis on the diversity of individual and group interests. The organization is regarded as a loose coalition which has just a passing interest in the formal goals of the organization.	Places emphasis on the oppositional nature of contradictory 'class' interests. Organization is viewed as a battleground where rival forces (e.g. management and unions), strive for the achievement of largely incompatible ends.
Conflict	Regards conflict as a rare and transient phenomenon that can be removed through appropriate managerial action. Where it does arise it is usually attributed to the activities of deviants and troublemakers.	Regards conflict as an inherent and ineradicable characteristic of organizational affairs and stresses its potentially positive or functional aspects.	Regards organizational conflict as inevitable and as part of a wider class conflict that will eventually change the whole structure of society. It is recognized that conflict may be suppressed and thus often exists as a latent rather than manifest characteristic of both organizations and society.
Power	Largely ignores the role of power in organizational life. Concepts such as authority, leadership, and control tend to be preferred means of describing the managerial prerogative of guiding the organization towards the achievement of common interests.	Regards power as a crucial variable. Power is the medium through which conflicts of interest are alleviated and resolved. The organization is viewed as a plurality of power holders drawing their power from a plurality of sources.	Regards power as a key feature of organization, but a phenomenon that is unequally distributed and follows class divisions. Power relations in organizations are viewed as reflections of power relations in society at large, and as closely linked to wider processes of social control, e.g., control of economic power, the legal system, and education.

Source: Based on Burrell and Morgan (1979: pp. 204–388).

practice. Some organizations tend to function like unitary teams, others as vibrant political systems with the kind of pluralist politics discussed earlier in this chapter, and others as battlefields where rival groups engage in ongoing warfare. Unitary characteristics are most often found in organizations that have developed a cohesive culture based on respect for management's right to manage, especially those that have a long and continuous history of paternalistic management. Organizations where there are sharp distinctions between different categories of employee, such as the division between blue- and white-collar workers found in many heavy industries, or where there has been a history of conflict between management and labor, tend to reflect the characteristics of the radical model. Organizations primarily made up of white-collar staff, particularly where there is room for employees to acquire considerable autonomy, often tend to fit the pluralist model. Sometimes the three models apply to different parts of the same organization. It is often a salutary experience for a person to ask: 'Which frame of reference applies to my organization?' By using the model presented in Table 1 to assess the general pattern of interests, conflict, and power one can often gain a useful initial grasp on the character of the political system with which one is dealing.

In addition to serving as analytical tools, the three frames of reference often serve as organizational ideologies. Thus managers or employees may encourage the idea that 'we're a team, let's work together,' or that 'we all want different things, so let's talk about and resolve our differences so we can all gain,' or that 'we're at war, I don't trust you, so we'll have to fight it out.' Clearly, the ideology in use will determine the character of the organization. If a manager believes that he or she is managing a team and can persuade employees to believe that this is the case, harmonious cooperation with a three-musketeers attitude of 'all for one and one for all' may gain ground. If the radical frame of reference provides the major context for interpreting organizational events, then a battle-torn organizational life is almost certain. These ideologies may emerge and be used as a means of shaping the organization to conform with the image that best suits specific ends. This, after all, is the role of ideology in organizations, as in society.

Each frame of reference leads to a different approach to management. If one believes that one is managing a team, one tends to expect and demand that people rally around common objectives, and to respect 'the right of the manager to manage and the duty of employees to obey.' Employees are expected to perform the roles for which they have been appointed. No less, no more. Conflict is seen as a source of trouble and as an unwanted intrusion. Hence the orientation of the unitary manager is usually to eliminate or suppress conflict whenever possible. Given this ideology, there is no room to recognize or accept the kind of organizational politics discussed earlier in this chapter. Unitary managers tend to see formal authority as the only legitimate source of power, and thus rarely acknowledge the right or ability of others to influence the management process. Unions are seen as a scourge, and the pursuit of individual interest through use of different kinds of power is viewed as a form of malpractice.

Though this unitary view may seem somewhat narrow and old-fashioned, it is often extremely pervasive and influential and is supported by many theories of management. For example, theories based on mechanical and organismic metaphors often encourage this unitary view, emphasizing the importance of designing or adapting the organization to achieve common goals. Hence they provide primary resources for the unitary manager who wishes to believe that an enterprise *ought* to possess the unity and shared sense of direction that we find in carefully designed machines or in the organisms in the natural world. The team idea is often much more attractive than the idea of a somewhat chaotic political system that wishes to move in many directions at once. Hence many managers often unconsciously take refuge in this team ideology rather than deal with political realities.

Also, unitary ideology can serve as a resource for a crafty manager who recognizes that in espousing the attitude that 'we're a team where conflict has no place,' he or she may have a means of creating unity among divergent elements. By identifying conflict itself as a *source* of trouble he or she may be able to unite the rest of the organization against those who are key actors in the trouble. This tactic is often used to unite employees and, through the media, the public in general against a group of workers or a union leader who are seen as disruptive elements in an otherwise harmonious and rational enterprise. The unitary frame of reference is a powerful ideology among the public at large, and managers can often use this public ideology as a strategy for mobilizing support and achieving control in the pluralist or radical power plays that characterize their organization. The fact that managers who at times espouse the unitary ideology may not actually believe in that ideology themselves, can make it difficult to determine which ideology has a controlling influence in an organization. However, the person who has an awareness of the role played by rhetoric and espoused ideology has a means of understanding when this form of power play is occurring. The unitary manager is often a pluralist in unitary clothing!

The hallmark of the pluralist manager is that he or she accepts the inevitability of organizational politics. He or she recognizes that since individuals have different interests, aims, and objectives, employees are likely to use their membership in the organization for their own ends. Management is thus focused on balancing and coordinating the interests of organizational members so that they can work together within the constraints set by the organization's formal goals, which really reflect the interests of shareholders and others with ultimate control over the fate of the organization. The pluralist manager recognizes that conflict and power plays can serve both positive and negative functions; hence the main concern is to manage conflict in ways that will benefit the overall organization or, more selfishly, in ways that will promote his or her own interests within the organization. The pluralist manager is, after all, not politically neutral. He or she recognizes the politics of organization and accepts his or her role as an organizational power broker and conflict manager.

For example, the pluralist manager seeks ways to use conflict as a means of promoting desired ends. He or she recognizes that various kinds of conflict can energize an organization. Conflict counters tendencies towards lethargy, stale-ness, apathetic compliance, and similar organizational pathologies by creating a 'keep on your toes' atmosphere where it is dangerous to take things for granted. In addition, conflicts can encourage forms of self-evaluation that can challenge conventional wisdom and theories in use. Such conflict may cause a certain degree of pain within the organization, but can also do much to stimu-late learning and change, helping to keep the organization in touch with what is going on in the environment. Conflicts can thus be an important source of innovation in that they encourage the parties involved to search for solutions to underlying problems, often to the benefit of all. This is particularly true in group decision-making situations, where the absence of conflict often produces conformity and 'groupthink'. The existence of rival points of view and of different aims and objectives can do much to improve the quality of decision making. Conflict can also serve as an important release valve that gets rid of pent-up pressures. It facilitates processes of mutual accommodation through the exploration and resolution of differences, often in a way that preempts more subversive or explosive resolutions. Somewhat paradoxically, conflict can thus at times serve to stimulate change, and at other times help to maintain the status quo.

One of the main tasks of the pluralist manager, then, is to find ways of maintaining just the right level of conflict. While too much conflict can immo-bilize an organization by channeling the efforts of its members into unproduc-tive activities, too little conflict may encourage complacency and lethargy. In the former case, the manager may need to employ conflict-resolution tech-niques or reorient conflict in more productive directions. In the latter case he or she may need to find ways of promoting appropriate conflicts, often by making hidden conflicts overt, or perhaps by actually creating conflict. While this may at times help to enliven the atmosphere and performance of an organization, it can also be perceived as a form of unwarranted manipulation, with disastrous results for relations between managers and their employees.

In approaching the task of conflict management, the pluralist manager is faced with a choice of styles, which hinge on the extent to which he or she wishes to engage in assertive or cooperative behavior. Though a manager may have a preferred style, all the different styles are likely to be appropriate at one time or another. Even in the realm of politics, contingency theory thus has an important place. On some occasions the manager may wish to buy time through various kinds of avoidance behavior. On others, head-on competition, collaboration, accommodation, or compromise may prove more effective. While some managers prefer to battle it out in a way that all can see, others prefer more subtle fly-fishing techniques that depend on an intimate knowledge of the situation and the skillful use of the right bait at the right time for the right people. The choice of the style and tactics to be used in a given situation is crucial, but unfortunately cannot be explored in detail here.

Regardless of style, successful pluralist management always depends on an ability to read developing situations. The manager must be able to analyze interests, understand conflicts, and explore power relations, so that situations can be brought under a measure of control. This requires a keen ability to be aware of conflict-prone areas, to read the latent tendencies and pressures beneath the manifest actions of organizational life, and to initiate appropriate responses. In general, the manager can intervene to change perceptions, behaviors, and structures in ways that will help redefine or redirect conflicts to serve constructive ends.

Many organizational conflicts can be fruitfully resolved through pluralist means, but not all. This is particularly true in radicalized organizations where conflicts between managers and employees run deep. Here, issues often have to be negotiated in fairly formal terms if progress is to be made, or else grind their way to a bitter end through the raw interplay of structural forces embedded in the economic and industrial structure of society itself. Disputes leading to head-on clashes between management and unions, such as those relating to the replacement of skilled employees by automation or the closing and relocation of plants, are obvious examples. The underlying power relations and bitterness between the parties involved often encourage a winner-take-all or fight-to-the-death attitude that makes compromise extremely difficult, often leading to painful outcomes such as unemployment or bankruptcy of the organizations involved. Though the intransigence that often accompanies such disputes can seem senseless to outside observers, it is intelligible in terms of the basic premises on which the radical frame of reference builds.

REFERENCE

Burrell, G. and Morgan, G. (1979) *Sociological Paradigms and Organizational Analysis*, London, Heinemann.

22

THE MANAGEMENT OF CHANGE

Peter Marris

Since it is not immediately obvious that understanding the nature of bereavement can lessen the pain of grief, nor that we would manage change differently if we were more sensitive to the element of loss, I want to suggest how this way of looking at change might influence what we do. I think there would still be a virtue in understanding, even if it changed nothing in our behaviour, just because we would then be better prepared to withstand the strain of change.

I am concerned here, not with the circumstances which demand change, or the ideals change should realise, but with the processes by which we come to terms with it. And once we turn our attention to this process, the articulation of its transitional stages appears crucial. The more radical the changes which evolve, the more important this is: we need to recognise the element of bereavement, above all, in the process of a major reconstruction. For then the whole purpose of change may be aborted by the mishandling of loss.

Whether the crisis of disorientation affects only an individual, or a group, or society as a whole, it has a fundamentally similar dynamic. It provokes a conflict between contradictory impulses – to return to the past, and to forget it altogether. Each, in itself, would be ultimately self-destructive, either by denying the reality of present circumstances, or by denying the experience on which the sense of self rests. But their interaction forces the bereaved to search to and fro, until they are reconciled by reformulating and reintegrating past attachments. If this process fails, life becomes mummified in a phantasy of the past; or empty and meaningless behind a façade of purposive activity; or obsessed by the unresolved conflict in a permanent crisis. The length and intensity of the crisis, the risk that its resolution will be abortive, can be reduced by the way the conflict is articulated and contained within a supportive structure. But though the underlying analysis applies, I believe, to any experience of loss, the implications are different when the experience is shared.

Collective losses

Once we turn from involuntary traumatic losses to situations where loss is an aspect of other kinds of changes, and from the isolation of private grief to the shared experience of disruptive change, the working out of the crisis takes on another aspect. For the ambivalence can now be projected in a social conflict, and though the situation may seem remote from any sense of personal tragedy, it still reflects in transmuted form the dynamics of grieving. Hence the conflict cannot be treated simply as a clash of interests: it expresses also a search for identity, whose demands are more ambiguous, evolving with the conflict itself.

The articulation of this conflict is therefore as crucial to assimilating social changes as mourning is to bereavement. Even if it were possible to foresee how interests might be balanced with the utmost fairness, everyone has still to work out in his or her own terms what it means to their particular attachments, gradually reorienting their essential purposes. No one can resolve the crisis of reintegration on behalf of another, any more than friends can tell the bereaved how to make the best of it. Every attempt to preempt conflict, argument, protest by rational planning can only be abortive: however reasonable the proposed changes, the process of implementing them must still allow the impulse of rejection to play itself out. When those who have power to manipulate changes act as if they have only to explain, and, when their explanations are not at once accepted, shrug off opposition as ignorance or prejudice, they express a profound contempt for the meaning of lives other than their own. For the reformers have already assimilated these changes to their purposes, and worked out a reformulation which makes sense to them, perhaps through months or years of analysis and debate. If they deny others the chance to do the same, they treat them as puppets dangling by the threads of their own conceptions. When liberal white people propose reforms on behalf of black, men on behalf of women, rich for poor, even the most honourable intentions can be profoundly alienating, if they assume the identity of those they seek to help and tell them what their lives should mean. The presumption is, I think, more intimately threatening than indifference or hostility, and is bitterly resented. To be told the meaning of your life by others, in terms which are not yours, implies that your existence does not matter to them, except as it is reflected in their own.

All this suggests three principles for the management of change. First, the process of reform must always expect and even encourage conflict. Whenever people are confronted with change, they need the opportunity to react, to articulate their ambivalent feelings and work out their own sense of it. Second, the process must respect the autonomy of different kinds of experience, so that groups of people can organise without the intrusion of alien conceptions. Third, there must be time and patience, because the conflicts involve not only the accommodation of diverse interests, but the realisation of an essential continuity in the structure of meaning. Each of these principles corresponds with an aspect of grief, as a crisis of reintegration which can neither be escaped, nor resolved by anyone on behalf of another, nor hurried.

These principles are seldom recognised in practice. The agents of change are preoccupied with the powers they must respect, and once they have negotiated a politically viable proposal, become impatient to implement it. They will, I think, most often try to save themselves the time and energy of further conflict – co-opting agreeable representatives of public opinion, outmanoeuvring attempts at organised opposition, fragmenting criticism and overwhelming it with expert knowledge. Legitimate discussion is to be contained within a co-operative framework, defined by their own conception of the common interest – costs, benefits, priorities of need, profitability, expansion. Not that their proposal need be unintelligent or unfair, nor their evasion of confrontation partisan. But people cannot reconcile themselves to the loss of familiar attachments in terms of some impersonal utilitarian calculation of the common good. They have to find their own meaning in these changes before they can live with them. Hence the reformers must listen as well as explain, continually accommodating their design to other purposes, other kinds of experience, modifying and renegotiating, long after they would like to believe that their conception was finished. If they impatiently cut this process short, their reforms are likely to be abortive.

Suppose, for instance, that the changes involve the reorganisation of a firm, or the teaching in a school system. Everyone in the organization has come to understand his or her job – the purposes it satisfied, its give and take, the loyalties and rivalries it implies – as a familiar pattern of relationships, on which they rely to interpret the events of the working day. This definition of their occupational identity represents the accumulated wisdom of how to handle the job, derived from their own experience and the experience of all who have had the job before or share it with them. Change threatens to invalidate this experience, robbing them of the skills they have learned and confusing their purposes, upsetting the subtle rationalisations and compensations by which they reconciled the different aspects of their situation. Most of these people have little part in the decisions which determine the policy of the organization; but collectively, they have great power to subvert, constrain or ignore changes they do not accept, because, after all, they do the work. If innovation is imposed upon them, without the chance to assimilate it to their experience, to argue it out, adapt it to their own interpretation of their working lives, they will do their best to fend it off. The changes may be tamed into conformity with familiar routines, or segregated as an extraneous adjunct to the organization. The reforms in the American school system, pioneered by community action agencies under the anti-poverty programme, were repeatedly emasculated by these tactics. Projects ramified around the system, in pre-school, after school, summer school programmes, without touching the heart of the reformer's intention – to draw teachers, pupils and parents together in mutual understanding and collaboration. Yet with rare exceptions, the teachers and those they taught were never involved in the preparation of these changes, or invited to argue out their merits (see Marris and Rein, 1967, pp.

58–70). Similarly, Tom Burns and G.M. Stalker here described how the attempt to convert small Scottish manufacturing firms to electronics foundered on the unwillingness to incorporate research and development laboratories within their structure. Like a thorn in the flesh, surrounded by inflamed antagonisms and a swollen tissue of mediators, the laboratories remained productively and often physically isolated (Burns and Stalker, 1961).

Reforms within organizations are vulnerable to these stultifying tactics, since the changes can only be carried out by those who resist them. People cannot so readily defend themselves against social changes which they are not required to promote. But if such changes, too, are imposed upon them without the opportunity to assimilate their meaning, the outcome may be even more damaging in the long run. People not only become alienated from the purposes of government, but from themselves. If the changes are disruptive and frequent, they must, I think, lose confidence that their own lives have a meaningful continuity of purpose. And this aimlessness or cynicism will still be provoked even if the changes are intelligent and necessary, so long as people cannot make sense of them in terms of their own experience.

The analogy between change and bereavement implies, then, a need to articulate conflict in subtler and more personal ways than the arbitration of interests can itself express. The process of change has to accommodate a politics of identity, which brings to that arbitration all the unresolved ambivalence of loss. If the evolution of the conflict is to help people work out some meaningful resolution, it must first make clearer to them and to others what crucial purposes and attachments seem threatened by change, and then explore how these purposes can be retrieved and reformulated in the particular context of individual experience. The conflict must therefore recognise the autonomy of experience, respecting the need of every group to find its own sense of continuity. There is, I think, in any important confrontation with disruptive changes, a hierarchy of conflicts, for each major division – between national and local, management and labour, organization and client, black and white – contains within it subdivisions, differences of experience and purpose which must also be argued out or segregated. If this hierarchy is not clearly articulated, conflicts at different levels confuse and weaken each other. So, for instance, a mayor may offer to negotiate with a community in his city, without allowing time for the community to resolve its internal differences apart from him, and then exploit this disarray to excuse the imposition of his own policy. I doubt if these tactics ever successfully forestall conflict, but they can stultify and demoralise it.

These inferences for the management of change are not at all specific – even conflict itself should be understood loosely, to mean any confrontation from outright opposition to argument or the assertion of a group identity. The forms in which internal tensions can be relieved and worked out through collective action will vary too much with circumstances for me to elaborate them here. But these kinds of conflict are, I believe, distinctively different from more obvious conflicts of interest, and fulfil a partly different need. They are concerned with the search for meaning; and meaning may be found in a fair settlement, in institutions which sustain conflicts of interest which have now become clear, in the definition of ideological opposition, or simply in under-standing that what must be given up is not, after all, vital. They merge into political action, but are also expressions of mourning, in the sense that they give meaningful structure to a process of transition whose outcome is still clouded by ambivalence.

REFERENCES

Burns, T. and Stalker, G.M. (1961) *The Management of Innovation*, London, Tavistock.

Marris, P. and Rein, (1967) *Dilemmas of Social Reform*, London, Routledge and Kegan Paul.

INDEX